Managing Cyber Risk in the Financial Sector

Cyber risk has become increasingly reported as a major problem for financial sector businesses. It takes many forms including fraud for purely monetary gain, hacking by people hostile to a company causing business interruption or damage to reputation, theft by criminals or malicious individuals of the very large amounts of customer information ('Big Data') held by many companies, misuse including accidental misuse or lack of use of such data, loss of key intellectual property, and the theft of health and medical data which can have a profound effect on the insurance sector. This book assesses the major cyber risks to businesses and discusses how they can be managed and the risks reduced. It includes case studies of the situation in different financial sectors and countries in relation to East Asia, Europe and the United States. It takes an interdisciplinary approach assessing cyber risks and management solutions from an economic, management risk, legal, security intelligence, insurance, banking and cultural perspective.

Ruth Taplin is Director of the Centre for Japanese and East Asian Studies, London, UK, Editor of the *Interdisciplinary Journal of Economics and Business Law* (www.ijebl.co.uk) and a Featured Author of Routledge.

Routledge Studies in the Growth Economies of Asia

Managing Cyber Risk in the Financial Sector

Lessons from Asia, Europe and the USA

Edited by Ruth Taplin

Routledge
Taylor & Francis Group

LONDON AND NEW YORK

First published 2016
by Routledge
2 Park Square, Milton Park, Abingdon, Oxon OX14 4RN

and by Routledge
711 Third Avenue, New York, NY 10017

Routledge is an imprint of the Taylor & Francis Group, an informa business

© 2016 Ruth Taplin

British Library Cataloguing in Publication Data
A catalogue record for this book is available from the British Library

Library of Congress Cataloging in Publication Data
Taplin, Ruth.
Managing cyber risk in the financial sector : lessons from Asia, Europe and the USA / Ruth Taplin. — 1 Edition.
pages cm. — (Routledge studies in the growth economies of Asia ; 129)
Includes bibliographical references and index.
1. Financial services industry—Security measures. 2. Financial institutions—Security measures. 3. Data protection. 4. Risk management. I. Title.
HG104.T37 2016
332.1068'4—dc23
2015030977

ISBN: 978-1-138-93546-4 (hbk)
ISBN: 978-1-315-67593-0 (ebk)

Typeset in Times New Roman
by Swales & Willis Ltd, Exeter, Devon UK

Contents

Illustrations

Figures

Tables

Contributors

Marcin Czech is Real World Evidence Principal for Eastern Europe at IMS Health. Dr Czech is a medical doctor holding a PhD in Medicine from the Medical University in Warsaw and also a doctorate in Management from the Warsaw University of Technology. He also has a Master of Business Administration from the Warsaw University of Technology, which includes the global affiliates of the London Business School; HEC School of Management, Paris; and Norwegian School of Economics, Bergen. Here he won the 'Best and Brightest' award from PricewaterhouseCoopers. Czech specialises in public health epidemiology. He is currently a university professor at Warsaw University of Technology, Business School and an adjunct at the Medical University of Warsaw, Faculty of Pharmacy, Faculty of Pharmacoeconomics where he was awarded the University President's Award 2008, and the Individual Degree University President's Award 2010. He was also the Health Economics Manager, Europe for Novo Nordisk's Health Economics and Outcomes Research Centre of Excellence.

Cint Kortmann was employed in several different organisations in human resources and other advisory roles and became a serial entrepreneur in 1997. Cint has built up (inter-)national businesses concerning the development and outsourcing of professionals (including Talent&Pro, Netherlands, Talent&Pro UK, Talent&Pro China, Talent&Pro Hong Kong, Ssense Advice, and Arrange) and handed over the last one in September 2014. He had offices in London (2002), Frankfurt (2004) and Copenhagen (2004). In 2012 Cint established Quant Base, a consultancy firm to analyse Big Data. His main markets are the finance industry, transport and retail. As a specialist for flexible labour, Big Data and business in China, he is a partner at Middenduin, a firm for accountancy, mergers and acquisition. Cint holds a Master's in Sociology from the University of Groningen, Netherlands. He contributed a chapter to *Outsourcing and Human Resource Management: An International Survey* (Routledge, 2007) edited by Ruth Taplin and has also published articles in *Gaaps Gazette*.

Monica Lagazio is a partner at Trilateral Research & Consulting, where she leads the security and services offering. Her work focuses on security and resilience, risk and foresight, data and information strategy, and policy development and evaluation, including compliance. Before joining Trilateral, she held senior executive positions as EMEA Head of Analysis and Insights at PayPal, Lead for Consumer Insights at Mouchel, and UK and Ireland Lead for Strategic Analytics and Insights at Accenture working on innovation, risk management, security, consumer insights and data strategy.

Malgorzata Skorzewska-Amberg is Assistant Professor of Law at Kozminski University, School of Law in Warsaw where she has been Head of the Centre for Legal Informatics since 2010. She holds a PhD in Law from the University of Warsaw (2006), which specialised in law and cyber law. Dr Amberg has an MA in Law from the University of Warsaw and an MSc in Computer Sciences from Warsaw University of Technology where she specialised in data security, information technology and cryptography. She has also been a senior lecturer at the Warsaw Institute of Technology, Faculty of Mathematics and Information Science where she taught and did research on data security, programming languages, algorithms and data structures. She has written a number of articles and contributed chapters to edited books including *Proceedings of the 10th European Conference on Information Warfare and Security* (Academic Publishing Limited, 2011) edited by R. Ottis.

Ruth Taplin studied Japanese at Durham University over 20 years ago as part of a special course for future leaders in the Japanese field in the UK. For 20 years she has provided translations particularly in Japanese as well as Chinese and Korean for financial, medical, clinical trial and legal documents. She received her doctorate from the London School of Economics and has a GDL in Law. She wrote freelance for *The Times* newspaper for nine years on Japan, Taiwan and Korea, and was a consultant to the Federation of Electronics Industry for nine years. The Centre for Japanese and East Asian Studies of which Professor Taplin is Director won Exporter of the Year in Partnership in Trading/Pathfinder for the UK in 2000.

Professor Taplin is the author/editor of 18 books and over 200 articles. Her books include: *Decision-making and Japan: A Study of Japanese Decision-making and Its Relevance to Western Companies* (reprinted by Routledge in 2003, first published by The Japan Library in 1995); *Exploiting Patent Rights and a New Climate for Innovation in Japan* (Intellectual Property Institute, 2003); *Valuing Intellectual Property in Japan, Britain and the United States* (RoutledgeCurzon, 2004); *Risk Management and Innovation in Japan, Britain and the United States* and *Japanese Telecommunications Market and Policy in Transition* (both RoutledgeCurzon, 2005); *Innovation and Business Partnering in Japan, Britain and the United States* (Routledge, 2006); *Outsourcing and Human Resource Management: An International Survey* (Routledge, 2008); *Intellectual Property and the New Global*

Japanese Economy (Routledge, 2009); *Intellectual Property, Innovation and Management in Emerging Economies* (co-edited with Professor Alojzy Z. Nowak, Routledge, 2010); *Mental Health Care in Japan* (Routledge, 2012); *Intellectual Property Valuation and Innovation: Towards Global Harmonisation* (Routledge, 2014). In 2010 she wrote 'Future developments in the Japanese exchanges' for the *Handbook of World Stock, Derivatives and Commodity Exchanges* for Mondo Visione. She visited Japan in July 2009 to carry out research and write a report on the future of Japanese securities and exchanges for this.

Professor Taplin was chosen by Routledge in January 2010 as the first author of the month for the whole of Asian Studies and continues to be a featured author. She is an honorary advisor to the Society for Interdisciplinary Business Research. Professor Taplin is occasionally invited by the United Nations to act as an innovation expert because of her entrepreneurial experience as an innovator.

Editor of the *Journal of Interdisciplinary Economics* for 20 years, she is now Editor of the *Interdisciplinary Journal of Economics and Business Law* (www.ijebl.co.uk) founded by her and colleagues. Professor Taplin has had a number of visiting affiliations with universities including Visiting Professor at Osaka City University, Visiting Professor at the Faculty of Management, University of Warsaw, Poland, Visiting Fellow at the University of Mumbai in January 2007 and in January 2008/April 2009 at the University of Bacheshir in Istanbul. In 2014 she was invited to lecture in Nepal. She has also worked for a number of law firms specialising in intellectual property around the world on a project by project basis.

Motohiro Tsuchiya is Professor of the Graduate School of Media and Governance at Keio University in Japan. Prior to joining the Keio faculty, he was Associate Professor at the Center for Global Communications (GLOCOM), International University of Japan. From March 2014 he has been a visiting scholar at the East-West Center in Honolulu, Hawaii. He contributed to the drawing up of 'Cyber Security Strategy' of the Japanese government in June 2013 as an expert member of the Information Security Policy Council. He is author of *Intelligence and National Security* (Keio University Press, 2007, in Japanese) and *Cyber Terror* (Bungeishunju, 2012, in Japanese), and co-authored *Cybersecurity: Public Sector Threats and Responses* (CRC Press, 2012) and 20 other books. His BA is in Political Science, MA in International Relations, and PhD in Media and Governance from Keio University.

Foreword

Cyber risk in terms of threat and attack to global financial services is increasing as witnessed by the recent US$1 billion hacked from banks since 2013. However, reporting by banks and insurance companies of such cyber attacks has been very slow. One type of cyber theft has been only for financial gain. The other that insurance companies are also grappling with increasingly is complex cyber-risk problems mainly in relation to data, some of which can be used maliciously against victims. Medical data theft is one of the most prevalent sectors that is linked to insurance-underwriting activities. Insurance companies often hold even more personal data than banks and this abundance of data means that insurance companies are often unaware of all the data they hold, which leaves them open to attack by cyber opportunists and criminals.

Cyber attacks can be undertaken purely for reasons of illegal financial gain or to obtain data for political and malicious purposes. Methods by which such illicit monetary gain and information is extracted are increasing in sophistication yearly. The forms and aims of cyber attack are broadening with damage through business interruption, theft of intellectual property rights and damage to reputation becoming the most widespread.

Such cyber threat and attack is occurring on an unprecedented scale and in the most complex global economies. Last year in Japan alone there were over 25 billion cyber attacks on Japanese institutions across the board. This was up from 310 million cyber attacks recorded in Japan in 2005. Although at least 40 per cent emanated from China, attacks also came from North and South Korea, Russia and the United States. This is why it is so important for this book to assess East Asia, Europe and the United States.

Yet, some of the most effective and malicious threats and acts of cyber attack come from within these countries, with China and the United States suffering large amounts of internal cyber threat and attacks. This is also true of financial sector organisations who find that the biggest risk is from employees who can either be financial opportunists, bear a grudge against the company or who wish to exploit easy access to data for a variety of reasons. Ruth Taplin in this book investigates all of these issues thoroughly and with great expertise from her contributors.

Finally, and perhaps most importantly, solutions largely within the context of risk management are explored extensively and with great rigour. The solutions are all interdisciplinary; an approach Ruth Taplin has written about extensively and adhered to throughout her long career. Solutions can range from having an internal risk-management team dedicated to understanding who within the internal company structure will betray trust invested in them and engage in illegal internal cyber attacks for personal gain to underwriters who can offer long-term protection for both cyber threat and attack in the financial sectors that can effect adversely both large and small companies. Yet, all disciplines from law, information technology, intelligence gatherers, forensic accountants, economists and risk-management specialists are needed to work together to combat the burgeoning area of cyber threat and attack, which can have both negative intangible and tangible physical outcomes for financial institutions and their customers alike.

Kuni Miyake
Foreign Policy Institute
Tokyo, Japan

Abbreviations

ADE	adverse drug event
ADR	adverse drug reaction
AEGIS	Associated Electricity and Gas Insurance Services
AIG	American International Group
APT	Advanced Persistent Threat
ATI	Allegheny Technologies Inc.
ATM	automated teller machine
BCP	business continuity plan
BGI	browser-generated information
CEPTOAR	Capability for Engineering of Protection, Technical Operation, Analysis and Response
CERT/CC	computer emergency response team coordination centre
CIIREX	Critical Infrastructure Incident Response Exercise
CISPA	Cyber Intelligence Sharing and Protection Act
CNCERT	National Computer Network Emergency Response Technical Team
CPS	cyber-physical systems
CSSH	Cyber Security Strategy Headquarters
CVC	card verification code
CYDER	Cyber Defence Exercise with Recurrence
DDoS	Distributed Denial of Service
DHS	Department of Homeland Security
DLP	data loss prevention
DNS	domain name server
DoD	Department of Defense
DoS	denial of service
DPA	Data Protection Act
DPRK	Democratic People's Republic of Korea
EMA	European Medicine Agency
ENCePP	European Network of Centres for Pharmacoepidemiology and Pharmacovigilance
ENISA	European Network and Information Security Agency
EU	European Union

FBI	Federal Bureau of Investigation
FFIEC	Federal Financial Institutions Examination Council
FISC	Center for Financial Industry Information Systems
FSA	Financial Services Agency
HIPAA	Health Insurance Portability and Accountability Act
HTA	Health Technology Assessment
ICT	information and communication technology
IoT	internet of things
IP	internet protocol
IPR	intellectual property rights
ISP	internet service provider
ISPC	Information Security Policy Council
IT	information technology
LAN	local area network
MHI	Mitsubishi Heavy Industries
NCUA	National Credit Union of America
NICT	National Institute of Information and Communications Technology
NISC	(formerly) National Information Security Center; (now) National Center of Incident Readiness and Strategy for Cybersecurity
NIST	National Institute of Standards and Technology
NSA	National Security Agency
NSF	National Science Foundation
PC	personal computer
PLA	People's Liberation Army
PRC	People's Republic of China
PwC	Price waterhouse Coopers
RIMS	Risk Management Society
ROK	Republic of Korea
RWD	real-world data
SEC	Securities and Exchange Commission
SME	small and medium-sized enterprise
SOE	state-owned enterprise
TSE	Tokyo Stock Exchange
USCYBERCOM	United States Cyber Command
USW	United Steel, Paper and Forestry, Rubber, Manufacturing, Energy, Allied Industrial and Service Workers International Union

1 Risk management and cyber risk in the financial services sector

An overview

Ruth Taplin*

Overview

Cyber risk and threat is all around us! While writing my chapters for this book and editing it, I had a phishing scam attack on my computer bombarding it with bogus emails. It was disruptive to my work and ironical as contributors were writing about this very type of cyber attack. However, this was a very small attack as chapters in this book underscore the enormity of damage both cyber risk and attack can cause at every level of the economy, business and society.

The financial sector was chosen along with data and medical data because the volume of such threats and attacks is expanding dramatically in these sectors and, until recently, has been largely underreported. This has been due mainly to fears that customers will lose confidence in the financial sectors as ever more personal data is hacked into and used for fraudulent and malicious purposes.

Is cyber threat and attack just an extension of ordinary criminal activities but in cyberspace as some argue, or is this a new form of attack crime that has its own peculiarities and cultural expression in different countries as others will put forward in this book?

Damage from cyber attack can range from business interruption, financial loss on a small or large scale, loss of reputation and even destruction of physical infrastructure through the hacking of smart machines. This book will cover the varied forms of possible cyber attack, explaining them, from where such attacks emanate and who is behind them.

Managing the risk of cyber threat and attack is central to this book as many of the technological-based 'solutions' are inadequate to deal with the ever-increasing volume of such attacks and all their many permutations. Managing risk can range from education of those in the company of how to spot it and deal with it to adequate insurance coverage to understanding who within the company would be prone to engaging in internal hacking and maybe even working with external collaborators.

It becomes clear from the subsequent analyses that effective internal company-based risk management must be multidisciplinary including in-house legal departments, finance, sales, traders in the banking sector and underwriters in the insurance sector. Human-resources input could also be invaluable in finding the disgruntled or revenge-bound employee or the employee with financial problems or a taste for luxury that their salary will not afford them.

In relation to the regional focus of this book, Asia, especially East Asia including Japan, China and South Korea, is an area of booming economies and also thriving communities of hackers. North Korea is not a thriving economy but has been politically implicated in numerous cyber attacks against South Korea, Japan and America. Japan has been using advanced technology to try and stop or manage cyber attacks while China holds hackers often sanctioned by the government to carry out external attacks and domestic hackers who are responsible for a good deal of damage within China.

Europe as an economic bloc is both wealthy and includes Eastern Europe where a good deal of cyber threat and attack emanates, especially from Russia whose hackers have been at the forefront of large financial and politically motivated attacks. Italy, for example, is a European country in which financially targeted cyber crime is soaring. A report that was published by DAS of the Generali Group stated that 22.3 per cent of Italians claimed to have been victims of cyber attack with 13.3 per cent having been victims of identity theft through social networks such as Facebook and Twitter. The report also highlighted that 70 per cent of users experienced cyber threat to their identity through social networks while 44 per cent feared that their financial data were being accessed for the purposes of illegal online purchases through their accounts and 38 per cent believed that hackers were using their personal information to commit fraud.[1]

The US, being a wealthy country, has experienced a great amount of financial cyber attack and medical-data hacking. Both banking and retail have seen millions of customer accounts hacked into and substantial damages paid out to victims. There has also been some reputational damage with the purported North Korean-derived hacking into Sony studios to damage reputations and relationships through email leaks in retaliation for the portrayal of the North Korean dictator Kim Jung Un as a buffoon who should be assassinated.

Recent phenomena

Awareness of cyber risk and management especially in the financial and medical-data sectors is so recent that much of the information that forms the basis of analysis is not derived from an extensive literature review but recent reports, newspapers, specialist cyber-risk companies and financial service associations including their briefing meetings and conferences. Experts from East Asia, Western and Eastern Europe and the US are also a unique and fresh source of information as they have been involved first-hand or in studies related to cyber risk.

As mentioned, the financial sector has been reluctant to divulge the extent of how much fraud and business interruption it has experienced because of fear of losing customer confidence and trust. Yet, the extent of this due to hacking is phenomenally high.

The *Financial Times*[2] noted that in summer 2014 JPMorgan Chase experienced a cyber attack compromising the personal account data of 76 million domestic users and roughly 2 million businesses. It was such a severe hacking that JPMorgan Chase doubled its spending on cyber defence.

The same article further reported that a leading bank in the UK was found to have 22 critical flaws, which could have given unhindered access to customer accounts. One of the major vulnerabilities would allow a hacker to take a user's identity and break in through the front door using 'cross site request forgery' by circumventing the bank's security procedures. The bank would see a normal transaction while the customer would be totally unaware of any malicious interference. Bronzeye, a cyber security company, had warned the Financial Conduct Authority of this loophole in July 2014. This flaw involved a hitherto unidentified problem of a two-step verification process of the bank in which customers received changing codes by mobile phone used in tandem with their passwords.

The changing mobile-phone code used for financial transactions is very popular in Eastern Europe where the Russian cyber security firm Kaspersky found that 100 mainly Eastern European banks had been subject to such attacks because of this cyber flaw, which could have lost the banks up to US$1 billion. It seems that such cyber-risk threat and attack is the tip of the iceberg in global financial sectors.

The insurance industry has only recently realised the importance of its role in managing the threat and attack of cyber risk. In a report published in March 2015 entitled 'UK cyber security: the role of insurance in managing and mitigating the risk',[3] former MP Francis Maude notes in the Foreword that 81 per cent of large businesses and 60 per cent of small businesses were the target of cyber attacks last year and the number of such cyber attacks has doubled since 2013. He highlights several important points concerning cyber risk and the need for more comprehensive insurance to deal with it. One is the need to value more accurately the cost of cyber risk and the real value of losses because of it. For years my books[4] have been arguing for a process of valuation of intellectual property intangible assets. In this report the first category requiring cyber-risk insurance protection is intellectual property. The ongoing problem with intellectual property is that although it is a lucrative target for global government and other business-derived hacking in particular, companies underestimate the value of their intellectual property and overestimate the coverage of their insurance policies. The above-mentioned report reflects the same problems that intellectual property insurance has faced over the years in that only 2 per cent of companies hold full cyber-risk insurance. This lack of take up of intellectual property insurance is as remarkable as the lack of demand for full cyber-risk insurance despite the growing amount of high-cost litigation in intellectual property and the increasing amount of high-value loss due to catastrophic single or multiple event cyber attack. The other salient point made in this report is that because most businesses do not fully understand cyber risk they have not put into place accountability or management structures to mitigate such cyber risk. In this book we will not only explain all manner of cyber risk but also how to manage it.

As we will discuss in this book, banks and particularly insurance companies cannot understand the amount of loss from cyber attack they are able to withstand because they are often unaware of the amount or variety of data they hold and therefore cannot understand the value of it and what value it can accrue to hackers. This is especially true in the City of London where many insurance companies still have paper archives and do not know the value of this information let alone what they hold in great volume in their internet-based records. I have been an observer of this after working for many years in the City of London.

This report chronicles many of the loss categories that businesses face and require insurance cover for.[5] They include: intellectual property theft; business interruption; data and software loss; cyber extortion; cyber crime/fraud; breach of privacy; information technology (IT) network failures; reputational risk/attack; damage to physical property; death and bodily injury; incident investigation; and response loss. Therefore referring to cyber risk in the financial sector as cyber crime shows an inadequacy of definition. Cyber threat and attack, which comprise the two main aspects of cyber risk, can cover all the above and more types of risk.

In this book we explore how as volumes of personal-data retention grow in banking and insurance coupled with the insurance sector becoming more integrally involved with providing coverage for cyber threat and attack, the more these sectors will become direct targets themselves of these attacks. This means that methods of risk management will need to change and grow with the cyber-risk threat and adapt to it. This has not occurred to date to any significant degree.

Insurance companies, in fact, while not being completely sure of the nature of the data they currently hold, are requesting even more data concerning their clients' health records. The Medical Protection Society, for example, which represents 290,000 medical professionals, said it discovered a sharp rise in concerns about data requests by insurers, with about 2,300 calls from doctors over the past year on the subject.

Medical records risk

Medical records are protected by strict privacy laws in Europe and the US but, despite this, hackers view such personal health information as a treasure trove. David Dimond, the Chief Technology Officer of EMC Healthcare based in Massachusetts, USA, noted that it is relatively easy for hackers using a birth date, health history and a social security number to open credit accounts. Using this information such thieves can then invoice US government healthcare programmes or insurance companies for fictitious medical care. He further pointed out that the value to unscrupulous hackers of personal health records and finances is three times that of financial information only.[6]

High tech leads to more healthcare hacking

The more healthcare relies on advances in high technology the greater the opportunities for hackers to steal and misuse medical information. Perry Hutton, a regional director of network security company Fortinet Africa, noted that the black-market value for healthcare personal patient data is 20 times higher than credit-card details stolen from mainly data lists of retail outlets. Cyber criminals are also aware that algorithms used in the credit-card financial industry make risk managers much more aware quickly of unusual activity taking place, which can be investigated immediately often through automated systems. The insurance sector of the financial services holds the majority of healthcare details for medical insurance but is less protected than banking with fewer internal risk-management strategies. He further adds that it can take up to a year for patients to realise that their personal healthcare information has been breached.

A recent study by Gemalto, a digital security company in the US, found that no other industry experienced so many data breaches as the healthcare sector with 391 incidents recorded for the year 2014. This accounted for one-quarter of all breaches for the year. In real terms this means healthcare organisations last year had 29.4 million data records compromised in these attacks, and the average records lost per breach for the healthcare industry was 75,152, up from 49,000 in 2013.

Gemalto listed that among the top data breaches in the healthcare sector in 2014 in relation to identity theft were the Korean Medical Association, with 17 million records; Community Health Systems, with 4.5 million records; and the State of Texas Department of Health and Human Services, with 2 million records exposed to identity theft.[7]

Data breaches in relation to medical records are growing steadily, especially in the US where healthcare and pharmaceuticals are big business. In 2011 and 2012 there were 458 big breaches of health data in total involving 14.7 million people, according to the federal Department of Health and Human Services. In 2013 and 2014, there were 528 involving 19 million people. A rough breakdown of stolen data showed that 10 per cent of breaches stem from hacking, while approximately half are physical thefts of records or computers. The rest are either inadvertent losses, disclosures without official authorisation or improper disposals of medical-record information.

As mentioned above it can often be the employees of a company who are the ones stealing internal company data. For example, in November 2013, an employee at US-based UPMC McKeesport was caught rifling through the electronic health records of 1,279 patients. Subsequently, the errant employee was dismissed, and hospital staff were retrained.

UPMC devised a management solution by programming its computer systems to monitor employee interest in patient health records, Therefore, if normal patterns of employees looking at medical records changes dramatically, perhaps rising, computers alert the employers about such unusual activity that often leads to evidence of hacking.

However, as data is spread further afield, managing cyber risk becomes more complicated. UPMC's security personnel are stretched as data are sent out to centres where clinicians can have access to the data through smartphones and tablets, which can be more easily accessed by hackers. To deal with hackers creating ever more sophisticated imitations of UPMC's web pages to 'phish' passwords from employees or even patients who use the online patient portal, the company uses fake phishing to test whether employees are careless with passwords.[8]

In March 2015 80 million people on the Anthem Inc. database had their identities put at risk with more than 750,000 Pennsylvanians, including 51,867 Highmark customers. This was a massive data breach. Yet, despite the Health Insurance Portability and Accountability Act barring healthcare providers, insurers, claims processors, data clearinghouses and contractors from transferring personal health information without the patient's permission, such data breaches continue unabated. Federal prosecutions fall short of what they should be and the internal systems that should be managing cyber threat and attack remain unchanged or inadequate with all strategies being seen to hold some risk.[9]

Bespoke cyber attack

Perry Hutton further notes that such criminal attacks on the healthcare industry are not new but the sophistication and success in obtaining patient data are a central feature of cyber threat and attack. Unlike the old smash and grab raids of paper records, cyber attack is much more complex as complete malware platforms can be made bespoke for hackers to address security systems developed for individual healthcare organisations. Today, everything from heart monitors to infusion pumps can be networked, automatically interfacing with electronic health record systems and providing real-time alerts to healthcare providers. From the perspectives of patient care and operational efficiency, this is a good thing. From a security perspective, it's a potential nightmare.

Hutton believes that most medical devices were never designed to take security considerations into account as many use standard operating systems such as Microsoft. Even those systems that are purpose built to collect specialised data are not designed to keep the data safe and can provide the hackers with unhindered access through devices with which they interface.

This medical example points to another theme explored in this book that cyber risk cannot be viewed as confined to attack solely within cyberspace but can result in an actual physical attack on people and infrastructure. Hutton notes that both terrorists and cyber criminals can, in theory and practice, manipulate actual medical device machines with the aim to shut down critical systems in hospitals or clinics or alter/stop critical-care machines for patients attached to life-saving machines. Hutton concludes:

> Healthcare security should not be addressed when medical records are breached. The time is now. The healthcare industry as a whole needs to be proactive and begin deploying systems with security baked in, protected at both the network and application levels. The stakes are simply too high to wait.[10]

Insurance: the answer to cyber risk?

Does a comprehensive solution to managing cyber risk lie with the insurance sector? Can it be so if insurance companies themselves are prime targets of hackers and have not developed their risk-management strategies to deal with such threat and attack?

Insurance seems to be at the centre of the quest for companies to find a risk-management solution as demand for cyber-risk insurance cover soars. At the RIMS conference in 2014, Daljitt Barn, the PricewaterhouseCoopers (PwC) cyber security director and former chairman of the Cyber Risk and Insurance Forum, noted that AIG's insurance policy, which compensates companies for cyber crime, was the first of its kind although London-based insurers have been discussing for some time how intangible losses could have catastrophic results on both business disruption and damage to employees.

He further stated that 'with the growing awareness on business to protect critical national infrastructures from cyber threats, we will see more clear and concise cyber policy wording over the next 12 months'. Today Daljitt Barn predicts that 'the generally accepted figure for the market (by the end of 2014) was £2bn globally. My view is that within 5 years that will have at least doubled to £5bn GWP.'[11]

AEGIS (Associated Electricity and Gas Insurance Services) is an insurance company that has branched out from its core energy-based insurance to offer a comprehensive cyber-risk insurance in the Lloyd's market. In April 2014 it launched a Cyber Resilience product, in this case for the energy sector, to cover both personnel information loss and threats/attacks on actual infrastructure. In relation to the energy sector, the infrastructure is mainly to do with generators, pumps and such like. Yet, such an idea could be used for medical insurance, which has both data/privacy and infrastructural vulnerabilities in relation to cyber risk.

To produce such insurance, AEGIS was the first Lloyd's syndicate member to recruit cyber security experts from both defence and security sectors as an integral part of its products and services.

David Croom-Johnson, an active underwriter of AEGIS London, speaking at the 2014 Electrical Industry Security Summit in April 2014, drew parallels between the insurance industry's reaction to the devastating 1906 San Francisco earthquake and the role insurance could have in preparing countries to manage future cyber terrorism and cyber warfare. In the cases of both the Titanic disaster and the San Francisco earthquake catastrophe, insurers' calls for safety improvements and their direct funding of initiatives led to improvements in wireless telegraphy, Marconi signal stations and building codes. Croom-Johnson called for the formation of a centralised body to take a holistic view of cyber security for the energy sector. The body could be based on the Institute of Nuclear Power Operations, which promotes safety in nuclear power facilities. He said:

> We need a unified industry response to risk management, security, incident response, threat intelligence and loss control. From our own discussions, we know there is growing regulatory and compliance fatigue over the question of cybersecurity. Yet critical infrastructure companies, more so than other sectors, are all too aware of the cyber spectre.

Croom-Johnson also said:

> Both the US and UK security agencies have offered alternative visions, but none are unified or consistent. Critical infrastructure companies would like unified guidance; no-one wants a repeat of the situation which occurred after US retailer Target was attacked, with regulators and shareholders becoming increasingly aggressive and militant.

He said that governments should understand that insurance cannot be the total solution to cyber risk:

> Governments tend to think there is unlimited capacity within the insurance market. This is far from the case. Insurers have only a finite capacity to respond, and indeed some will not wish to respond at all. Governments need to work with us with the objective of increasing cyber risk management and risk modeling capabilities and of improving security.[12]

Also related to the financial-sector cyber risk of both banking and insurance is the oldest insured area of maritime and transport in general and the newest area from the digital age, which is termed 'the internet of things' (discussed in more detail later in this chapter).

Maritime industries, which are increasingly becoming digitally connected like the internet of things in the home, are becoming the next target of hackers and subject to cyber threat/attack. Maritime and transport are integrally linked to the financial sector through insurance policies and bank loans for new container ships.[13]

Roughly 90 per cent of goods is moved around the world on container ships and oil tankers, which are increasingly connected by computer networks. Hackers have been busy recently exploiting the weaknesses in these networks as they closed down a floating oil rig by tilting it while infecting another rig with so much malware that it took 19 days to make it seaworthy once more. Other hackers infiltrated computer networks connected to the Belgian port of Antwerp, so they could locate certain containers laden with their smuggled drugs, take the drugs and delete the records. Somali pirates target the online navigational data that ships use to avoid capture by providing misleading data or by turning off their navigational devices, causing ships to unwittingly stray into dangerous waters.

Insurance brokers Willis found the maritime industry vastly underinsured in the area of such cyber attack, which could cost the industry dearly. By 2018, it is estimated that cyber attacks against global energy infrastructure will cost energy companies approximately US$1.9 billion. The UK government estimates that cyber attacks already cost energy companies roughly £400 million per annum.[14]

While speaking at TOC Europe's Container Supply Chain Conference in London, freight insurance specialist TT Club's (insurance provider for international transport and logistics) Mike Yarwood highlighted the increasing dangersposed by hackers targeting carriers and transport operators. Yarwood, an insurance-claims specialist, has made a study of the fast-growing trend. 'We see incidents which at first appear to be a petty break-in at office facilities. The damage appears minimal – nothing is physically removed', reported Yarwood in his TOC presentation. 'More thorough post-incident investigations however reveal that the 'thieves were actually installing spyware within the operator's IT network.'

Often it is the individuals' personal devices that are the targets of hackers because cyber security is less adequate. Hackers also target operational personnel through social media. Truck drivers who travel a good deal are tracked by hackers to ascertain routing and overnight parking patterns.

Yarwood also noted that the type of information being sought and extracted may be release codes for containers from terminal facilities or passwords to discover the delivery instructions. The focus is often on specific individual containers in attempts to systematically track the units through the supply chain to the destination port so the terminal's IT systems can be compromised. As mentioned above, cyber criminals can, through gaining access or releasing codes of containers holding their illegal drugs, evade the law enforcers. They also use these methods to steal high-value cargo and engage in human trafficking.

Mike Yarwood and the TT Club are unequivocal in their advice to operators. As argued in this book, it is vital that the first step in managing cyber risk is to identify the value of the data held by an organisation or individual when assessing potential exposure to cyber threat/attack. 'Awareness is often the first step', noted Yarwood. 'Education of employees across all disciplines of the organisation is crucial. Making them aware of robust risk management policies designed to defend the organisation from cyber-crime. Often the level of threat is dependent on an organisation's own culture', concluded Yarwood.[15]

It becomes ever more clear from the advice of expert practitioners, including those who have contributed to this book, that managing cyber risk can only be effective whatever the technology utilised, the insurance policy held or new electronic gadget employed if the following is addressed initially. This includes first understanding the value of the data held by the company, ensuring that employees are educated across all disciplines as to the value of the data held and how it can be subject to cyber risk both threat and attack. It is important then to further educate company employees from all parts of the company such as the legal department, human-resource management, economists, managers, etc. to understand signs that another colleague may be in collusion with hackers. As mentioned above, unusual patterns of employee behaviour in relation to data can be detected and enquiries made. Cyber risk is generated by human beings not computers or electronic devices, which are only vehicles. Yet, when managing such risk, it is important to know how human manipulation of digital technology makes the threat and attack of cyber risk a new digital-age form.

Big Data and Open Data

In my last book, *Valuing Intellectual Property and Innovation: Towards Global Harmonisation*,[16] a number of chapters written by various experts dealt with whether data should be open source or committed to a strict copyright/privacy legal regime. Data are being termed Big Data because of the huge amounts of information held in the realms of cyberspace. A new aspect of this debate is whether allowing for Open Data in the knowledge economy will only serve to exacerbate cyber risk allowing cyber criminals to obtain masses of personal data with fewer encumbrances. Or will it lessen the challenges to hackers who will feel less triumphant because anyone can have access to such data easily? Or will it produce a combination of the two? Intellectual property rights (IPR) by their very nature protect those with inventive minds and talent in society by allowing innovators to be rewarded. If IPR were done away with as some of the open-source persuasion suggest, will cyber crime also diminish as there will be no trade secrets to steal and make money from? Yet, if innovators are not rewarded, where is the incentive to innovate and how will companies be encouraged to have a competitive edge over others if all new innovations are open to everyone? What is now broadly seen as the European Big Data opportunity is getting an enthusiastic hearing in Europe. In the wake of the US National Security Agency (NSA) and Edward Snowden's revelations it's thought that Europe could end up with the best and most harmonised set of regulations and requirements around Big Data, user privacy and network security, making it the jurisdiction of choice for multinational corporations anxious to store their data and anchor their clouds in the best, and most risk-free, environment.

According to Dr Richard Benjamins, director of Big Data at Telefónica, which has recently published a report on Big Data and their role in Europe, the next innovation after Big Data is Open Data. He asserts that Open Data from governments could power major innovations in many sectors such as healthcare, transport, education and public administration. He also argues that creating an Open Data business culture is more likely to be successful in Europe than in other countries perhaps partly because it can be encouraged and part-funded by the European Union (EU). This can be seen with the massive funding provided for now seventh-stage research projects and for example the recent E-Crime funded project. Government initiatives and organised programmes seem to be more popular in Europe than in the US, which has the wealth to support large-scale research project funding but has anti-government interference strongly felt within the US population. However, to stop the intrusion of federal government there are funds available at state and local levels and mainly from the private-company sector. Yet, many private companies may be very much against supporting Open Data as it will undermine their IPR and open their data to cyber threat and attack. Yet, Benjamins insists that what is needed most of all is open ecosystems based on Open Data, which will allow new ideas and help new businesses to start up.

Benjamins is supported to some degree in his supposition by Wayra, Telefónica's start up accelerator, which now hosts more than 317 new digital businesses in 13 cities in Europe and Latin America. Telefónica was awarded €7 million in new funding from the European Commission so that the project was able to support and fund between 50 and 100 new Open Data businesses.

Telefónica has also produced a large study to understand some of the European sentiments surrounding Big Data, charting those who are frightened or indifferent, and those who are avid supporters. The report shows that the great majority of 18–30-year-olds believes they are in control of their personal online data with three-quarters stating that they fully understand the types of information and data that companies collect and share about them. Yet, this same group also expressed concerns about digital privacy and security with eight out of ten worried about having their personal data hacked into or stolen.

There has been a call, as announced at the Brussels European Voice 'Data: the New Currency?' summit, for European policy makers to extend the level of confidence found in younger people to the broader population. Benjamins noted:

> We all agree that data is the lifeblood of digital technologies. It is therefore vital that the reform of the legal framework for data protection results in a trusted digital environment. Policy makers should take a risk-based approach which considers not only how data is collected but also how it is used. They should aim to protect people first, rather than data, and must prevent the use of data in ways that might negatively impact individual people's lives.[17]

Changes to Data Protection Act

A landmark decision by the Court of Appeal in the recent case of *(1) Vidal-Hall (2) Hann and (3) Bradshaw* v. *Google Inc.* (hereafter referred to as *Vidal-Hall et al.* v. *Google*) has reversed an important part of the UK 1998 Data Protection Act (DPA), which had an article that militated against financial compensation being awarded for a non-damage court decision in the event, for example, of distress being caused without pecuniary loss. The DPA was a UK attempt to ameliorate the European Directive (Directive 95/46/EC) 'on the protection of individuals with regard to the processing of personal data and on the free movement of such data', which allowed, like in the US, damage to be interpreted by the court as non-pecuniary in a number of cases such as under the general rubric of 'distress'. Huge sums of money may be awarded in US courts if it can be proved that the claimant has suffered undue stress because of the harmful or neglectful action of others. The current claimants in the *Vidal-Hall et al.* v. *Google* case have argued that the DPA did not properly implement the above-mentioned European Directive. This issue had already been considered in a prior case, *Johnson* v. *Medical Defence Union*, in which the presiding judge, Lord Justice Buxton, had stated that there was 'no compelling reason to think that "damage" in the Directive has to go beyond its root meaning of pecuniary loss'. This decision was based on Article 13 of the DPA, which states:

> (1) An individual who suffers damage by reason of any contravention by a data controller of any of the requirements of this Act is entitled to compensation from the data controller for that damage.

> (2) An individual who suffers distress by reason of any contravention by a data controller of any of the requirements of this Act is entitled to compensation from the data controller for that distress if –

(a) the individual also suffers damage by reason of the contravention, or

(b) the contravention relates to the processing of personal data for the special purposes.

In the *Vidal-Hall et al.* v. *Google* case, the Court of Appeal has overridden Article 13 of the DPA because the claimants have argued that Google collected private information concerning their internet usage through its Safari browser without their knowledge and consent. Cookies were used that collated 'browser-generated information' (BGI), which has been used by Google as part of its commercial deal with advertisers. BGI allowed advertisers to place bespoke advertisements mirroring the claimants' interests on the screens of their devices. This then revealed private information about the claimants that was or might have been seen by third parties. The argument rested on Google's publicly stated position that this would not happen to Safari users unless they had expressly given permission for this to occur.

There was much referral to DPA Article 13 and past precedents but, in the final judgment by the Court of Appeal, the Act was seen to be not in keeping with the European Directive and was dismissed. This has opened the floodgates, as termed in legal language, meaning that damage can be applied to, for example, all alleged breaches of privacy due to data loss, theft and so forth. This can have enormous consequences for cyber risk as the bulk of financial and medical data storage is now digital and involves millions of possible claimants. Such legislation makes an even more compelling case for understanding the extent of data loss, its value and how it can be protected through managing cyber risk in the ways discussed in this book. The need for managing cyber risk becomes even more compelling when viewed from a global, cross-cultural perspective.

Variation according to country and culture

In this book, we also try to demonstrate that cyber risk will inevitably be managed in different ways according to country and culture. European regulation in relation to protecting personal data or those who are promoting Open Data will have little or no effect on countries and cultures that hold different views and regulatory practices.

Although the nature of cyber threat/attack/risk may be similar, globally regulations on how to deal with the data breaches that underpin the bulk of cyber attacks vary widely. The US and Europe, which will be explained in subsequent chapters, have differing regulations and fines. The former requires data-breach notification by law and levies fines, while the latter has focused on rights to data access, not notification, or specify any pecuniary penalties. The maximum penalty for breach of the DPA is £500, for example, in the UK. These regulatory laws are also changing with draft law, for example, on a comprehensive cyber security law at the federal level, now before the US Senate Intelligence Committee, and the EU working on proposals for data-protection regulation and a cyber security directive.

Data privacy in Europe and the US

A regulatory area in which the EU and the United States are moving further apart is in relation to data privacy. Unnerved by the Snowden leaks from when he was contracted to the US NSA, the EU is working on legislation concerning the manner in which US companies can handle European consumer data information.

The draft legislation to replace various national laws concerning data privacy would require explicit individual consent before US companies could share their personal data. It will also include the right to be forgotten. The EU has also rid itself of the 'safe harbour accord', which allows US companies to collect data generated by their European customers. Currently, all 28 private authorities could bring cases against US companies such as Facebook, which has three separate cases pending, for breach of data privacy.

Giovanni Buttarelli, the European Data Protection Supervisor and a leading figure in coordinating EU policy for data protection, said in an interview in March 2015 that he disagreed with President Obama, who implied recently that some European efforts to protect consumer data in light of the Snowden data theft leaks were actually intended to protect national commercial interests:

> 'Isolating a national cloud from the rest,' [Buttarelli] said – referring to regulations mandating that Internet-borne information pertaining to Europe be stored in Europe – was not about slowing innovation or cross-border flow of data but allowing people to control sensitive information. Some countries have discussed proposals to keep EU personal data in Europe as a way to enforce European privacy rules.[18]

Chinese control of data

In the People's Republic of China, for example, it has been reported that those who use internet chat rooms and blogs will not only have to register their names with operators but also make a written promise that they will not challenge the communist political system. Non-Chinese technology companies have been noting that officials have attempted to block virtual private networks, which are used to circumvent extensive internet filters in China. Despite China having the largest population of internet users (649 million), increasing censorship has limited the use of social media. Since 2012 regulators in Beijing have required that internet companies obtain the real names of online users. Compliance has been uneven and there had been a lack of clarity concerning the requirement. The latest announcement, however, makes it clear that registration of real-name usage be extended to blogs, microblog services such as the popular Sina Weibo and website comment sections. These settings often offer many Chinese their only opportunity to express themselves in public in a society in which all media are controlled by the ruling Communist Party.

The rules also requires that first-time users of online sites sign a contract that includes a pledge to refrain from 'illegal and unhealthy' activity. This supports earlier rulings that any material posted online that is considered a threat to national security – meaning Communist Party rule – is prohibited and any violators will have their accounts deactivated.

While the ruling Communist Party encourages internet use for business and educational purposes, it attempts to block material deemed subversive or obscene. The Cyberspace Administration of China said the latest rules are also needed to combat 'username chaos'. In a statement, the agency said users had taken inappropriate online names such as Putin and Obama, which promoted a 'vulgar culture' and committed fraud with users pretending to be Communist Party officials or agitating for separatist causes.

Related to such Communist Party censorship, police in China have raided the office of US car-sharing company Uber after the country's government banned drivers of private cars offering the service through apps. The Guangzhou Municipal Transport Commission has stated that police suspected Uber was operating an illegal taxi service without the proper business registration required in China. Police had accordingly seized thousands of iPhones and other IT equipment used to run the business in the raid in the city of Guangzhou. The Commission also said it was cracking down on other car-sharing apps in the region. Uber stated that it was cooperating with the Chinese authorities while continuing to offer the service to Guangzhou residents.[19]

Japan and cyber risk

Japan, the world's third largest economy, will also be discussed at length in a number of chapters in this book, with one chapter explaining how Japanese companies are managing cyber risk.

The Japanese government and companies are now viewing cyber risk as one of their major priorities as they experienced over 25 billion cyber attacks in the year 2014 and these were only the ones that were logged. The figure, from the National Institute of Information and Communications Technology (NICT), which has a network of a quarter of a million sensors, cited on Kyodo News, includes attempted attacks at testing the vulnerability of the software used in servers. The NICT survey was first carried out in 2005 when only 310 attacks were recorded. It stated that increasingly targets were attempted take overs of security cameras, routers and other systems connected to the internet. The NICT was able to trace some of the attacks, with 40 per cent originating in China, while others were traced to South Korea, Russia and the United States. Therefore, how often a country is attacked depends on their culture and wealth or ease with which hackers believe they can be targeted.[20]

Japan has a reputation for being a trusting society. It was not long ago that when visiting London or other cities Japanese businessmen were known for leaving their briefcases and umbrellas outside the post office or bank they needed to visit and when they returned to collect their belongings they had been stolen. This led to advice being given to Japanese businessmen that they must not leave their belongings unattended. It was also well known by businessmen visiting from the

UK that Japanese company members were not as well acquainted with new digital technology as they should be and Japanese colleagues often relied on *gaiguin* (non-Japanese) to deal with the running of IT systems.

The internet of things

A whole new dimension has been added to the complexity of cyber risk and that is the interconnectness of all systems through the internet known as 'the internet of things' (hereafer IoT), which is affecting the insurance value chain. According to James Tuplin, Portfolio Manager TMT, Financial Speciality Markets at the London-based European operations of Australian insurance company QBE, the IoT is comprised of four components that are interdependent: things that have networked remote sensors that link machines to buildings to automobiles to people or any other permutation; data stores that are local networks or in the cloud; analytics engines that can be the traditional mechanical types such as Scada or the newest digital types; and action/results such as switches being tripped or potentially insurance premiums going up or down. The IoT offers a new way for insurers to collect data as IoT infrastructure sensors embedded in objects collect and transmit data concerning their internal states or environment to their users in real time where they are then analysed or fed into models. Feedback is then directed back to the users or objects and this offers new opportunities for insurers who understand and use IoT technology. In other words, the feedback offerred by the IoT is instantaneous and direct from someone who, for example, is using a smartphone, plugged into social media or has a sensor tracking device attached. The latter could be sensors in trucks that would show if the driver was driving recklessly as we have seen with recent telematics capabilities or an IoT fitness tracker such as smartwatch, which can track people's heart rates and distance/speed travelled and hence feedback to insurers if people are keeping up their fitness routine in relation to health insurance. Users today are giving so much information concerning their personal choices and behaviours that insurance companies can utilise this information in the above ways and consequently offer better pricing and underwriting terms. Embedded sensors can collect graphics and text, which can, in the cases of companies, feed back to the insurers details of exposures and risks that the policyholders are facing allowing underwriters to provide a more accurate and cost-efficient insurance policy based on real data. Valuation of risk as mentioned in this chapter is still the most difficult aspect for brokers and underwriters so the IoT can assist with this process.

Both policyholders and insurers can benefit with the former having lower premiums and the latter reduced costs and expenses. Yet, this must be balanced against the cost of running an IoT infrastructure. Adoption depends on the efficiency and cost of maintaining such remote sensor-based data networks, which can also be affected by the size of the company or the number of subjects being monitored as a very large corporation would require a much larger IoT system. James Tuplin believes these costs are currently prohibitive, as the whole IoT genre is still in its infancy, but sees costs coming down in the near future following Moore's Law, which will allow insurers to reduce costs and increase efficiencies.

The difficulty in running effective IoT remote-sensor networks is that every remote-access sensor is an exit that has to be secured as every new route opened offers another opening to hackers. There are also four other potential problems that James Tuplin points to concerning uptake of the IoT and the results it produces. First is the time element. IoT data collection or cyber-risk data in general is so new, maybe 10 years old in the US and 4–5 years old in the UK, there has just not been sufficient amounts of time to understand long-term trends, which are used to calculate risk. The second is the factor of culture, which affects risk calculation. An example would be that because there is a tendency in the US to sue and be involved in high litigation costs, which are less likely in the UK, the costs of risks would be valued differently in the two countries. Third is the process of standardisation of data collection and interpretation according to company requirements, which again affects premiums and coverage. Fourth, and linked to all of the above, is the possibility of data sharing so that risk can be calculated based on wide and comprehensive data collection. These problems will be dealt with throughout the book but particularly in Chapters 4 and 8 by Ruth Taplin who assesses these issues in an American and Japanese context. Finally, James Tuplin believes that the future of the IoT used to manage cyber risk and better provide cyber insurance will not be a stand-alone policy but part of a comprehensive underwriting policy.[21]

Big Data analytics based on IoT sensor networks is very new and will be discussed in particular in one of this book's chapters as noted in the following chapter overview. It is a potentially important development but offers skilled hackers a potential treasure trove of personal data on a massive scale that can be exploited for nefarious purposes. Potential loss related to cyber risk and attack needs to be taken into account when adopting such a complex and technologically invasive system.

Another aspect of insurance that needs to adapt to the complexities of cyber-risk insurance is the conditions-precedent clauses found in the small print. This means an insurance policy can become null and void if any of the items in the small print is not adhered to. Marsh has removed the conditions precedent from its policies and other insurance companies will most likely follow, which will make for more comprehensive policies that can cover most of the eventualities of data loss, theft and all the other forms of cyber threat/attack.

Overview of the chapters

In Chapter 2 Monica Lagazio defines the concept of cyber risk and cyber crime, which, she argues, is fraught with difficulties because of the explanations and interpretations based on the social, political, practical and scientific. Her definitions and explanations of what are the main forms of cyber risk, threat and attack apply to the whole book. The majority of definitions of cyber risk/crime take into consideration the utilisation and mediation of cyberspace in the perpetration of criminal activity, while distinguishing those criminal activities that are heavily dependent on cyberspace from those that are not. However, in relation to specific categories of cyber crime, existing taxonomies tend to vary greatly in the criteria adopted to develop the key categories of cyber-criminal activities. This chapter initially reviews existing definitions and taxonomies of cyber crime in the financial sector, identifying both difficulties with them and areas for improvement. It then puts forward a taxonomy of cyber crime for the financial sector, which focuses on the nature of cyber crime and makes use of cognitive mapping. This new taxonomy concentrates on the different motivations and objectives of cyber crime and places more emphasis on the nature of the crime than on the technical means employed by its perpetrators. Lagazio argues that this more inclusive taxonomy could help both in the management of cyber risks in the financial sector and in the development of integrated operational countermeasures.

Chapter 3 takes us back to the above-mentioned new process that involves the IoT and how Big Data analytics are being employed in companies such as the cutting-edge one developed by the author of this chapter Cint Kortmann, in which he attempts to define Big Data analytics and answer questions about responsibility, cost, transition, transparency and development. In doing so, his aim is to give insight into the importance of this development and to provide context to the issues relating to cyber risk/crime. In describing how such Big Data analytical tools are used in his company he provides three case studies of how both the policyholder and insurer can benefit from the use of such tools. To manage cyber risk in both terms of threat and attack, he explains how the IoT is used in practical terms, which gives an idea of the potential cyber risks in this new process and ultimately how they can be managed.

In Chapter 4 Ruth Taplin looks at the state of cyber risk in the United States through giving examples of how the financial sector has been hit by both cyber threat and attack in almost every way. The United States is still the largest economy in the world and there is no reason it will not continue to be so in the future. It is also a world leader in producing world-class technology, which, combined with its wealth, makes it a prime target for hackers. The losses that the financial business sector has faced because of cyber attack are huge. The variation in losses is wide from purely pecuniary to business interruption to reputation and to infrastructural. Managing risk within this context is difficult but this chapter assesses different strategies.

Motohiro Tsuchiya, a Japanese national, provides the background in Chapter 5 for the rise of the internet and increasing cyber risk in Japan and East Asia. Within this context he assesses how the financial sectors in Japan, South Korea, North Korea and People's Republic of China have all been targeted by cyber attacks, with China, for example, facing an internal domestic threat as well as directing attacks against the other East Asian countries. He argues that the main reason why East Asia is one of the most active cyber battlegrounds in the world is because it is the most dynamically developing area of the internet. East Asia holds the world's second- and third-largest economies, China and Japan. It is not only immensely wealthy but also has more people online than any other region globally. He assesses how and which areas in the financial sector, mainly banking, have been hardest hit by cyber threat and attack and how cyber risk is being managed in this region.

In Chapter 6 Marcin Czech assesses the fastest-growing area of cyber risk, which is medical data as mentioned above. He explains from a mainly European and United States perspective what medical Big Data entails and the different ways and why such data is becoming a major focus of cyber crime. The main part of the financial sector that is involved with medical data is insurance and he explores how insurance is affected by cyber attack. As this is a very recent phenomenon and is a rapidly evolving one, managing cyber risk in relation to medical data is not that advanced, so Czech argues that more conventional methods of dealing with fraud are being used, but to what effect? He offers his own personal risk-management strategy.

Malgorzata Skorzewska-Amberg in Chapter 7 reviews the law with regard to protection Polish people and companies have in relation to cyber crime. She also provides a thorough list of ways individuals and companies are being attacked by hackers in Poland. Poland is the largest Eastern European country in terms of economy and population within the EU. It experiences cyber risk and attack from domestic cyber criminals and its large Slavic country neighbour Russia from where a good deal of cyber crime derives. She charts provisions in Polish law as the way in which cyber risk is being managed in Poland and the fact that the law must adapt to the changing technology. Management of cyber risk in the financial sector is viewed within the context of dealing with criminal behaviour in general in Poland with few or no solutions outside of this framework.

Chapter 8 by Ruth Taplin looks at the official council experts' response to cyber attacks in Japan. This is an important if not lengthy document that defines cyber attack, how it is manifested in the Japanese financial sector and how to manage such risk. It is a comprehensive institutional response from the Center for Financial Industry Information Systems created by experts within the financial services industry to counter cyber attacks on both financial services customers and financial institutions. The countermeasures are extensive and show how seriously the Japanese government and those in Japanese financial institutions are treating cyber threat and attack to the lifeblood of their economy.

Notes

* James Brewer who was insurance editor of *Lloyd's List* assisted with some of the research in this chapter and must be thanked for his general contribution. Thanks also goes to Peter Sowden, Routledge.
1 Distributed for DMeurope.com via M2 Communications, www.m2.com (25 April 2014).
2 Sam Jones and Caroline Binham, 'Cyber security loophole found at bank', *Financial Times* (3 March 2015), p. 1.
3 Published by HM Government and Marsh, March 2015.
4 For example, Ruth Taplin (ed.) *Valuing Intellectual Property in Japan, Britain and the United States* (Abingdon: RoutledgeCurzon, 2004) and *Intellectual Property Valuation and Innovation: Towards Global Harmonisation* (Abingdon: Routledge, 2014).
5 Published by HM Government and Marsh, March 2015, p. 11.
6 'Health care files a rich trove for identity thieves', *Pittsburgh Post-Gazette* (16 March 2015) cited in *Cyber Risk Network News* by Advisen Ltd.

7　ITWeb (online) 'Patient data turns goldmine for hackers' (3 March 2015).

8　'Health care files a rich trove for identity thieves'.

9　Ibid.

10　ITWeb (online) 'Patient data turns goldmine for hackers'.

11　'Reporting from RIMS: demand booms for cyber cover', shown on A.M. Best TV episode and distributed by Miranda Ward of PwC/Financial Services PR London UK. RIMS is the Risk Management Society™. It is a global not-for-profit organisation representing more than 3,500 industrial, service, non-profit, charitable and government entities throughout the world, see www.RIMS.org. The prediction of growth in the cyber-risk insurance market was given directly to me by Daljitt Barn in conversation and writing.

12　London AEGIS Conference Press Release, 'Insurers have bigger role to play in fighting cyber terrorism, Croom-Johnson tells security chiefs' (30 June 2014).

13　See Taplin (ed.) *Valuing Intellectual Property and Innovation* for the chapter on container ship risk, IPR and the valuing of these tangible assets.

14　'Maritime industries vulnerable to cyber attacks', Reuters, Cape Argus, South Africa (24 April 2014).

15　TT Club news release through ISIS Communications, London (26 June 2014).

16　Taplin (ed.) *Valuing Intellectual Property and Innovation*.

17　AEGIS press release (14 April 2014).

18　'EU seeks to tighten data privacy laws', Dow Jones News Service, Elizabeth Dwoskin (10 March 2015).

19　'Operators will be required to assign an employee to review and keep track of user details to ensure they comply, the agency said', Press Association (5 February 2015).

20　'Japan sees 25 billion cyber attacks in 2014: government agency', Agence France Presse World News (17 February 2015).

21　Permission given from James Tuplin, Portfolio Manager TMT, Financial and Specialty Markets, QBE European Operations in an interview with the editor of this book (Ruth Taplin) on 12 May 2015 and from a part of his presentation given at the Association of British Insurers conference on cyber risk on 5 May 2015 at their offices.

2   A taxonomy of cyber crime in the financial sector

A comprehensive approach to countermeasures

Monica Lagazio

Introduction

Cyber crime today operates at the scale of and with the sophistication of a global industry. The activities of modern cyber criminals often appear to have clear business objectives. Cyber crime has various aspects: attack planning, development and sale of tools, execution and generation of personal gain for the criminals. Cyber crime is complex. As a result of this complexity, in order better to understand cyber crime while developing and deploying measures to fight against it, it is important to understand its core mechanics as well as the thought processes and activities that characterise its cycles.

While nobody disputes the importance of protecting business operations from criminal activities, our understanding of cyber crime and its nature is still limited. The literature on cyber crime, though vast, remains theoretically underdeveloped. The existence of so many different perspectives has led to a lack of consensus on many fundamental aspects of cyber crime. The lack of consensus extends to definitions, classifications and countermeasures. Understanding of cyber crime can also be fragmented when spread across the different levels of the value network[1] with the different players involved in each level holding only part of the overall 'puzzle' and often unable or unwilling to share their knowledge for fear of perceived negative consequences.[2] Because of this fragmentation and multiple perceptions of cyber crime, more flexible approaches are needed in order to appreciate the complexity of cyber-crime activities in the financial sector. Better and more inclusive understanding will lead to the development of more effective countermeasures to reduce cyber-crime risk for financial businesses.

As part of the emerging debate about the need to embrace a comprehensive views of cyber crime, this chapter focuses on developing a taxonomy for cyber crime in the financial sector that takes account of the nature of the crime, its motivations and the interactions among different types of cyber crimes. I argue that the more encompassing and comprehensive taxonomy I advocate could assist with the management of cyber risks in the financial sector and aid the development of integrated operational countermeasures. In order to capture and map the complexity of cyber-criminal activities I have used cognitive mapping to further analyse the initial taxonomy. Although cognitive maps are neither a panacea nor always appropriate, I nonetheless believe that they provide a useful methodology that has not to date been sufficiently exploited in the context of cyber-crime analyses. The structure of this chapter is as follows: the second section briefly reviews the existing debate and research on the definition and taxonomy of cyber crime, while identifying existing research challenges and gaps; the third section introduces the taxonomy of cyber crime in the financial sector based on the nature of the criminal activities and briefly discusses the data and methodology used for the taxonomy including the key motivators for and main players in cyber crime; the fourth section integrates the key findings from the previous sections and identifies their relevance for the development of more comprehensive countermeasure to fight cyber crime in the financial sector. Many of the issues covered in this chapter are still under development and are the subject of continuing dispute among specialists. My aim is to contribute to the ongoing debate about these issues. I do not claim to provide conclusive answers.

Existing definitions and taxonomies

In order to understand and combat cyber crime in the financial sector, it is necessary to have a robust framework in which different aspects of cyber crime can be classified and categorised. In this section I present a short analysis of the existing attempts to develop such a taxonomy and consider how useful such classifications are, given the range of approaches that have been followed to capture the rapidly evolving nature and extent of cyber crime.

At the most basic level, cyber crime can be simply interpreted as types of crime involving the use of computers. However, this is a broad description that does not help our understanding of and response to this growing problem. Already in 2005 Moitra discussed the issues involved in developing policies in respect of cyber crime. He defined five key questions that need to be answered in order to develop 'effective, efficient and equitable polices'.[3] These questions are:

1   What is cyber crime?
2   Who commits cyber crime?
3   How much cyber crime is there?
4   What are its impacts?
5   How can we respond effectively, efficiently and equitably?

Moitra, together with other security researchers such as Williams,[4] sees a robust taxonomy as an essential starting point to addressing these questions. Moitra argues that while there is a consensus that the internet has become an arena for deviant behaviour, there remain questions about the extent to which it has facilitated criminal activity, and the nature of these crimes.[5] Following a similar line of thought, Williams discusses the need for 'recourse strategies' to be adopted and implemented by organisations to address cyber crime, featuring in particular proactive measures based on coherent taxonomies that enable easy and efficient information sharing.[6] Both Moitra and Williams argue that a taxonomy of cyber crime is required as a practical measure to respond to cyber crime: without a disaggregation of cyber crime by crime type, meaningful policy responses cannot be developed.

Following Moitra and Williams, a number of divergent approaches to creating a cyber-crime taxonomy has been proposed in the literature. Some of these approaches stand alone, while others are hybrid or can be combined to present more nuanced and focused classifications. Below I have classified these attempts into six groups and then briefly discussed them in the following sub-sections:

1   approaches based on traditional criminology;
2   approaches based on technologies, adversaries and threats;
3   approaches based on cyber criminals;
4   approaches based on the impacts on victims;
5   approaches based on legal frameworks;
6   approaches based on multi-dimensional categories.

Approaches based on traditional criminology

Some sources draw on the long and well-established traditions of criminal justice, viewing computers and the internet as a tool with which existing crimes are facilitated and therefore viewing cyber crime as an extension of traditional criminality. For example, Wall bases his analysis of cyber crime on the idea that the internet is an additional, new tool to commit crimes. Following this argument he develops a high-level definition of three different types of cyber crimes: traditional crimes that are now to be regarded as 'cyber' because they are also conducted online and are exploiting cyberspace as providing more opportunities for crime (e.g. traditional fraud, piracy, espionage, stalking, trading sexual material); 'hybrid' cyber crimes, which are traditional crimes whose effectiveness, nature and modus operandi have significantly changed as a result of new opportunities provided by the internet (e.g. ID theft, hacking, 'hacktivism', illegal sex trade); and new cyber crimes consisting of opportunities created purely by the internet and carried out only within cyberspace (e.g. spams, denial of service, phishing, online gambling, cyber sex).[7]

Although this approach has overcome the limitations of the common working definition of cyber crime as 'a crime committed on a computer network'[8] by expanding what constitutes cyber crime, it has also opened up new problems. For instance, the dividing line between cyber crime and cyber terrorism is unclear unless motivations for cyber crime are taken into account. A key distinction suggested that crime is 'personal' while terrorism is 'political'.[9] An additional complication is added by the existence of cyber warfare, i.e. the conduct of military operations by virtual means. It 'consists of nation-states using cyberspace to achieve the same general ends they pursue through the use of conventional military force'.[10] The techniques and some of the results will be identical to certain instances of cyber crime, but cyber warfare clearly, however, falls outside the scope of the criminal justice system. These questions have a clear significance for judicial investigation and law enforcement. Procedures are needed to allow the police and other government agents to pass the information they are receiving in respect of cyber threats and actual cyber attacks and then respond appropriately. For instance, in the case of a sequential attack on financial systems such as ATMs (automated-teller machines), how can the authorities efficiently distinguish between cyber crime, cyber terrorism, hacktivism and cyber warfare? Historically warfare and terrorism have been relatively easy to identify as they have involved physical actions carried out by military forces or militants. Cyber warfare, cyber terrorism and hacktivism are far less clear as fundamentally any attacks will consist of individuals or groups seeking either to disrupt or take over communications and information systems. Analysts and legislators are thus faced with the problem of understanding the motivations of those carrying out cyber attacks in order to better differentiate among cyber crimes and determine how the perpetrators should be prosecuted.

Approaches based on technologies, adversaries and threats

Other sources focus primarily on the technological aspects of the crimes being committed and the nature of the cyber adversaries, seeking to differentiate cyber crimes based on how the crimes are carried out and which aspects of computer and network infrastructure are the targets or vectors of attack. Work on cyber taxonomies by Howard,[11] Hansman and Hunt,[12] and Kjaerland[13] all follow this approach.

From the survey of computer emergency response team coordination centres (CERT/CCs) data on security incidents, Howard proposed in 1998 a five-category taxonomy of such incidents:[14]

1   attackers (hackers, criminals, terrorists, vandals);
2   tools (scripts, toolkits, user commands);
3   access (implementation or design vulnerabilities, access permissions);
4   results (corruption, deletion or disclosure of data, theft of resources, denial of service); and
5   objectives (intellectual challenge, peer status, financial gain, damage).

Hansman and Hunt extended this initial attempt by introducing multiple tiers of threats and further levels in the descriptions via four additional categories: attack vectors (the means by which the target is reached); targets (hardware, software, network, data); specific vulnerabilities and exploits (security flaws); and payload (the outcome and effects).[15] Kjaerland added a quantitative component to the classification of attacks, using four new sub-groups: source sectors (top-level domains); method of operation (resource theft, social engineering, malware, denial of service); impact (disruption, distortion, destruction, disclosure); and target services (commercial or governmental).[16]

Although providing useful information, these approaches tend to focus on the direct use of computers in committing crimes and the cyber aspects of the crime. However, this is just a part of the full picture. Many techniques and tools are common across a range of cyber-criminal activities, which are quite different in nature (i.e. cyber warfare, cyber terrorism and hacktivism, etc.). Understanding these differences together with the motivation for the cyber crime is important in order to make clear and useful distinctions. As a result, these approaches tend to support technological countermeasure rather than the development of more comprehensive defence strategies.

Approaches based on cyber criminals

Here the characteristics of attackers are used as key differentiators for developing classifications. This approach has a long history, with roots in the analysis of hacker culture as this phenomenon began to draw academic and public attention.[17] An example of such a taxonomy is provided by Rogers and Meyers. Their taxonomy of cyber criminals includes eight groups:[18]

1   script kiddies, newbies, novices;
2   hacktivists, political activists;
3   cyberpunks, crashers, thugs;
4   insiders, user malcontents;
5   coders, writers;
6   white-hat hackers, old guard, sneakers;
7   black-hat hackers, professionals, elite; and
8   cyber terrorists.

These categories are distinguished on the basis of the cyber criminals' skills (in ascending order in this list), maliciousness, motivations and methods. Clear contrasts are drawn between the ends of the spectrum. At one end there are the unskilled and inexperienced adversaries, those with minimal technical skills whose activities are distinguished by their naivety, lack of focus and use of widely available scripts and basic techniques. In the middle are those who might exploit their legitimate access rights to systems and data in order to damage, steal or embarrass. At the far end are the professionals, security experts and experienced hackers who might choose to employ their skills for good or for bad and who might have their motivation backed up by significant resources.

Although addressing the lack of criminal motivations of the previous approaches, the single focus on criminal characteristics and the simplified generalisation for the categories of cyber criminals make these classifications not easily adaptable and therefore date very quickly. Furthermore, overlaps and similarities among cyber criminals are downplayed together with cooperation activities that might potentially involve different types of cyber criminals in the pursuing of a common cyber crime. For instance, this could refer to black-hat hackers recruited by cyber terrorists or criminal organisations for infrastructure attacks having as the primary objective the collection of a ransom from the target. Finally, identifying and classifying cyber criminals can in practice be difficult because techniques for anonymisation and for routing attacks through intermediaries prevent the correct identification of the attackers or the origins of a cyber attack. In addition, the nature of the target or of the attack will not in every case allow the recognition of the motivation of the perpetrators.

Approaches based on the impacts on victims

A further approach to classification is to identify the impacts of criminal activities on the victims. These impacts can be both tangible and intangible. The first systematic study of the costs of cyber crime was presented by Anderson et al. in 2012.[19] This work was commissioned in part as a consequence of a report published by Detica in February 2011,[20] which estimated the annual cost of cyber crime to the UK to be £27bn. Experts and the media viewed this figure with widespread scepticism and a counter-study was then prepared by Anderson et al. In respect of the communications sector, the European Network and Information Security Agency (ENISA) publishes an annual report on security incidents due to malicious and other non-malicious causes, which have been reported by national regulatory authorities through ENISA's CIRAS (confidential reporting system) tool.[21] This report includes the impact on victims.

Quantifying the impacts of cyber crime is a complex and difficult task. Lack of reliable data and common specifications affect this approach.[22] In order to use these taxonomies, their scope needs to be carefully defined and understood; the quality and completeness of the data need to be appreciated; and the maturity of the information-gathering process needs to be taken into account.

Approaches based on legal frameworks

The taxonomies proposed by legal conventions' international bodies are significant because of their visibility and influence in shaping opinion, promoting research and providing a framework for legislation aimed at combating cyber crime. The best-known legal framework for cyber crime is the Council of Europe Convention on Cybercrime.[23] This Convention remains the main (and only) international treaty that defines the substantive elements that lead to some cyber activities to be classified as crimes, and that has procedural provisions that allow for the prevention, detection and prosecution of these activities. The Convention proposes four large categories covering a wide range of cyber-criminal activities: offences against the confidentiality, integrity and availability of computer systems and data; computer-related offences (forgery, fraud); content-related offences; and offences related to infringements of copyright and related rights. These four categorises are further subdivided in subsequent sub-groups.[24] Indeed, the Convention serves as a general model by which to understand what constitutes cyber crime, educates people about what is right and wrong behaviour on the internet, and also acts as a general legal framework for the European and international countries in the development of countermeasures against cyber crime. Although providing an important legal reference on cyber crime, the taxonomy in the Convention can still be interpreted in different ways and remains too generic for sector-specific in-depth assessments.

Approaches based on multi-dimensional categories

A number of authors has proposed multi-dimensional taxonomies of cyber crime, with variations on the nature and degree of specificity of these dimensions.

Generally these taxonomies tend to start with two primary categories of cyber crime: cyber crimes where the computer, computer network or electronic device is the target of the criminal activity; and cyber crimes where the computer, computer network or electronic device is the tool used to commit or facilitate the crime. Several sub-classes are then added under the two main categories. The categorisation by the UK Audit Commission,[25] the Australian High Tech Crime Centre[26] and Foreign Affairs and International Trade Canada[27] all share this approach. From the academic side, Alkaabi et al.[28] have proposed one of the most comprehensive multi-dimensional categorisations including seven further sub-classes decomposed in a variety of third-level groupings (see Figure 2.1).

Classification based on the different characteristics of cyber crimes can yield valuable insights when seeking to design and implement preventive measures and thereby reduce the vulnerabilities to, and the rate of success of, any attacks. The multi-dimensional aspect also ensures that both general and more specific information is provided in the multi-dimensional taxonomies taking into account the variety of the characteristics of the crime. However, what is apparent from this short review is that cyber crime can be viewed in different ways reflecting different multi-dimensional taxonomies. This is problematic for two main reasons. First, it makes it difficult to draw conclusion and comparison among different taxonomies. Second, even within the same taxonomy, categories are not necessarily exclusive as, in some crimes, computers or networks play multiple roles, meaning that one crime could be classified under multiple types and sub-classes. This makes it difficult to classify cyber crimes and position them within the multi-dimensional taxonomy. What is missing is a relational dimension where interactions among the key categories and concepts are analysed and captured in the taxonomy. Instead of focusing on mutually exclusive categorises, overlaps and fuzzy boundaries should be considered.

A taxonomy of cyber crime in the financial sector based on the nature of crime

To address some of the issues underlined in the previous section, here I propose a taxonomy of cyber crime for the financial sector based on the nature of the crime. I briefly discuss the main data and methodology used to develop the taxonomy. The initial key motivators and players for cyber crime are also analysed and used to develop and finalise the taxonomy.

Data: interviews

In order to develop the taxonomy of cyber crime in the financial sector I initially needed to capture both the number of specific incidents affecting financial companies on a yearly basis and industry perceptions on the importance of different types of cyber crime. Reliance on previous studies and statistical publications was not enough. As a result, in addition to the data from the literature I sought

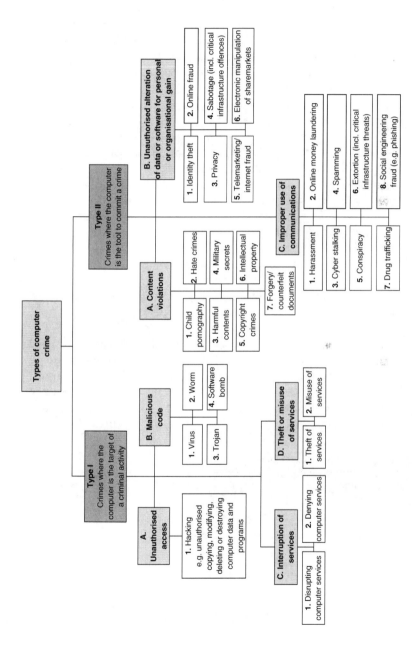

Figure 2.1 Example of multi-dimensional taxonomy.

Source: Alkaabi et al., 2010.

additional primary data from a sample of industry representatives through surveys and interviews.

The financial sector is heavily affected by cyber crime.[29] However, the competitive nature of the industry leads to practices such as under-reporting and lack of information sharing.[30] There is a tendency for financial institutions not to share information about cyber-crime incidents in order to protect their reputation and market share. Given these well-known difficulties in gaining information from the sector, I decided to follow a qualitative approach, combining the insights from the literature with an initial small number of surveys followed up by in-depth interviews. I also restricted the data collection to the UK financial sector. The UK provides an informative single-country view, since it has a mature online economy with a sophisticated and regulated financial sector, which is well-informed about the risks of cyber crime.[31] This approach allowed me to build a more detailed and informative, albeit less representative, picture of how the financial sector experiences and perceives cyber crime. Table 2.1 shows both the number of surveys and interviews I sought and the number of responses I received.

On the one hand, the response rate for both surveys and requests for interview was relatively low (6 out of 59 replied). On the other hand, those I was able to interview held roles that gave them an overview of potential and actual cyber crime in the sector. Consequently, I was still able to identify six key observations from the survey and interview data. These were then used to develop the taxonomy and the mind map. These key observations are summarised below. While I believe them to be a valuable starting point, further work and data collection on a wider sample will confirm or amend them:

1   Overall, industry representatives make no clear distinction between fraud more generally and fraud that has a cyber aspect. They see fraud as something that could happen even without the existence of cyberspace. Thus they include cyber fraud within their overall fraud statistics without identifying instances of fraud involving cyber crime while separately reporting other kinds of cyber crime (e.g. cyber attacks by so-called 'hacktivists').

Table 2.1 Number of surveys sent and responses received

Industry sub-sectors	Survey and interview requests	Responses received
Banking	32	2
Cards	6	1
Insurance	4	0
Retail	5	0
Online payment providers	3	0
Financial services	8	3
Government fraud service	1	0
Total	**59**	**6**

2   Four respondents reported that compromised cards and accounts were the most common cyber-crime incidents bringing maximum financial losses to the company.

3   Three respondents said that attacks to information technology (IT) infrastructures occur often, while three said they occur only occasionally.

4   Four respondents said there is a focus on preventive measures to avoid compromised customer accounts and online scams targeting customers. This indicates the importance for financial companies of protecting customer trust in their business, products and services.

5   Two respondents stated that so-called 'hacktivist'-motivated attacks against the financial sector and leaks of sensitive information have been common in current times. Most of the time, hacktivists want their attacks to be discovered and reported so they can use a successful attack as a platform to disseminate their propaganda against financial organisations.

6   Perception of the occurrence of cyber crime within the financial sector remains fragmented and, at times, contradictory. While the banking and cards sub-sectors claim that the overall number of cyber incidents is very low, the financial advisory services sub-sector argues that cyber incidents happen on a consistent basis. This fragmented view might be due to under-reporting or might simply reflect the fact that, for large companies, even a few hundred incidents only cause negligible losses. The tendency of the industry to consider fraud and other types of cyber crime as two separate and mutually exclusive types of crime and risk may also have a part to play in this.

Broad motivators

In sub-categorising the differing types of cyber crime, it is important to understand the factors that drive the growth of cyber crime in the financial sector. In general, cyber crime, like most crimes, has four broad motivations:[32]

1   To obtain intrinsic benefits: self-satisfaction, peer-approval, status, feeling of revenge, etc. are examples of such benefits.

2   To obtain intrinsic benefits coupled with enjoyment: for example, when cyber crimes are committed for the sheer fun of the activities involved.

3   To fulfil intrinsic motivations based on perceived organisational/community obligations: this ranges from acts of hacktivism to committing cyber crimes while either working for a government organisation (the National Security Agency – NSA or the UK Government Communications Headquarters known as GCHQ, etc.) in the furtherance of national interests or as private individuals acting out of a sense of national pride/obligation.

4   To obtain extrinsic financial benefits: for example, direct monetary gain or information that may later be monetised.

These motivations are, of course, not mutually exclusive.

The growth of IT has presented individuals and groups with many opportunities to satisfy these motivations. Lack of employment opportunities coupled with low wages in certain countries has driven many highly qualified programmers to work for cyber-criminal organisations. In countries such as Russia, working with criminal organisations offers better upward mobility and higher wages. As a result, many programmers have turned to the Russian mafia as an employer. In the case of rogue states, corruption can create alliances between criminal organisations, the political system, and law and order. Individuals within such states may be encouraged to commit crimes of their own because of impunity.[33]

Arguably, the most important reason for the growth of cyber crime is the problem with its attribution, i.e. ascribing the blame to a particular entity or person. In the case of cyber crime such attribution has been proven to be extremely difficult. On the one hand, this is due to the lack of available, reliable data tracing responsibility for the crime back to its ultimate source. On the other hand, it is due to the reluctance in the financial sector and the industry overall to share data and information on cyber attacks. This leads, among other things, to under-reporting. According to Chris Hoofnagle[34] the problem of under-reporting of cyber crime could be attributable to a number of reasons. As mentioned above, it may be that most banks and credit-card companies consider fraud and cyber crime as two separate and mutually exclusive types of crime and risk. Fraud and cyber crime losses are reported separately following the rationale that fraud could happen through any means and not just through cyberspace. Furthermore, the competitive nature of the industry has led to the tendency not to share information about cyber-crime incidents in order to protect the company reputation and market share.[35] The fact that criminals can get away unscathed after a successful act of cyber crime has encouraged more and more people to become involved in it. In the case of recreational hacking, one of its prime attractions may be the relatively low risk of being caught or, at least, prosecuted.

Cyber criminals also take advantage of jurisdictional arbitrage, i.e. the various issues relating to which law applies to the crime and whose law enforcers are responsible for detecting and prosecuting it. Most crimes are initiated from countries with poor cyber laws or inefficient law-enforcement systems. In some countries, the police have other more pressing problems to take care of than cyber crime. Therefore, legal actions against criminals may be difficult and the cross-border nature of crime can also make attribution very difficult in terms of data availability as well as jurisdictional limitations to accessing data. An international legal framework is required to overcome this problem.

Methodology: cognitive mapping

In order to map the relationships and interactions among different concepts of cyber crime, I have used cognitive mapping. Cognitive mapping is a type of 'visual thinking' approach. Visual thinking approaches focus on two things: making ideas explicit and exploring the relationships between ideas. Cognitive mapping was initially developed by Eden and Ackermann[36] and is based on Kelly's[37] work on personal construct theory. Its first application was in the field of strategic management and, although its uses have spread more widely, strategic management remains the widest area of application.

Cognitive mapping can be described as a qualitative analysis tool in that it deals solely with qualitative data (ideas). Its objective is to help researchers play with ideas while structuring them and exploring the relationships among them and, in so doing, moving understanding forward. In practical terms, cognitive mapping is used to generate a visual representation of a researcher's, an interviewee's or a group's ideas about a particular issue by providing a means of capturing and structuring ideas. Ideas are captured in terms of 'concepts'. These are short phrases expressing an idea; single words are not used. The aim when developing these short phrases is, where appropriate, to incorporate an active verb into the idea to give a sense of action and direction. Concepts may be mono- or bi-polar. Bi-polar concepts are important because they add richness to the ideas in the map, capturing the 'shades of grey' and nuances in peoples' thinking. The concept 'long queues at X-ray rather than 3 minutes or less' is an example of a bi-polar concept. Another concept might have expressed a different idea, such as 'long queues at X-ray rather than no X-ray at all'. Both statements give us more insight into a person's preferences. 'Long queues at X-ray' is the emergent pole of the concept and the statement after 'rather than' is called the 'contrast' or 'opposite pole'. In cognitive mapping the 'rather than' phrase is represented by three dots (. . .). As further indicated in Figure 2.2, in order to structure ideas, cognitive mapping links short phrases appropriately to express their relationship to one another. Most links are directional, representing causal relationships and are read as 'may lead to'. Negative links can be used. These switch the relationship between the concepts, so that the emergent pole of the tail concept (the concept at the start of the link) relates to the contrasting (or opposite) pole of the head concept (the concept at the arrowhead of the link). Concept reference number can be turned off, becoming 'hidden link'. Hidden links show links to other concepts, not shown in the map.

Differently from mind mapping,[38] in cognitive mapping one does not have to work with a central idea, from which all others stem (unless one wants to). Instead, cognitive maps may have several focuses. This allows a researcher to build-up a database of relationships and then to use the tools at his or her disposal to explore the model that has been created, elaborating the model and developing the thinking about the problem or issue under consideration. This allows researchers to see the connections between ideas they already have, to connect new ideas and to organise ideas in a logical but flexible structure. Flexible structures make use of 'hierarchy'. Cognitive mapping encourages the search for a 'hierarchy' in the ideas being mapped. The hierarchy is one of cause/effect, means/ends, how/why, working towards identifying desired outcomes. The terminology used to refer to the outcomes depends on the setting in which the approach is being used. They might be referred to as goals/not goals, aspirations/fears and so on. Figure 2.2 shows an example of cognitive map, which was developed within a marketing department of a company, looking at ways of improving service levels within their organisation. What is shown is only a part of a larger map.[39]

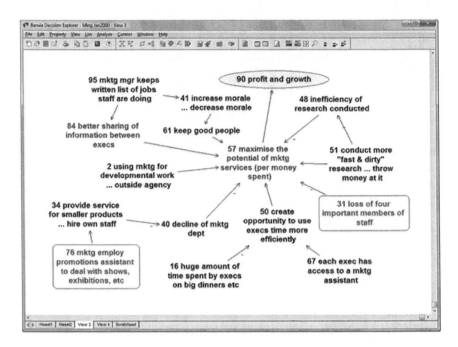

Figure 2.2 Example of cognitive mapping (taken from Explorer user guide).

As is shown by the example in Figure 2.2, in cognitive mapping, as with the other forms of mapping, the full meaning of the ideas is given by the 'whole picture'.[40] Links between ideas add further contextual information to the concepts themselves. Meaning is generated through the content of the ideas – the way in which they are expressed as short phrases – as well as through the context within which they sit. This is suitable for cyber crime in the financial sector for a number of reasons. First, cognitive mapping is widely recognised as a clear method for communicating ideas and complex structures to those with little working knowledge of the particular problem involved. This is relevant to cyber crime in the financial sector since different financial players might have some knowledge of the problem at stake but they hold only a small part of the picture. Second, based on more recent analyses[41] cyber crime appears to be highly flexible and interconnected. These integrated relationships can be well represented by a cognitive map. Finally, given the lack of comprehensive and robust data on cyber crime, cognitive mapping can offer a useful alternative to more data-driven models. In particular, it is possible initially to develop a cognitive map for cyber crime with partial data and then discover new insights via the connections and full picture that the map is representing. These additional insights can then be further analysed when more data become available. Mapping the initial framework for cyber-crime relationships with cognitive mapping will therefore, facilitate and direct further analyses in the light of more data, while providing, in the meantime, new insights into the problem.

The cognitive map of cyber crime in the financial sector

The information from the literature review, the initial motivators and the insights from the interviews were used to build the cognitive map model. The map was developed using the Decision Explorer software. Figure 2.3 shows the cognitive map presenting observed clusters of certain concepts of cyber crime organised in a visual representation of the structure of cyber crime in the financial sector. The map has been developed by breaking the problem down into concepts expressed in terms of a few words and then linking them to form a hierarchy of means and ends. Each link from one concept to the other would then read as a causal link, i.e. 'may lead to'. Certain concepts can be described as having two poles, for example, from the map in Figure 2.3, the concept 'motivation to obtain financial gain through illegal means . . . legal means', the ' . . . ' reads as 'rather than' and the two concepts on either side represent two opposites poles of the same concept. Therefore, the concept would be the presence of a motivation to obtain financial gain through illegal means rather than through legal means, which shows the two polar opposite motivations. Negative links on the map, indicated with the symbol '−' on the arrow, show a negative direction of movement from the cause to the effect, for example, the concept 'Use the account associated with the ID . . . use the stolen ID for further fraud' has a negative causal link with 'Get mortgage or loans', which implies that 'using the account associated with an ID' leads to fewer chances of getting a mortgage or loan. This automatically implies that the other pole, 'use the stolen ID for further fraud' may lead to more attempts at getting mortgage or loans. Similarly, positive links, indicated by the absence of any symbol along the arrow, show a positive direction of movement. For example, the concept 'Go for an extreme impact approach . . . go for a minor impact approach with less damage to lives' has a positive link with the concept 'Take on cyber terrorism . . . take on hacktivism'. In this case, going for an extreme-impact approach leads to more cyber terrorism and going for a minor impact approach leads to more hacktivism.

By facilitating continuous questioning of logical flows among concepts and allowing analyses of the hierarchy of means and ends, the cognitive map has helped bring about the following key insights on the nature of cyber crime:

1   The model revealed that there is quite a bit of overlap between hacktivism and cyber terrorism. Depending on the scale of the damage caused, one could classify a disruptive attack as either cyber terrorism or hacktivism. The methods used to cause disruption also show overlaps for the two type of crime. Therefore, instead of using separate concepts to represent the two, they were made two poles of the same concept. Ultimately, it is the final impact or damage caused that would determine if the cyber crime is perceived as an act of hacktivism or terrorism.

2   Hacktivists can also commit espionage in order to leak sensitive information. This is shown in the model through a link between hacktivism and espionage.

3   'Demanding political and social change' was added as the end motive to cyber terrorism and hacktivism.

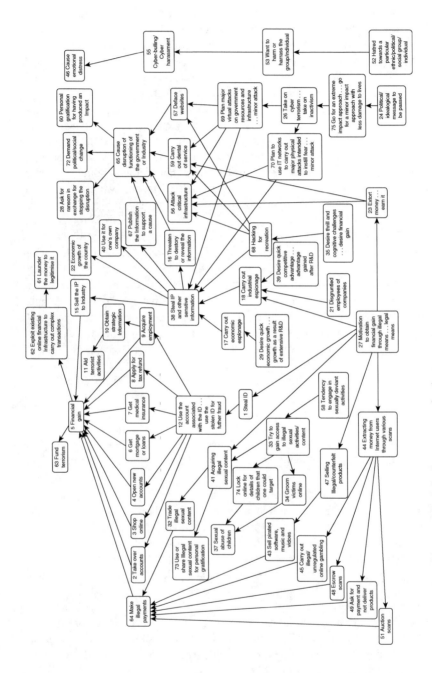

Figure 2.3 Cognitive mapping of cyber concepts for the taxonomy.

4   The current model makes a distinction between planning a purely virtual attack on key infrastructures and planning a physical attack by taking over the control systems of the target infrastructure. The latter is more damaging to life and property. The two attacks have very different impacts and therefore illustrating this difference in the model was important.

5   Child sexual abusers can use the internet as an aid to do two things: online grooming or getting details of children so that they could meet them in person to groom them in the physical world. This distinction was added in the model.

6   Money laundering through electronic transfers is an issue that is often over-looked. However, it is a growing problem within the financial sector and as such I added it to the model.

By observing two emergent properties of the cognitive map, i.e. clustering and hierarchy, further considerations for the taxonomy were extracted. Observing how concepts cluster around one another helps classify cyber crimes of a similar nature into the same category. Analysing the hierarchy of concepts helps understand the drivers and objectives of these crimes. Therefore, it helps find overlaps in certain types of crimes related to common motivations and common impacts.[42] The final cognitive map reveals the following about the different types of crime in the financial sector. By observing the emerging clusters alone, the following were the broad categories of cyber crime identified in the map:

1   ID theft;
2   espionage;
3   cyber terrorism and hacktivism;
4   online scams;
5   use and distribution of illegal sexual content and sexual offences;
6   hate crimes.

When, however, I added the output of the hierarchical analysis considering the interaction of clustering of concepts, I identified the following similarities in motivations and/or end results of certain types of cyber crime:

•   Both cyber terrorism and hacktivism have similar motives and end results, only the severity of the impact and the means chosen to commit them differed. In this regard, recreational hacking is motivated by factors other than financial gain, yet might produce the same result as terrorism, i.e. disruption to normal life. Extortion could also cause disruption but this tends to be more limited. In addition, it is mainly motivated by financial gain.

•   ID theft was a core concept in the map and has two key motivations: one is financial gain; the other is to use the stolen ID to fake one's identity to obtain a visa or employment. This difference therefore leads to two sub-categories of ID theft. Within the sub-category of ID theft motivated by financial gain, the three major categories of ID theft are: direct crimes committed on the user accounts; indirect crimes by using the stolen details for further fraud that involves financial gain (such as obtaining loans); and tax-refund fraud.

- Online scams where end-users are unaware of the trap placed in front of them are different from selling counterfeit products where a good percentage of end-users are aware that they are being sold a fake product at a cheaper price. However, both types of crime lead towards a common end, i.e. making illegal payments and therefore misusing financial products.
- Both hate crime (through cyber bullying and cyber harassment) and child sexual abuse are targeted at individuals or small groups. Both of them involve exchange of illegal content on the internet by targeting certain types of individuals. Hence, the two are similar in the means used. The trading of illegal sexual content has financial motivations and is different from the previous two, but can still be considered as an offence involving distribution of illegal content. These crimes can then be classified based on those that are only obscene and illegal in content and those that are targeted against and cause harm to individuals.
- Economic espionage and industrial espionage are similar in the way they are carried out, but different in the final objectives. While economic espionage aims at using the stolen information for large-scale changes such as economic growth and military advantage, industrial espionage can be carried out for direct financial gain, competitive advantage of one's own company and for other petty things such as payback from unhappy employees.
- Money laundering was observed to be very high up in the hierarchy. This indicated that several of the cyber crimes at the bottom of the map could be committed to lead up to money laundering. This called for treating it as a separate category of cyber crime altogether.

With the help of the above emergent concepts, clusters and hierarchies, I have developed in the following section the final taxonomy of cyber crime in the financial sector identifying the key categories and sub-categories of cyber crime based on the nature of the crime.

A taxonomy based on the nature of crime

As underlined earlier in the chapter, criminals have many broad motivations to commit cyber crime: financial, political, economic or even recreational. Depending on their capabilities and the loopholes they can find in the technological and social systems, they choose various 'criminal channels' to achieve their ends and satisfy their motivations. Cyber crime, in the present era, has provided new opportunities to meet these ends. This section deals with the classification of cyber crime in the financial sector based on the channels that criminals choose in order to meet their broad and primary motivation using such resources and skills as they possess. These channels can be collectively referred to as the nature of the crime. Technology is only a means and, at most, a proxy[43] within these channels. It plays the mediator role in one or more criminal activities leading to the achievement of the criminal's main objectives. Understanding these channels offers greater insights into what criminals will target and how they will execute their crimes in the financial sector given a set of resources and means available to them. Hence this understanding, if properly applied, could lead to the development of more effective and comprehensive countermeasure strategies.

Using the findings from the cognitive mapping, I have developed and presented a taxonomy for financial cyber crime based on the nature of crime. This taxonomy is aligned with the European Convention on Cybercrime (2001).[44] I have selected the European Convention on Cybercrime as the starting point for the taxonomy since it is an established legal instrument, provides the foundation and the initial minimum standards for the criminalisation of cyber crime, and is widely recognised. Furthermore, its four large categories can be adapted for different sectors and recent cyber-crime developments.[45]

Before turning to the classification based on the nature of cyber crime, it is, however, necessary to identify some of the main means of carrying out cyber crimes in the financial sector. The following is a list of the most commonly used means. The list is not meant to be comprehensive. Rather, it provides a selection of what the literature and our interviewers think are the most common methods of carrying out cyber-criminal activities in the financial sector. Although the list is less useful in relation to countermeasures (since it mainly focuses on technology rather than dealing with further criminal objectives), it does, at least, provide an indication of the starting point of the crime (i.e. phishing can lead to ID theft) and the kind of specialised skills that individuals or groups need in order to carry out certain types of crime.

Unauthorised and unlawful access, alteration of data or software: The obtaining of unlawful access to a computer system and/or IT systems, data and software by an unauthorised person. Such unauthorised users would include employees, spies and cyber criminals.[46] It would also include attacks on critical infrastructures such as the blocking of payment systems and, therefore, of financial transfers. Process-control systems that control critical infrastructures can be manipulated if the authentication for these devices is obtained or hacked into. Moreover, control systems of infrastructures are connected to the internet for better remote access. Therefore, access to these systems is becoming easy for attackers.[47]

Misuse of devices: The possession, production, sale, procurement for use, import, distribution or otherwise making available of a device (hardware or software), designed or adapted primarily for conducting a crime constitutes misuse of a device.[48] Cyber crime can be committed using only fairly basic equipment since criminals may make use of a device's computing power for crypto-currency mining or to break into digital right management systems.

Malware: 'Malware is a general term for a piece of software inserted into an information system to cause harm to that system or other systems, or to subvert them for use other than that intended by their owners.'[49]

Keystroke loggers: These are used to record passwords that are entered into the computer.[50] They can be installed in a system via email and are mostly used for ID theft by capturing passwords from systems.[51]

Virus: A virus is a computer program that replicates itself from one file to another within a computer or from system to system without the user's knowledge. A worm is a type of virus that makes copies of itself from computer to computer.[52]

Trojan: A Trojan is a virus that infiltrates a system without the user's knowledge and remains in the system. The victim may never realise that his or her system has been infected. Trojans either destroy or modify system data or they transfer sensitive data to another system.[53]

Denial of service: A denial-of-service attack occurs when access to a network or system is blocked or disrupted intentionally. It works by sending large traffic into a network from multiple computers to disrupt its functioning.[54]

Phishing: It is the main means of identity-related crime.[55] It involves tricking victims into revealing personal information through emails and websites that appear to be legitimate.[56] In a 'phishing' attack, fraudsters pretend to be calling from the bank and ask the customer for account or other details.

Spam: 'Spamming is the distribution of unsolicited bulk emails that contain invitations to participate in ways to earn money, obtain free products and services.'[57]

Botnets: Malware is used to infect computers and organise them into a network of thousands of computers under the hacker's control[58] to carry out different types of attacks such as denial of service, phishing, fraud, spam, etc. These networks are called botnets.

As discussed in detail earlier, the development and application of a useful and reliable taxonomy of cyber crime is a complex matter. Many approaches have been proposed with a variety of starting points. That described below is the taxonomy of the broad types of cyber crime in the financial sector based on the nature of the crime committed. As I have argued throughout this chapter, attention to the nature of cyber crime is useful for the development of more effective countermeasures to reduce the risk of cyber crime in general. Furthermore, my taxonomy has been developed with both a focus on the financial sector as main reference and a recognition of the need for a more comprehensive approach. For this reason, cyber crimes that do not directly target financial products, organisation institutions or financial customers have also been included. These types of cyber crime might have a lower level of relevance for the financial sector, but they could still be important to understand how to fight cyber crime targeting the financial sector. This is for several reasons. First, financial products (i.e. credit card, online payment systems, etc.) might be used to monetise the output of these less relevant cyber-criminal activities. Second, these less relevant cyber crimes might be connected with and/or be enabling more relevant financial cyber crime therefore highlighting the need to intervene on other cyber crimes as additional countermeasures. Ignoring the interplay between cyber-criminal activities risks overlooking opportunities to fight back.

For each broader category in the taxonomy I have developed sub-categories when relevant and provided a short description for each of them. Table 2.2 later in the chapter presents the taxonomy based on the nature of the cyber crimes involved in the form of a table while also overlaying the key categories in the ways discussed here.

Identity-related crimes

Identity theft is a growing problem that has been affecting consumer confidence in online businesses globally.[59] ID theft is usually carried out via credit-card numbers, passwords, bank account details, etc. The information gathered this way is either sold to those who are able to commit direct financial fraud on the account or to data brokers who collect the information and sell it to criminals. Compromised private information obtained through ID theft is highly profitable, serving as the prime motivation behind the steadily increasing number of ID-related criminal activities.[60] ID theft is usually a precursor of further crime such as financial fraud or even terrorism after gaining strategic access to gov-ernment agencies using a false identity. Major motives behind identity theft are financial fraud (in most of the cases), selling the stolen information and hiding one's own identity.[61] The personal information can be used in tax-refund fraud, insurance fraud and even illegal immigration, where the criminal attempts to hide his or her original identity.[62] In this chapter, all the crimes involving ID theft can be referred to using the broad term 'ID-related crimes'.

Phishing is the most common method used to obtain personal details. Although, as described earlier, the term 'phishing' generally refers to a social-engineering scheme in which cyber victims are tricked into revealing personal information by receiving fake emails or being lured into fake websites, it can include the use of phone calls that trick victims into revealing sensitive information.[63] Malware is another method whereby the security of the system is compromised and the data from the computer are forwarded to the attackers.[64]

There are several sub-categories of identity-related crimes. Ali Hedayati described some of the most common identity theft types of crime and they are listed below.[65]

Account-related fraud

Personal information is obtained through various social-engineering methods including redirecting internet users to fraudulent websites in order to acquire their personal information.[66] Using the stolen information, fraudsters usually take over existing accounts and withdraw money before they can get caught. Sometimes, they open new accounts under the victim's name and then change the billing information in order to hide their activities from the victim. Online businesses can also be defrauded through payments made using stolen or forged credit cards. Online shopping is one such activity where the fraudster uses the victim's information from a different location to makes a purchase and delivery to another, anonymous, location.[67]

Acquiring financial products

Criminals use the victim's personal information to obtain mortgages and loans. This could also be done using fictitious personal details. The insurance industry faces significant amount of ID-related crime involving the theft of customers' information in order to make false insurance claims.[68]

Acquiring employment and key positions or immigration status

International criminals, terrorists and illegal immigrants use stolen or fake identities to obtain a passport to cover up their past records. Government institutions carry out criminal-record checks. In order to evade such checks, fraudsters use stolen identities when obtaining employment. Terrorists may attempt to get employment in strategic organisations using false identities, posing a serious threat to national security.[69]

Tax-refund fraud

ID fraudsters use victims' identities such as employment records or social-insurance numbers to file their income taxes to receive victims' tax refunds.[70]

ID-related frauds can vary greatly in impact, ranging from the loss on a single bank account to infiltration into strategic government agencies. Although the majority of ID-related cases are financially motivated, the increasing number of cases suggests that the ease of stealing identity could be exploited to aid terrorism and threaten national security.

Disruptive attacks

Another category of cyber crime involves attacks that cause disruption to financial businesses, government activities or the normal functioning of society. The motivations for these crimes are different depending on their intended impact on the financial sector and society overall. However, all such attacks have one thing in common: the need to cause disruption in order to draw attention to the attacker's objectives. This section discusses the disruptive forms of cyber attacks that we see today across the globe and which are relevant for the financial sector.

Recreational hacking

The term 'hacker' was originally used to describe a person who was capable of coming up with 'technically elegant software solutions'. However, the usage of the term has evolved now to most often describe individuals who 'deliberately attempt to gain unauthorised access to computer systems'.[71] Over time, the term 'hacker' has developed negative connotations. Nowadays, hackers are even perceived as a threat to national security.[72]

Many hacking activities stem from a sense of cognitive challenge felt by the hacker. Studies showed that hackers are eager to understand the complexities of the systems they work with and ready to take up challenges while pushing limits.[73] Winning respect in the hacking community is also a strong motivation of hackers.[74] There is another class of hackers called the 'thrill-seekers' who derive pleasure from the risks and the chase associated with hacking activities.[75] Such hackers commit crimes not only for the fun of it but also because they feel they can emerge unscathed because of the vastness of the internet. After the first anti-malware programs were released, there were hackers who developed viruses just for the sake of exploring the weaknesses in security systems rather than for financial gain. There are fewer such hackers today and more of the financially motivated ones. The few hackers who still search only for security loopholes generally do so to inform manufacturers of the need to develop better security.[76] Apart from these recreational hackers, who mostly work alone or as part of small hacking communities, there are financially motivated hackers who are hired by international criminals or terrorist organisations to carry out various tasks that only specialised individuals can perform.[77] Financially motivated hacking, on the one hand, is addressed within this category of our taxonomy because it is normally only an initial step in various other types of cyber crime such as ID fraud or espionage. Recreational hacking, on the other hand, is an objective in its own right for hackers who seek thrills and cognitive challenges. Regardless of the motivation, such hacking causes major disruption and costs to businesses and infrastructure.

Hacktivism

The word hacktivist combines 'activist' and 'hacker'. Hacktivists are created when activists try to spread their political or social message by hacking into business and government networks and revealing sensitive information. Unlike for the majority of present-day hackers, financial gain is not the primary motive of hacktivists. Their motivations are mostly political or ideological. For example, there are many hacktivist groups that fight for the freedom of information and, therefore, attack business and government systems in order to reveal sensitive information.[78] Hacktivism uses techniques such as web-defacement, distributed denial of service, email bombs and viruses to publicise its various ideological causes.[79] Hacktivism is usually carried out through denial-of-service attacks, web-defacement and unauthorised access to system and data. Certain hacktivists also hack into industry systems to reveal lax security on the part of the company.[80] There is a clear distinction between hacktivism and terrorism. Terrorism is more extreme and generally aims at a larger and more damaging impact than hacktivism. While hacktivism's usual objective is to draw attention to a cause through relatively minor disruption, terrorism strives both to instil fear and cause maximum damage and destruction. Nonetheless, what may be an act of hacktivism to some, may be an act of terrorism to another. A terrorist could also carry out cyber terrorism while, at the same time, spreading propaganda on the web in much the same way as a hacktivist.[81]

Extortion

A denial-of-service attack can cause severe disruption in the functioning of financial organisations, not to mention loss of business and reputation. Some cyber attacks are carried out in order to ask for a ransom in exchange for ending the attack or the public dissemination of sensitive information on the attack and/or the business.[82]

Cyber terrorism

Some cyber terrorism strives to destroy critical infrastructures, causing breakdown of payment systems nationally and globally, economic market functioning as well as the compromise of government networks and data.[83] The remote-attack capabilities of the internet can facilitate the takeover of infrastructures critical to the financial sector and state, using this control to cause widespread disruption and damage. An example would be taking control of a stock exchange's IT infrastructures globally to immobilise market functioning, using this control to make terrorists' political (as opposed to merely financial) demands.

Espionage and stealing of intellectual property

Stealing sensitive information from companies and organisations in the financial and/or other sectors as well as from government has become easier with the digitisation of data and growth of IT technologies within organisations. A US Counter-Intelligence Executive report stated that, for the cyber attacker, sensitive information of interest may be business information about scarce resources or new products or information that would help foreign competitors gain an edge in order to win private and public contracts in the targeted nation. Of course, information relevant to national security such as military technologies is also extremely valuable for espionage purposes. Technologies within fast-growth sectors such as the financial, energy and pharmaceutical sectors are also targets for espionage. Furthermore, a target that is considered to be critical is information and communication technology since it is the 'backbone of every other technology' and is used across many other sectors and in the military. Trade-secret theft affects corporate job creation, revenues, growth, innovation and national security.[84]

The US Economic Espionage Act of 1996 distinguishes between economic espionage and industrial espionage. Economic espionage refers to state-sponsored espionage carried out for purposes related to national security. However, some countries believe that, since national security depends on economic security, it is the government's role to develop and nurture indigenous industries by stealing the intellectual property of other countries. However, since such stealing of intellectual property leads to an economy where innovation is not encouraged, it can, in turn, lead to slow growth of the national economy.[85]

According to a report issued by the US Counter-Intelligence Executive, China has been the biggest player in industrial espionage with many intrusions into private networks suspected to originate from China. Intelligence agencies in Russia are also suspected of carrying out economic espionage against both European countries and the United States.[86]

By industrial espionage, hackers try remotely to gain unauthorised access to the digitally stored intellectual property of business competitors in order to gain a competitive advantage.[87] The main objectives of industrial espionage are to undermine a marketing campaign, save money on research and development and obtain a competitive advantage in winning contract bids.[88] Hacktivism differs from cyber espionage not in the means but in its final objective. The objective in this case is to hack into government or corporate systems in order to reveal sensitive information to the public for political reasons. WikiLeaks was a typical example of such a modus operandi.[89]

Exploiting existing financial structures

Money laundering and financial exchange

Money laundering is a method of legitimising money obtained through illicit means. It tends to follow a three-step process, which is mainly used by large criminal organisations, including terrorist groups. The first step is called 'placing' and involves the depositing of illegally obtained funds in financial institutions. Next comes 'layering', the distancing of illicit proceeds from their sources using a series of complex financial transactions. The final step is called 'integrating', making the money appear legitimate through further, legitimate, transactions.[90]

Online financial services provide the means of making multiple, worldwide financial transactions very quickly, without any need for physical monetary transactions. The development of online payment systems has made it easier to carry out cross-border monetary transactions in poorly regulated jurisdictions with complete anonymity and where all that is required from a new customer is an identification code.[91] Some e-payment systems even allow the opening of anonymous accounts. Prepaid payment cards can also be used to carry out anonymous transactions. The lack of clear governance and understanding of all the main components and intervening actors in cross-border online payment services also make it difficult fully to track these activities. Jurisdictional arbitrage (discussed earlier in this chapter) is another means that has been exploited by e-payment service companies that register their business in countries where e-payments are lightly regulated. Online gambling and shopping sites also provide the means for money laundering. Furthermore, human so-called 'money mules' are recruited online through spam mails and made to open accounts and make transfers to required accounts in different places. These money mules open bank accounts and receive funds from compromised accounts (as a result of ID theft) or in the form of cash or wire transfers. They then transfer money to the ultimate recipient's account through traditional financial structures.[92]

Content-related offences

The term 'content-related offenses' was proposed by David Wall.[93] There are two broad areas of concern relating to content-related cyber crimes: so-called cyber obscenity and violent behaviour online. Cyber obscenity involves trading in illegal sexually expressive materials, including child pornography, in cyberspace. What may be illegal in one country might not be so in another country. Both criminal groups and individuals engage in the distribution and/or use of illegal sexual material. On the one hand, the criminal groups are motivated by financial gain and lure people through spam mails. On the other hand, individuals who indulge in such activities are usually sex offenders.[94] Sex offenders or child abusers sometimes try to locate child victims online through different means: targeting young people through chatting and social networking, sharing material with like-minded people or by identifying countries to which they can travel in order to abuse or exploit children.[95]

Cyber violence refers to the violent impact of the cyber activities of individuals or groups on other individuals or socio-political groups. Even though cyber violence may not physically harm the victim, it can cause long-term psychological damage. Cyber violence is done through cyber stalking, cyber bullying and hate-speech.[96] Cyber bullying is targeted at minors, whereas similar activities carried out against adults are termed as cyber harassment or cyber stalking.[97] Hate-speech, harassment or the dissemination of extremist political messages may be carried out online by individuals as well as various activist organisations.[98]

Although content-related and cyber violence-related offences do not directly affect the financial sector, they could create opportunities for more financially relevant crime to happen. For instance, small criminal groups might start with less complicated crimes before moving on to more complex criminal operations. Small criminal groups in Russia initially started with child pornography and used online casinos as an easy way to launder the money earned from child pornography.[99] Furthermore, financial products, offline and online, could unknowingly facilitate the perpetration of this type of cyber crime when payments for the provision of the illegal services (i.e. child pornography) are required. Finally, the perpetration of content-related cyber offences can provide a forum to groups and individuals involved in such crimes for soliciting, offers and incitement to commit other cyber crimes.

Online scams and piracy

The market for online gambling was estimated at US$12 billion in 2005, accounting for nearly half of the global market. Out of all online gaming sites, unlicensed sites represent 90 per cent of the relevant market.[100] Among the vast array of online gambling sites, there are many fictitious gambling companies engaging in money laundering and fraud. They are registered anonymously and carry out transactions via offshore accounts or electronic payment companies such as PayPal. These bogus sites do not pay out winners on any fair basis. Some organised criminal groups manipulate the game or pay out at predetermined and artificial rates in order to make money. Russian criminal groups, such as Russian Business Network and Yambo Financial, began criminal activities through child pornography and online casinos. Fictitious online gambling is considered to be a very profitable criminal activity.[101] Apart from these types of criminal activity, online auction scams are also a common activity. Online auction sites such as eBay have warned customers of account takeovers and fake auctions carried out under the compromised account holder's name.[102] Common methods employed by criminals for online auction scams include the so-called 'travelling salesman'. The seller will tell the victim that he/she has to leave the country for an emergency and, therefore, the victim will have to wire the money to an overseas account. The wire transferred money is never recovered. The fraudsters will always try to get the victim to wire transfer the money. In some cases, they offer losing bidders of legitimate auctions a chance to buy the item but on condition of having to wire transfer the money. After the victim makes the wire transfer, the fraudster disappears.[103] These scams seem to be carried out by criminal groups rather than individuals due to the coordinated effort required in order to lure victims and beguile them into successfully transferring the money.

Many online sites sell counterfeit products to gullible customers at attractive prices.[104] Online vendors also sell fake passports, cheques and diplomas.[105] Criminals sometimes make payments with fake cheques for more than the transaction amount. The victim is then asked to wire the excess amount back.[106] Selling of fake anti-virus software and codes that often infect the victims' computers is another widespread criminal activity in Russia.[107] Spam is often used to advertise products that are fake or of poor quality. Among the many sales offers contained in spam mails, there are a lot of advertisements for hazardous or fake pharmaceutical products that may cause severe harm to the buyers.[108]

As with content-related fraud, although these online-scam offences do not directly affect the financial sector, they could create opportunities for crime of more relevance to the financial sector to happen. Furthermore, the use of financial products, both online and offline, is necessary to monetise the illegal activities.

Table 2.2 illustrates the taxonomy of cyber crime based on the nature of crime overlaid with the main methods used to commit the crime.

Table 2.2 Taxonomy of financial cyber crime based on the nature of crime

Channel based on nature	Means
1. ID related fraud	Unauthorised and unlawful access, alteration of data or software, misuse of devices, phishing, malware, trojan, virus, keystroke loggers

Account related financial fraud
    Account take-over
    Opening new account
    Online shopping
Acquiring financial products
    Mortgage fraud
    Insurance fraud
Acquiring employment, key positions or immigration status
Tax refund fraud	

2. Disruptive attacks	Unauthorised and unlawful access, alteration of data or software, misuse of devices, denial of service, web defacement, botnets
Recreational hacking *Hacktivism* *Extortion* *Cyber terrorism*	
3. Espionage and stealing intellectual property	Unauthorised and unlawful access, alteration of data or software, misuse of devices, phishing, malware, trojan, virus
Economic espionage *Industrial espionage*	
4. Exploiting existing financial infrastructures	Complex legitimate transactions exploiting the online financial infrastructure
Money laundering	
5. Content related crime (indirectly related to financial cyber crime)	Spam, web-redirection
Obscenity Trading illegal sexual material Trading illegal sexual services	Spam, web-redirection
6. Online scams and piracy crime (indirectly related to financial cyber crime)	Spam, web-redirection

Piracy
Selling counterfeit products
    CD and software pirating
    Scams
Online gambling fraud
    E-auction scams	

Key players in cyber crime

As initially brought to attention by the Confederation of British Industry in 2000, attackers in the most serious cyber crimes were: hackers (44.8 per cent); former employees (13.4 per cent); organised criminal groups (12.8 per cent); current employees (11.5 per cent); customers (7.9 per cent); competitors (5.8 per cent); political and protest groups (2.6 per cent); and terrorists (1.4 per cent).[109]

Bearing this in mind, cyber criminals can be broadly classified into four general types, often interacting with each other:

1   international criminal organisations;
2   foreign intelligence agencies (i.e. states);
3   individuals and small criminal groups (opportunistic or planned attacks); and
4   legitimate organisations.

International criminal organisations

Many international criminal organisations, some backed up by rogue states, have specialised IT departments run by hired hackers to bring in revenue through a wide array of cyber-criminal activities. An example is the Russian mafia. Following the 1998 financial crisis, which left many programmers and highly qualified individuals out of work, there was a hacking boom in Russia. This, coupled with a rampant corruption in Russia, led several of these highly IT skilled individuals either to start their own cyber-crime businesses or to join traditional criminal organisations. These companies are protected by the Federal Security Service against extradition in return for their agreement not to attack government IT infrastructure. In recent years, more than 75 per cent of science and technology graduates from Russia have been unable to obtain employment. This has led to the opening of so-called 'hacker schools' that provide hacking lessons and direct the students towards various criminal organisations.[110]

Another example of traditional international criminal organisations involved in cyber crime is the Chinese triads. They have started to use specialists in IT pirating. These specialists are also hired to carry out distributed denial-of-service attacks against commercial sites for ransom.[111]

Within this type of cyber criminal grouping, I have also included virtual criminal networks. This is a more recent phenomenon. Such virtual criminal networks can have thousands of members. Ordinarily, however, this kind of cyber crime involves 10 to 30 network members specialising in different areas such as hacking, spamming, denial of service, etc. These core members supervise the activities in their area of expertise and settle member disputes. Virtual cyber-criminal networks are different from traditional organised crime groups in that the members do not meet in person but, rather, meet in a web forum where members are only known by their cyber nicknames. Sophisticated virtual networks carry out thorough background checks before accepting a new member to ensure that they are not connected to law enforcement. Highly sophisticated and elite criminal networks that are highly secretive operate within a cellular structure and do not solicit new potential members online.[112]

Finally, there are also many international hacker groups such as the Lizard Squad and the Cult of the Dead Cow. These should be regarded as international criminal organisations. These hacker groups tend to believe in the free flow of information and uncensored communication. They carry out defacement of sites to pass on their message. Their ultimate aim is to deregulate the copyright system, abolish patenting and reduce internet surveillance. These international groups can be large but their life span is often limited with such hacker groups splitting up once their common purpose has been served.[113]

Foreign intelligence agencies

Stealing intellectual property is considered by some governments as a helpful means of boosting national economic output without the cost of research and development.[114] Intellectual property may also be stolen with the specific objective of helping the home-country bidders win international contracts.[115] For this purpose, foreign intelligence agencies of countries such as China and Russia, and also those of some western democracies, have been engaging in industrial and military espionage. Several cyber experts believe that the Chinese intelligence agency is using Chinese citizens in the US with corporate insider connections to carry out economic espionage.[116]

In addition, covert intelligent cyber operations, organised and/or sponsored by national agencies, may themselves cross grey lines. As the Snowden revelations[117] indicate, information warfare can reach levels that are questionable from both national and international legal standpoints.[118] Less democratic governments are also heavily involved in legally debatable cyber attacks. For instance, one large-scale state-sponsored instance, called Titan Rain,[119] occurred over a three-year period commencing in 2003.[120] The attacks seemed to be targeted at US defence-contractor websites and were widely alleged to be the work of the Chinese military. While the stories of 'Unit 61398' of the Chinese Army are numerous, a larger and more legally insidious example of state-sponsored cyber attacks is that undertaken by Russia (on the Russian attacks see Chapters 1, 4 and 5).[121] More recently the US Department of Homeland Security (DHS) issued a bulletin to cyber security insiders reporting that a destructive malware program known as 'BlackEnergy' had been placed in key US infrastructure systems that control everything from telecommunications and power transmission grids to water, oil and natural gas distribution systems and some nuclear plants. The DHS bulletin added that a group of Russian cyber spies known as 'Sandworm' inserted or attempted to insert the same 'BlackEnergy' malware this year in systems belonging to NATO and several European energy and telecommunication firms.[122] All these examples demonstrate the blurring of the line between cyber warfare and cyber crime: 'It really is more murky, the difference between where a cyber criminal hack ends and where some type of state or state-sponsored event begins'.[123] Indeed, criminal prosecution of state players might not be far away.

In May 2014, US Attorney for Western Pennsylvania, David Hickton, brought indictments against five members of China's People's Liberation Army, alleging that they had stolen documents and internal communications from companies such as US Steel, Alcoa and Westinghouse as well as the United Steelworkers of America.[124]

It also appears that the main customers for cyber-crime malware writing are often governments.[125] For instance, serious doubts have been raised about the collaboration of the US and Israeli governments with the cyber underworld in the case of Stuxnet.[126] Several security experts are convinced that two different Ukraine-based malware factories were behind the coding of Stuxnet, acting as effective 'sub-contractors' for the US and Israeli governments.[127]

Finally, I could not rule out the possibility that a government-built malware and/or cyber weapon will run out of control. Again this has already happened with Stuxnet, which infected IT systems in different countries, not just the particular systems it was designed to target.[128]

Individuals and small groups

Individuals and small criminal groups commit cyber crime mostly for financial gain. However, individual cyber criminals can also include paedophiles, recreational hackers or hacktivists. These attacks may be planned or opportunistic. They may or may not be sophisticated depending on the individual's or small group's resources. However, their influence and size will grow relative to the individual's or group's cash inflow.[129] Common cyber crimes committed by these groups and individuals include financial fraud including ID theft, extortion, data theft, online scams, etc. As already argued, small groups might start with less complicated crimes to move to more complex criminal operations.[130]

More recently, socially/politically motivated and/or recreational hacking is also growing among individuals and small groups. In many countries, hackers have managed to find legitimate employment, even after getting caught, as their expertise is often indispensable. Although hacking may be viewed in a negative light by law-enforcement agencies, the general public's perception of hackers is that of a 'positive delinquent'. In a survey conducted in China in 2005, it was revealed that people view hackers with the same respect as that of rock stars. In Russia, where violent crimes are rampant, people are least bothered about online crimes as they do not cause bloodshed.[131]

Legitimate organisations

Certain legitimate organisations, such as private companies, commit intellectual property theft or industrial espionage in order to increase their competitive advantage. Although most organisations would not engage in such activities due to the heavy reputational damages such activities can entail, increasing competition and poor market conditions could put certain companies under pressure to increase performance in the global market and to use illegal means to do so.[132]

In general, large criminal organisations have the resources (including often support from the state) to carry out all the key steps involved in cyber crime, whereas individuals or small groups may only be able to carry out a single step, such as data theft before selling on the data to a data broker. Evidently, there is a hierarchy of potential criminal players with international criminal organisations and states having the best resources to support and coordinate the activities of local organisations, which in turn control small criminal groups and individual hackers. All these players and/or groups can also exist independently without having to depend on a bigger organisation. For instance, 'hacktivists' might exist independently and promote their cause without involving themselves with large criminal networks. The pyramid in Figure 2.4 shows the hierarchy of cyber-criminal players. The area of each horizontal section gives an idea of the proportion of such players potentially involved in cyber-criminal activities. For example, a single state can have affiliations with two criminal organisations and each of them can employ five to six small organisations, which in turn might employ ten hackers each. Therefore, one large-scale criminal activity can be committed through the efforts of a large number of hackers, a few criminal organisations and one rogue state. Remove the rogue state and the international criminal organisation from the picture, and we might be left with a large number of unemployed hackers. It is unclear how many of them would shift to committing crime alone once they are no longer employed by a rogue state and/or criminal organisations.

To extract additional insights from our taxonomy, I have overlaid it with reference to the key players (individuals, small groups, international criminal organisations or the state) that tend to commit such a crime in Table 2.3. Two ticks against a player indicates that this player is, most of the time, merely a pawn in the crime, employed by the higher player in the pyramid (Figure 2.4). The final categorisation of each crime will then be related to the highest-level player and not the pawn who is merely hired to provide technical expertise or support.

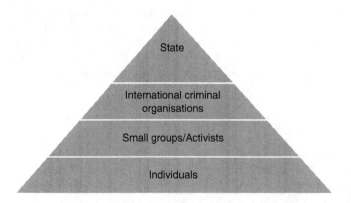

Figure 2.4 Key players in cyber crime.

Table 2.3 Matrix of taxonomy of cyber crime vs cyber players

Types of crime / Criminal entity	State	International criminal organisation	Small criminal groups	Individuals
1. ID related fraud				
Account related financial fraud				
Account take-over		✔	✔	✔
Opening new account		✔	✔	✔
Online shopping			✔	✔
Acquiring financial products				
Mortgage fraud		✔	✔	✔
Medical insurance fraud		✔	✔	✔
Acquiring employment, key positions or immigration status	✔	✔	✔	✔
Tax refund fraud		✔	✔	✔
2. Disruptive attacks				
Recreational hacking			✔	✔
Hacktivism			✔	✔
Extortion		✔	✔	✔
Cyber terrorism	✔	✔	✔	✔ ✔
3. Espionage				
Economic, political and military espionage (traditional intelligence)	✔	✔	✔ ✔	✔ ✔
Industrial espionage		✔	✔	✔
4. Exploiting existing financial infrastructure				
Money laundering		✔	✔	✔ ✔
5. Content related crime				
Obscenity				
Trading illegal sexual material		✔	✔	✔
Sexual services		✔	✔	✔
Cyber-violence and harm				
Hate speech			✔	✔
Cyber bullying			✔	✔
Conspiring to commit crime through social networking and other internet services		✔	✔	✔ ✔

(continued)

Table 2.3 (continued)

Types of crime \ Criminal entity	State	International criminal organisation	Small criminal groups	Individuals
Cyber stalking			✔	✔
Child Abuse		✔	✔	✔
6. Online scams and piracy				
Piracy				
Selling counterfeit products		✔	✔	✔
CD and software pirating		✔	✔	✔
Scams				
Online gambling fraud		✔	✔	✔
E-auction scams		✔	✔	✔

Notes

✔ Indicates that the end channel/objective of that crime is the driving motivation for the criminal player that commits the crime.

✔ ✔ Indicates that the criminal player is merely a rent player in the larger criminal activity. Here, the criminal player has no direct relation to the end channel /objective of the crime.

What does all this mean for countermeasures and managing risk?

Given its complex nature, there is currently uncertainty about the effectiveness of existing responses to cyber crime in the financial sector and other key sectors of our society. Existing attempts to fight cyber-criminal activities have been deemed only partially effective and have usually provided only short-lived results. Efforts tend also to focus only on single-domain measures, whether legislative, technological and social or organisational and cultural in nature. Given the interdependent and multifaceted nature of cyber crime, anti-cyber-crime responses need to be based on multi-actor cooperation, which will enable a full range of integrated responses to cyber-crime threats.[133] This implies the need for a comprehensive and integrative approach to cyber security that cuts across traditional boundaries between the international and domestic and between the private and public spheres.

From a legislative perspective, the development and effective implementation of common and international legal frameworks have proved difficult. After a few years of preparatory work, the 2001 European Convention on Cybercrime, as it has come to be known, finally came into force in 2004. The document attempted to develop policies to prevent computer-related crimes and to aid extradition procedures. The Convention serves as a framework for international policies on cyber crime and is the first document that addresses cyber crime from a global perspective.[134] It also gives the police powers to investigate crimes committed across national borders. Additional protocols, added later, address transmission of racist and xenophobic materials. However, as of December 2014, the Convention has been ratified by only 44 states and signed by 9 others. So-called 'problem countries' (e.g. Yemen and North Korea) have not signed the European Convention. It is just these countries that most need to sign the Convention in order for it to be effective. Otherwise, cyber criminals will simply route their activities through problem countries or rouge states.[135] In addition, the provisions of the Convention have not really been implemented in half of the states that have ratified it.[136] What is more, definitions of cyber crime still vary from one jurisdiction to the other. For example, 'identity theft' is not criminalised in many European Union (EU) Member States.[137] Cyber criminals take advantage of this lack of harmonisation of relevant legal definitions between different legal jurisdictions. Most crimes are initiated from countries with poor cyber laws or inefficient law-enforcement systems.[138] Therefore, legal action against cyber criminals remains problematic. So far, there has been no effective international legal framework developed to overcome this problem.

Enforceability is also an issue. Although transnational law-enforcement units such as Interpol, Europol and Eurojust cooperate closely, their respective responsibilities need to be better defined.[139] Lack of harmonised legal definitions and legislation also has a negative impact on enforceability. Furthermore, some countries will investigate crimes more vigorously than others and not every country has the resources to enforce the laws. Many nations have not given priority to fighting cyber crime as they regard other issues as more important.[140]

In relation to anti-cyber-crime technologies and organisational responses, best practices and technological measures are often short-lived and fragmented, addressing only a part of the problem or a piece of the puzzle and neglecting to address interaction among different cyber crimes and players. Because cyber threats are relatively (although not entirely) new, financial organisations and institutions have not yet developed mature and comprehensive responses, developed and tested over time, which focus on the different channels and types of cyber crime. In addition, in accordance with the prevention or avoidance paradigm, which has dominated information security and security at large in the past decade, great emphasis has been put on preventing cyber crime.[141] The desire to pre-empt criticism of a financial organisation's poor security measures after a cyber attack has also contributed to a concentration on prevention. For instance, high-end security measures allow financial organisations to respond to any post-attack criticism with the argument that they did everything right but still could not prevent the breach of their cyber security systems. Being more protected than their competitors is often perceived as a means of marketing an organisation and its products as being safe. Any financial company that can afford high-end IT security systems will install them irrespective of whether they face serious cyber threats and/or of whether these measures are effective in fighting cyber crime.[142] However, as it has been said:

New threats will appear overnight that can't be predicted or easily prevented. Traditional risk management is insufficiently agile to deal with the potential impacts from activity in cyberspace. Enterprise risk management must be extended to organisational risk and cyber resilience.[143]

This move from a traditional risk management to an enterprise-management approach in cyber security is required for several reasons. First, traditional risk management tends to focus on pure risks, with each risk viewed separately, whereas enterprise risk management encompasses all risks across an enterprise both pure and speculative. The latter approach is much more appropriate in a cyber context where threats are speculative and unpredictable and in addition might affect the entire business due to their potential impact, ranging from direct (i.e. loss due to fraud, legal costs, etc.) to indirect losses (i.e. reputational damage, etc.). Indeed, cyber-risk management is no longer just a matter of protecting data and intellectual property, instead it should include the protection of brand and reputation – and ultimately stock price. Second, cyber threats are fast-moving and constantly changing; this calls for risk management approaches to become more resilient, based on a foundation of response preparedness. If risk cannot be avoided, greater attention should be given, within the risk-management frame-work, to fast recovery and quick responses based on a comprehensive response plan, which prioritises resilience assessment and adjustment capacity. Within the cyber sphere, the need for organisations to be resilient in the face of cyber attacks requires a move from fixed systems to dynamic, responsive infrastructures and new risk-management approaches. Harmonisation of EU resilience legislation and effective enforcement of such legislation across Europe is also required.[144] Other suggestions include: cyber security measures that combine biometrics and identity management for enhanced security; financial organisations and/or inter-net service providers (ISPs) requiring a clean up of malicious software from the users' systems as a requirement of user agreements.[145] Educating consumers in ID-related crime is another suggested approach.

Another important issue is the lack of coordination in the development of coun-termeasures. The presence of significant overlaps among different cyber crimes and players, as indicated in the above taxonomy, calls for greater coordination among financial companies and other key stakeholders in the public and private sectors. Effective protection of the cyberspace and its infrastructure requires the involvement of several stakeholders. No single financial organisation can make a significant impact on cyber crime by itself. Ad-hoc efforts work only partially and are typically short-lived. Instead, a coordinated, multi-stakeholder approach is required to share information, strategies, actions and post-action evaluation. Ideally, companies in the financial sector and beyond should share clear, concise records of threat information that pinpoint the 'who, what, why, where and how' of attacks with detailed information about impact, implemented actions and ex-post evaluation. Ex-post evaluation of the implemented actions and security poli-cies should be carried out and shared. Such evaluations will inevitably include a short-term view. However, they should also present some conclusions concerning the medium term, taking into account the specific nature of the cyber crime and source of the threats.[146] A typical example of collaboration would be establishing knowledge and data sharing among financial companies, law-enforcement agencies, network and hosting service providers, and domain registrars, in order to identify suspected domains. Such domains could then be shut down helping to stop cyber criminals upstream. This type of data and knowledge sharing would also facilitate criminal charges and arrests.[147] The need for cooperation has become even more prominent within cyber security studies. In a recent article, the suggested scope of this cooperation has been enlarged so as to include both voluntary cooperation as well as that legally required or encouraged through incentives for cooperation within the private, public and third sectors. It is hoped that consumers themselves might also play a role in fighting cyber crime but it is still unclear what and how. At this point in time, most consumers do not play an active role in fighting cyber crime as most crimes go unnoticed and/or unreported.[148] Mostly their role is limited to recouping their own individual financial losses, regaining control of lost identities and reclaiming hijacked bank accounts. These processes are themselves often mediated through other organisations (banks, ISPs, etc.).

Some coordination efforts have been building momentum but more cooperation is still needed.[149] Issues of trust and awareness, fears of losing control and competiveness, uncertainty about violating privacy legislation, and lack of incentives are all well-known barriers to multi-stakeholder cooperation in the financial sector. Above all, many industry players continue to believe that they might lose more as the result of loss of competitive edge by sharing their knowledge and data than they stand to lose as a result of cyber crime itself. Indeed, there is a tendency in the financial sector not to share information about cyber-crime incidents in order to protect reputation and market share. Furthermore, most financial companies are not incentivised to report cyber-crime attacks (e.g. ID theft). For instance, cyber crime is often written off as a cost of business due to lack of awareness of cyber-insurance products, perceived insurance cost, embedded practices or lack of flexible insurance options.[150] This distorts awareness of the real nature and dangers of cyber crime as well as implementation of effective responses. The existence of these barriers means that a better strategy for cooperation among the private sector, as well as among public and private sector, civil society and individuals, is still needed.[151] Of importance to the success of this strategy is the requirement to work out how to develop 'community building for information sharing'. This means working out how to build trust across similar and diverse stakeholders.

Finally, it is also paramount that security standards and guidelines should not stop or slow down the positive impact of cyberspace (e.g. economic growth and technological development) or reduce the trend towards resilience. There is the danger that an exaggerated concern with cyber security could reduce the generative potential of the internet – the ability to put information technology to many different, initially unforeseen, uses that has been identified as central to the development of the online economy.[152] Financial executives need to find the right balance between implementation of regulation, security, flexibility, cost–benefit considerations, resilience and openness of cyberspace.

Acknowledgements

This chapter draws on research performed as part of the E-CRIME project funded by the EU's Seventh Framework Programme for Security under grant agreement no. 607775. The author ran some of the analyses for research on behalf of Trilateral Research & Consulting LLP in collaboration with the London School of Economics and with the help of Nazneen Sherif.

Notes

1 Value networks are any web of relationships that generates both tangible and intangible value through complex dynamic exchanges between two or more individuals, groups or organisations. Any individual, organisation or group of organisations engaged in both tangible and intangible exchanges can be viewed as a value network, whether individual consumer, private industry, government or public sector.

2 Bauer, J.M., Van Eeten, M.J.G. and Chattopadhyay, T., 'ITU study on the financial aspects of network security: malware and spam', *ITU Report*, 2008. Available at: www.itu.int/ITU-D/cyb/cybersecurity/docs/itu-study-financial-aspects-of-malware-and-spam.pdf.

3 Moitra, S., 'Developing policies for cybercrime', *European Journal of Crime, Criminal Law and Criminal*, 13(3): 2005, pp. 435–64.

4 Williams, L., 'Catch me if you can: a taxonomically structured approach to cybercrime', Forum on Public Policy, 2008. Available at: http://forumonpublicpolicy.com/archivespring08/williamsly.pdf.

5 Moitra, 'Developing policies for cybercrime'.

6 Williams, 'Catch me if you can'.

7 Wall, D., 'Mapping out cyber crimes in a cyberspatial surveillant assemblage', in F. Webster and K. Ball (eds), *The Intensification of Surveillance: Crime, Terrorism, and Warfare in the Information Age*, London: Pluto, 2003, pp. 112–36.

8 Brenner, S.W., 'Cybercrime, cyberterrorism and cyberwarfare', *Revue Internationale de Droit Penal*, 77: 2006, pp. 453–71.

9 Ibid.

10 Ibid.

11 Howard, J., 'An analysis of security incidents on the internet, 1989–1995', Carnegie Mellon University, 1997. Available at: www.cert.org/archive/pdf/JHThesis.pdf.

12 Hansman, S. and Hunt, R., 'A taxonomy of network and computer attacks', *Computers & Security*, 21: 2005, pp. 31–43.

13 Kjaerland, M., 'A classification of computer security incidents based on reported attack data', *Journal of Investigative Psychology and Offender Profiling*, 2: 2005, pp. 105–20.

14 Howard, 'An analysis of security incidents on the internet'.

15 Hansman and Hunt, 'A taxonomy of network and computer attacks'.

16 Kjaerland, 'A classification of computer security incidents'.

17 Landreth, B., *Out of the Inner Circle: A Hacker's Guide to Computer Security*, Bellevue, WA: Microsoft Press, 1985.

18 Rogers, M., 'A two-dimensional circumplex approach to the development of a hacker taxonomy', *Digital Investigation*, 3: 2006, pp. 97–102; Meyers, C., Powers, S. and Faissol, D., 'Taxonomies of cyber adversaries and attacks: a survey

of incidents and approaches', Lawrence Livermore National Laboratory, Report No. LLNL-TR-419041, April 2009.

19 Anderson, R., Barton, C., Böhme, R. et al., 'Measuring the cost of cybercrime', *WEIS 2012*, Berlin, Germany. 2012. Available at: http://weis2012.econinfosec.org/papers/ Anderson_WEIS2012.pdf.

20 Detica, *The Cost of Cyber Crime*, London: Cabinet Office, 2011.

21 ENISA, *Annual Incident Reports, 2013*, ENISA Publications, 2014. Available at: www.enisa.europa.eu/activities/Resilience-and-CIIP/Incidents-reporting/annual-reports/annual-incident-reports-2013.

22 Lagazio, Monica, Sherif, Nazneen and Cushman, Mike, 'A multi-level approach to understanding the impact of cyber crime on the financial sector', *Computers & Security*, 45: September 2014, pp. 58–74.

23 The Council of Europe, Convention on Cybercrime, Budapest, 2001.

24 Ibid.

25 UK Audit Commission, *Ghost in the Machine*, 1998. Available at: http://collections. europarchive.org/tna/20121114095218/http://audit-commission.gov.uk/subwebs/ publications/corporate/publicationPDF/1246.pdf.

26 Australian High Tech Crime Centre, 'Fighting the invisible', *Platypus Magazine: Journal of the Australian Federal Police*, 80: 2003, pp. 4–6.

27 Foreign Affairs and International Trade Canada, Cybercrime, 2015. Available at: www.international.gc.ca/crime/cyber_crime-criminalite.aspx?lang=eng.

28 Alkaabi, A., Mohay, G., McCullagh, A., Chantler, A., 'Dealing with the problem of cybercrime', *Conference Proceedings of 2nd International ICST Conference on Digital Forensics & Cyber Crime*, Abu Dhabi, 2010.

29 Ponemon Institute, *Global Report on the Cost of Cyber Crime*, Traverse City, MI, 2014.

30 The *Economist*, 'A spook speaks', June 2012. Available at www.economist.com/ node/21557817.

31 European Commission, 'Towards a general policy on the fight against cyber crime', communication from the Commission to the European Parliament, the Council and the Committee of the Regions, 2007, pp. 2–3. Available at: http://eur-lex.europa.eu/ legal-content/EN/TXT/?uri=URISERV:l14560.

32 Kshetri, Nir, 'Pattern of global cyber war and crime: a conceptual framework', *Journal of International Management*, 11: 2005, pp. 541–62.

33 McAfee Labs, *Cyber Crime and Hacktivism*, white paper, 2010. Available at: www. pdfdrive.net/hacktivism-and-cyberwars-hacktivismsu-home-e5454010.html.

34 Hoofnagle, C., 'Identity theft: making the known unknowns known', *Harvard Journal of Law and Technology*, 21(1): 2007, pp. 98–122.

35 The *Economist*, 'A spook speaks'.

36 Eden, C., 'Cognitive mapping', *European Journal of Operational Research*, 36: 1988, pp. 1–13; Eden, C. and Ackermann, F., *Making Strategy: The Journey of Strategic Management*, London: Sage Publications, 1998; Ackermann, F., Eden, C. and Cropper, S., 'Getting started with cognitive mapping'. Available at: http://www.banxia.com/pdf/ de/GettingStartedWithCogMapping.pdf.

37 Kelly, G.A., *The Psychology of Personal Constructs*, New York: Norton, 1995.

38 Buzan, T., *The Mind Map Book*, London: BBC Books, 1993.

39 Decision Explorer, 'Gain insight into your critical thinking', user guide, 2014.

40 Ausubel, D., *Educational Psychology: A Cognitive View*, New York: Holt, Rinehart, and Winston, 1968.

41 Detica, *The Cost of Cyber Crime*; Information Security Forum, 'Cyber security strategy'. Internal paper, London.
42 Eden, C., 'Analyzing cognitive maps to help structure issues or problems', *European Journal of Operational Research*, 159: 2004, pp. 673–86.
43 Anderson, R., 'Why information security is hard. An economic perspective'. Annual Computer Security Applications Conference, New Orleans, Louisiana, 2001.
44 The Council of Europe, Convention.
45 Marion, Nancy, 'The Council of Europe's Cyber Crime Treaty: An exercise in symbolic legislation', *International Journal of Cyber Criminology*, 2(1–2): 2010, pp. 699–712.
46 United Nations Office on Drugs and Crime, *Handbook on Identity-related Crime*, English, Publishing and Library Section, United Nations Office, Vienna, 2011.
47 Moore, T., 'The economics of cyber security – principles and policy options', *International Journal of Critical Infrastructure Protection*, 3(3–4): 2010, pp. 103–17.
48 Sonntag, Michael, 'European Cybercrime Convention', conference presentation, Institute for Information Processing and Microprocessor Technology (FIM), Austria, 2012. Available at: www.sonntag.cc/teaching/Security_and_WWW_SS12/3_IR_and_legal_day/Cybercrime.pdf.
49 OECD, 'Scoping paper on online identity theft', report presented at the Ministerial-level meeting organised by the ICCP, Seoul, Korea, 2008. Available at: www.oecd.org/sti/40644196.pdf.
50 Sommer, P. and Brown, I., 'Reducing systemic cybersecurity risk', report from the Future Global Shocks programme, OECD, 2011. Available at: www.oecd.org/gov/risk/46889922.pdf.
51 Moore, 'The economics of cyber security'.
52 Ibid.
53 Microsoft, 'Defining malware: FAQ'. Available at: https://technet.microsoft.com/en-us/library/dd632948.aspx.
54 Sommer and Brown, 'Reducing systemic cybersecurity risk'.
55 Jaishankar, K., 'Identity-related crime in the cyberspace: examining phishing and its impact', *International Journal of Cyber Criminology*, 2(1): 2008, pp. 10–15.
56 OECD, 'Scoping paper on online identity theft'.
57 Wall, D., 'Digital realism and the governance of SPAM as cyber crime', *European Journal on Criminal Policy and Research*, 10: 2004, pp. 309–35.
58 Sommer and Brown, 'Reducing systemic cybersecurity risk'.
59 www.identitytheft.org.uk.
60 OECD, 'Scoping paper on online identity theft'.
61 Hedayati, A., 'An analysis of identity fraud – motives, related frauds, techniques and prevention', *Journal of Law and Conflict Resolution*, 4(1): 2012, pp. 1–12.
62 OECD, 'Scoping paper on online identity theft'.
63 Symantec, 'How to report suspected phishing sites'. Available at: https://support.symantec.com/en_US/article.TECH195146.html.
64 UK Home Office, 'Cyber crime strategy', presented by the Secretary of State for the Home Department to Parliament, London, 2010. Available at: www.official-documents.gov.uk/document/cm78/7842/7842.pdf.
65 Hedayati, 'An analysis of identity fraud'.
66 Sommer and Brown, 'Reducing systemic cybersecurity risk'.
67 UK Home Office, 'Cyber crime strategy'.
68 Ibid.
69 Ibid.
70 Ibid.

71 Furnell, S.M. and Warren, M.J., 'Computer hacking and cyber terrorism: the real threats in the new millennium?', *Computers Security*, 18(1): 1999, pp. 28–34.

72 Turgeman-Goldschmidt, O., 'Meanings that hackers assign to their being a hacker', *International Journal of Cyber Criminology*, 2(2): 2008, pp. 382–396. Available at: www.cybercrimejournal.com/Orlyijccdec2008.pdf.

73 Backmann, M., 'The risk propensity and rationality of computer hackers', *International Journal of Cyber Criminology*, 4(1–2): 2010, pp. 643–56.

74 United States Government Accountability Office, 'Cyber threats facilitate ability to commit economic espionage', testimony before the subcommittee on Counterterrorism and Intelligence, Committee on Homeland Security, House of Representatives, 2012.

75 Backmann, 'The risk propensity and rationality of computer hackers'.

76 McAfee Labs, *Cyber Crime and Hacktivism*.

77 Ibid.

78 Ibid.

79 Denning, D.E., 'Activism, hacktivism, and cyberterrorism: the internet tool for influencing foreign policy', in John Arquilla and David Ronfeldt (eds), *Networks and Netwars: The Future of Terror, Crime, and Militancy*, Santa Monica, CA: RAND Corporation, 2001, pp. 239–88.

80 Ducklin, Paul, 'DHS website falls victim to hacktivist intrusion', *Naked Security*, 7 January 2013. Available at: https://nakedsecurity.sophos.com/2013/01/07/dhs-website-falls-victim-to-hacktivist-intrusion/.

81 Denning, 'Activism, hacktivism, and cyberterrorism'.

82 Detica, *The Cost of Cyber Crime*.

83 Matusitz, J., 'Cyberterrorism: postmodern state of chaos', *Journal of Digital Forensic Practice*, 3(2–4): 2010, pp. 115–23.

84 Office of National Counterintelligence Executive, 'Foreign spies stealing US economic secrets in cyber space', report to Congress on Foreign Economic Collection and Industrial Espionage, 2011.

85 Microsoft Corporation, 'Rethinking the cyber threat. A framework and path forward', 2009. Available at: www.microsoft.com/en-gb/download/confirmation.aspx?id=33754. Microsoft, 'Defining malware: FAQ'.

86 Office of National Counterintelligence Executive, 'Foreign spies stealing US economic secrets'.

87 Moore, 'The economics of cyber security'.

88 Sommer and Brown, 'Reducing systemic cybersecurity risk'.

89 Office of National Counterintelligence Executive, 'Foreign spies stealing US economic secrets'.

90 McAfee Labs, *Cyber Crime and Hacktivism*.

91 Council of Europe, 'Criminal money flows on the internet: methods, trends and multi-stakeholder counteraction', research report, February 2012. Available at: http://www.coe.int/t/dghl/cooperation/economiccrime/Source/Cybercrime/CyberCrime@EAP/2523_2467_IWS_actrep%20Kyiv%2027-29%20FEB_%20V5a.pdf.

92 Ibid.

93 Wall, D., 'The internet as a conduit for criminals', in April Pattavina (ed.), *Information Technology and the Criminal Justice System*, Thousand Oaks, CA: Sage, 2005, pp. 77–98.

94 UK Home Office, 'Cyber crime strategy'.

95 European Commission, 'Tackling crime in our digital age: establishing a European cyber crime centre', Communication from the Commission to the Council and the European Parliament, Brussels, 2012.

96 Wall, D., 'The internet as a conduit for criminals'.

97 New York State Senate, 'Cyberbullying: a report on bullying in a digital age', The independent democratic conference, 2011. Available at: www.nysenate.gov/files/pdfs/final%20cyberbullying_report_september_2011.pdf.

98 UK Home Office, 'Cyber crime strategy'.

99 McAfee Labs, *Cyber Crime and Hacktivism*.

100 Ibid.

101 Ibid.

102 eBay, 'How to avoid eBay fraud'. Available at: www.ebay.co.uk/gds/How-to-Avoid-eBay-Fraud-/10000000000825523/g.html.

103 FBI, 'Online auction fraud don't let it happen to you', FBI news, 2009. www.fbi.gov/news/stories/2009/june/auctionfraud_063009.

104 Norton, 'The latest in online auction scams', Your Security Resource article, 2013. Available at: http://uk.norton.com/yoursecurityresource/detail.jsp?aid=Online_Auction.

105 McAfee Labs, *Cyber Crime and Hacktivism*.

106 Norton, 'The latest in online auction scams'.

107 McAfee Labs, *Cyber Crime and Hacktivism*.

108 Yu, S., 'Email spam and the CAN-SPAM Act: a qualitative analysis', *International Journal of Cyber Criminology*, 5(1): 2011, pp. 715–35.

109 Kshetri, 'Pattern of global cyber war and crime'.

110 McAfee Labs, *Cyber Crime and Hacktivism*.

111 Ibid.

112 UK Home Office, 'Cyber crime strategy'.

113 Ibid.

114 Office of National Counterintelligence Executive, 'Foreign spies stealing US economic secrets'.

115 Detica, *The Cost of Cyber Crime.*

116 Office of National Counterintelligence Executive, 'Foreign spies stealing US economic secrets'.

117 In June 2013 Edward Snowden, an American computer professional, leaked classified information from the NSA to the mainstream media.

118 European Parliament, Resolution on the US NSA surveillance programme, surveillance bodies in various Member States and their impact on EU citizens' privacy, 2013/2682, 4 July 2013.

119 Titan Rain was the designation given by the Federal government of the United States to a series of coordinated attacks on American computer systems started in 2003. The attacks were labelled as Chinese in origin, although their precise nature, e.g. state-sponsored espionage, corporate espionage or random hacker attacks, and their real identities – masked by proxy, zombie computer, spyware/virus infected – remain unknown.

120 Bodmer, S., Kilger, M., Carpenter, G. and Jones, J., *Reverse Deception: Organized Cyber Threat Counter-Exploitation*, New York: McGraw-Hill Osborne Media, 2012.

121 Davis, Dai, 'Hacktivism; good or evil', *ComputerWeekly*, 2014. Available at: www.computerweekly.com/opinion/Hacktivism-Good-or-Evil.

122 Conte, Andrew, 'Line dividing hacker cyber crime, state-sponsored terror attack murky', *TribLive News*, 2014.

123 Ibid.

124 Ibid.

125 Paganini, Pierluigi, 'Raoul Chiesa – from cyber crime to state-sponsored hacking', *Security Affairs*, April 2014. Available at: http://securityaffairs.co/wordpress/23956/cyber-crime/raoul-chiesa-bad-actors-cyberspace.html.

126 Stuxnet is a computer worm discovered in June 2010, which was designed to attack industrial programmable logic controllers. Different variants of Stuxnet targeted five Iranian organisations, with the most probable target widely suspected to be uranium-enrichment infrastructure in Iran. On 1 June 2012, an article in the *New York Times* reported that Stuxnet was part of a US and Israeli intelligence operation called 'Operation Olympic Games', started under President George W. Bush and expanded under President Barack Obama.

127 Ibid.

128 Ibid.

129 Detica, *The Cost of Cyber Crime.*

130 McAfee Labs, *Cyber Crime and Hacktivism.*

131 Ibid.

132 Detica, *The Cost of Cyber Crime.*

133 Sofaer, Abraham D. and Goodman, Seymour E., 'Cyber crime and security: the Transnational Dimension', in *The Transnational Dimensions of Cyber Crime and Terrorism*, Stanford, CA: Hoover Institute, 2001, pp. 1–34.

134 Marion, Nancy, 'The Council of Europe's Cyber Crime Treaty'.

135 Congressional Research Service, 'Cyber crime: the Council of Europe Convention, Report for Congress, 2006, pp. 3–4. Available at: www.ipmall.info/hosted_resources/crs/RS21208_060928.pdf.

136 Marion, Nancy, 'The Council of Europe's Cyber Crime Treaty'.

137 European Commission, 'Towards a general policy on the fight against cyber crime'.

138 Kshetri, 'Pattern of global cyber war and crime'.

139 European Commission, 'Towards a general policy on the fight against cyber crime'.

140 Marion, Nancy, 'The Council of Europe's Cyber Crime Treaty'.

141 A recent development in security has been the idea of the prospective nature of security. This means the movement towards a pre-threat/pre-crime approach, where the emphasis is on prevention rather than punishment after the threat has materialised or the crime has occurred. Zedner, Lucia, *Security: Key Ideas in Criminology*, London: Routledge, 2009.

142 Excessive spending on protection against cyber crime could add to the costs caused by cyber crime. This spending could be significantly more than the losses incurred due to cyber crime. Lagazio et al., 'A multi-level approach'.

143 Information Security Forum, 'Cyber security strategy'.

144 ENISA, *Economics of Security: Facing the Challenges*, Publications Office of the EU, 2012.

145 Sharp Sr., Walter Gary, 'The past, present, and future of cybersecurity', *Journal of National Security Law & Policy*, 4(1): 2010, pp. 13–25.

146 ENISA, *Economics of Security.*

147 Trend Micro, 'The business of cyber crime. A complex business model', white paper, January 2011, pp. 12–13.

148 Sofaer and Goodman, 'Cyber crime and security'.

149 Examples of these organised efforts include the Conficker Working Group, a task force comprised of security researchers, ISPs, domain-name registries, universities, law-enforcement agencies and other cross-industry stakeholders. The group was formed recently to combat the Conficker worm, which is believed to have originated with the same Russian and Ukrainian cyber-criminal networks behind many other profitable criminal operations, such as the RBN, Atrivo/Intercage, McColo, the Storm botnet, the Waledac botnet, rogue anti-virus campaigns and other criminal activities. Additionally, the Anti-Phishing Working Group created an initiative that includes civilian network operators and researchers who have volunteered to try

to bridge the cyber-crime data-sharing gap between public law enforcement, private network security, investigative intelligence, network measurement and experimentation, and related policy. An organisation named FIRST (Forum of Incident Response and Security Teams) also provides a global forum to share information. Finally, the network of CERTs is an example of local and regional groups formed to combat cyber crime.

150 Lagazio et al., 'A multi-level approach'.
151 European Commission, 'Towards a general policy on the fight against cyber crime'.
152 Zittrain, Jonathan, 'The generative internet', *Harvard Law Review*, 119:2006. Available at: http://dash.harvard.edu/bitstream/handle/1/9385626/Zittrain_Generative%20Internet. pdf?sequence=1.

3 Big Data analytic tooling and cyber-risk management

Cint Kortmann

In this chapter, I will attempt to define Big Data analytics and answer questions about responsibility, cost, transition, transparency and development. In doing so my aim is to give insight into the importance of this development and provide context to the issues relating to cyber risk and crime.

What is Big Data?

Definitions of Big Data vary widely and serve to illustrate the challenges of defining a new concept. The *Oxford Dictionary*, for example, defines Big Data as 'data of a very large size, typically to the extent that its manipulation and management present significant logistical challenges; (also) the branch of computing involving such data'. The online Oxford Dictionaries point towards extremely large data sets that may be analysed computationally to reveal patterns, trends, and associations, especially relating to human behaviour and interactions. Meanwhile, the popular Wikipedia suggests that Big Data is an all-encompassing term for any collection of data sets so large and complex that it becomes difficult to process using traditional data-processing applications.

What is clear from the definitions is that the adjective 'big' is always subjective. Indeed, Big Data has a very different meaning for scientists at CERN or those working with IBM Watson, than, for example, the local supermarket. What these definitions have in common, however, is Big Data's ability to encompass the world of plain figures into the realm of behaviour. While sensors in a machine can guide the production process, the data from these sensors can be processed for us to learn more about machine behaviour. In short, Big Data allows us to understand unexpected downturns, and therefore be used to optimise the production process. Analysis of the data trail can also help us to observe patterns in human behaviour. In the context of cyber crime, analysis of Big Data provides the information we need to fight cyber crime from the source.

Of course, the first issue when implementing Big Data analytics is not centred around hardware equipment or software tools. First, we must be able to identify what and how much information we are looking for, and in what timeframe. Clearly a 24/7 flow of information will require a different set of tools than those needed to produce a yearly overview. Furthermore, the ability to capture and analyse human data requires a very different approach to that of machine data.

Some may say that data is the new oil, and that Big Data analytics is likely to become the new source of energy in a new information age. Just as the discovery of oil brought us comfort and convenience, it also became a trigger for global warming and a source of corruption, suppression and war. In turn, data will no doubt bring about a similar combination of positive and negative effects. One example of the positive might be improved and personalised medical care. At the negative extreme is cyber war and the impact this could have on our society.

Who is responsible for the data in an organisation?

The most popular information technology (IT) shares on the stock market, such as Google, Twitter, Alibaba, Facebook and Amazon, have given data a central place in their operations. Data is their resource and data mining their profession. In many public and private organisations, the data hidden inside a cavern of archives is still not treated professionally or with the respect it deserves. Data can be spread across the entire company, with every department housing its own so-called 'archives'. The result is often that such departmental archives can contain extra insights and personal interpretations that do not fit and are not tailored for the data warehouse. One could even go as far as to say that it is a misappropriation that detracts key insights from colleagues and one that keeps such data outside the company control systems, making the company extra vulnerable to data crime. Historically, most Chief Information Officers have focused predominantly on software and hardware issues. Few have made the transition towards taking responsibility for the data and information that are harvested. In such an instance, data has no central role and one needs well-developed social skills to persuade department heads to make appropriate use of their 'personal' data archive. Indeed, to enrich and check content demands, an internal risk-management solution led by a dedicated Chief Data Officer or Chief Data Scientist who has influence on the board as well as in the organisation is required.

Why Big Data?

Continuing with the analogy of data becoming the new oil suggests that there can never be too much. That said, everything needs its own scale. E-commerce has access to an unlimited flow of data relating to customer behaviour. Recognising all elements opens the way towards being able to make personalised offers to clients and thereby influencing their purchasing power at the right moment.

Privacy regulations in Western society make collecting and maintaining data a far greater challenge for physical stores. Smartphone users, however, have become accustomed to handing over numerous personal details in order to install an application for a game, video or web store. In short, online customers are willing to give up their privacy rights, making them vulnerable to identity theft and other forms of cyber crime.

Within the health industry, personalised medicine and treatment is without limits. However, costs can be high and the gap between rich and poor looks set to become ever more substantial. Developments in the collection of individual healthcare data may well present ethical questions in the future: some people will just die, whereas others may choose to die.

The benefits of the optimisation of production processes are clear. With the availability of more knowledge about the customer or user, there are more opportunities than ever before to create a product suited to an individual's unique and exact requirements. The more knowledge we have based on the output of sensors, the better we can program the machines to avoid waste and to speed up the production process. That said, machine data presents yet another opportunity for cyber crime. Market competition may well intervene in the process, but governments will also have the ability and resources to hack systems within a cyber-war setting. Examples include the assumed hacking of the atomic program of Iran and the rumoured hacking of the Sony film systems by North Korea. In January 2015, for example, the *Financial Times* published an article that detailed a case in Germany. The case appeared to be similar to cyber attacks involving the Stuxnet worm, which in itself was considered to be the first known cyber weapon, created by the US and Israel to attack Iran's nuclear programme:[1]

> Security will need to be improved to ensure that internet-connected objects cannot be hacked and hijacked. Physical attacks over the Internet are happening. At the end of last year, the German federal office of information security revealed that machinery at a German steelworks was severely damaged when hackers gained access to control systems via the internet. When everything from traffic lights and cars to home heating systems are linked online, the potential for harmful hacks increases further. However, the simple, low-power devices used for the Internet of Things might not be able to handle heavy encryption, or may not be patched and updated if a security flaw is discovered.[2]

Others expect the Internet of Things (IoT) to offer advanced connectivity of devices, systems and services that goes beyond machine-to-machine communications and, in turn, that it will cover a variety of protocols, domains and applications.[3]

What is clear is that the more dependent we are on the way processes are guided by sensors, the more vulnerable these systems will become.

Established organisations and Big Data

What can established organisations do with their data, and how can Big Data analytics bring these organisations and their processes back on track? Established organisations have a choice. They can make their data work for them or they can head down the path towards bankruptcy. Kodak and Nokia are just two examples of companies that waited too long to learn from their available data. In the end they became the players in their own liquidation. Of course, there were people in these organisations who wanted to use data to their advantage, but they could not prove the benefits and failed in their internal argumentation. In established organisations, people make a dash towards the financial bottom line, or focus their efforts towards an updated customer survey. However, these are not true examples of how to best utilise Big Data analytics. After all, it is hard to dig for gold in an environment where success and career advancement were made using traditional models. Indeed, in the past, few ventured into looking to the archives for answers, and those who did were not earmarked for future management. Certain legal requirements ensured that departments scanned important documents into PDF files, but these files were rarely updated. At the end of the day, hidden data was stored in a mixture of paper files and outdated software, or locked up inside the chasms of unknown software. Not only was data hard to access, but it was also hard to protect from those who knew the key. Actions, even those that were well intended, were not always completed as reorganisation and cost-reduction programmes destroyed whatever was started. What becomes clear is that new data warehouses are sometimes so rigid that the most important data is kept inside the department in a well-hidden shadow file, accessible only by a privileged few. Maintenance and security can also be a huge problem. The question is what investment an organisation is willing to make if it has the choice to invest in a huge clean-up operation or in new security measures.

What are the developments in Big Data analytics globally and what can we expect in the future?

The total amount of data is now doubling every 15 months. However, Alibaba, Amazon and Japan's Rakuten are among the minority of less than 5 per cent of e-commerce companies that use predictive data analytics.[4] We can predict significant development in this area and that China, with its growing and relatively under-researched middle class, is set to become one of the world's most important data markets.[5]

As the market is still led by the IT industry, we can assume that machines and tooling will be used to handle the growing amount of data and that spinoff consultancy firms, such as Quant Base, will be established to guide the whole process. What we do know is that not all data is based around e-commerce activity, which has to be analysed on a 24/7 basis. Some companies will require data analytics only once a year or less. What is clear is that while data can be infinite, those who know their constraints will succeed.

It will come as no surprise then that the next big revolution is expected to come from a combination of smartphones and Big Data. Wi-Fi tracking and GPS will make it possible to tell more about the user of a smartphone than ever before. For privacy reasons, however, it is not necessary to know the identity of the person behind the collected data. The industry is interested in smartphone behaviour rather than human behaviour, despite the human maintaining control by providing the data destined to be analysed. Data on smartphone behaviour can be combined with data on place, time, weather and multiple other elements. Indeed, it is this combination of human and machine data that may well lead commercial and political influencers to the smartphone, just as the smartphone guides the actions of its anonymous user. My prediction is that the frontrunners will be the companies that win the battle for what I will refer to as 'screentime', or the time people spend on their smartphones. Put simply, the smartphone has progressed the data world into a new era.

I would define the four key drivers of development as follows: (1) the producers of smartphones who want to expand the number of smartphone users; (2) the telecommunication companies who want to maximise the amount of time people spend on their smartphones; (3) the builders of applications and platforms whose focus is to maximise the amount of time users spend on a particular application or platform; and (4) the data collected from web behaviour.

For application and platform developers, the goal is to attract the biggest share of screentime. These companies are doing their utmost to attract users to the platform and to keep them there. We have moved a long way from the simplicity of online chatting. E-stores, movies, taxis, games and online banking are just some of the applications attracting screentime. Asian companies, mostly Chinese, are taking the lead in this battle to attract the right shops, advertising, movies and the like. Tencent's WeChat is taking the lead as Western companies, such as Facebook with its purchase of WhatsApp, vie for second place. Alibaba, meanwhile, is investing its initial public offering money into video in a simple bid to gain more screentime. Companies such as Japan's Line, Apple and Google in the US, and Xiaomi in China are working hard to connect everyone using their own hardware and software. The idea of warning users via cookies about the collection of data drawn from their behaviour on their PCs and laptops never really worked out. Users have proved to be unconcerned, or perhaps ignorant, about safety or privacy issues and have become accustomed to accepting cookies in return for accessing a particular website. Applications on smartphones go one step further by asking users to accept certain terms and conditions. That said, the rejection of cookies and the refusal to accept terms and conditions are other signals of behaviour that in the end becomes part of the data. Indeed, analysis of smartphone usage will help e-commerce sites and political organisations to learn even more about user behaviour, with information such as location, movements and preferences being the prize. Analysis of screentime provides the hosts with more and more information about the smartphone and its user at any given moment. Ultimately, the more you know, the more you can influence the behaviour of the user, making campaigns run by political organisations, non-governmental organisations and government all the more effective. Through their collection of data, they will know when the smartphone user is most vulnerable for which formulation of a message embedded at a certain place. Just as Twitter played an important role in the last US presidential elections, the question may well be whether or not the next US presidential elections will be won by the candidate whose team is able to optimise screentime information. However, while this fourth driver disconnects the individual from the device as the name of the holder of the smartphone becomes less important, it is not too great a challenge to connect a variety of devices used by one person. Organisations will aim to communicate with the smartphone in a bid simply to influence whoever reads the message. In short, the numbers game overtakes the individual and most will follow the stimulus of their device. It is a scenario that gives solid ground to warnings from Stephen Hawking,[6] Elon Musk and many others in January 2015 that humans must remain in control of machines.[7]

Cyber crime and transparency: who knows what and why?

Perceptions of privacy vary across the globe. In some countries, privacy is something that must be bought; in others it is a right. Some regions limit the use of personal medical and financial data but are quite liberal in the way other forms of data are collected, stored and used. Users of technology in the Western world are inconsistent in the way they look at data and privacy issues. Privacy has been hyped in the West since the 1970s, and the way the National Security Agency has been perceived as the world police has not helped to define this logic. That said, people are seduced by details of the personal lives of others, just as they are attracted to media gossip and reality shows. While some users may be uneasy about handing over their bank details, they may willingly provide what they believe to be anonymous and intimate details about themselves for the sake of enjoying the advantages of a certain application.

Meanwhile, as Big Data becomes an essential resource and respectable data miners invest in bringing the 'new oil' to market, there will always be those of a criminal persuasion who will seek to misuse advances in technology. Eventually, regulations will no doubt be put in place as instances of cyber crimes such as identity theft become all the more commonplace. However, regulations on privacy issues are unlikely to control the situation as criminals have already taken the lead in an unlevel and ambiguous playing field in which it is difficult to take legal action. A more offensive legislation focusing on transparency could help, and ultimately people should be able to trust in the 'three Ws' – simply the 'Who' knows 'What' about me and 'Why'. Allowing civilians to restore corrupted data requires regulation in a world where the need for transparency could hamper cyber criminals more than outdated privacy laws harking back almost 50 years. Indeed, just as Big Data can be a source of cyber crime, so too should it be able to accommodate the war against it, with patterns of behaviour leading us to the source of the crime. One such example is that since 2007 the US Department of Justice has used Big Data to detect fraud in Medicare. In just five years it was able to recover US$19.2bn,[8] but while the fight for public freedom continues, the reality is far more complex. Everyone wants the criminals who hack into your bank account or use your cyber identity to mislead your contacts to be accountable for their crimes, but no global entity currently exists to enforce justice. Without global cooperation, local governments will continue to use their own intelligence for their own agenda. In practice it seems that divulgence of information, led by cyber criminals or governments, only feeds mistrust by civilians. Meanwhile industry experts are warning that companies will need as much as US$1bn or more in cyber insurance coverage each as the costs of hacking attacks mount. However, some businesses are struggling to secure even a tenth of that,[9] with the maximum available now set at US$500m.[10]

Conclusion

In this chapter, I have written about just some of the issues relating to Big Data. In our use of technology, we create a data trail that can provide us with discounts in online stores and create custom-made services. Production becomes more efficient and medical treatment is personalised for our individual needs. The bridge between human data and machine data is distinct, yet also provides us with tools required for integration. The IoT will enter our private lives and soon we can expect it to handle the needs of our household. The smartphone is entertaining and the use of applications that have the ability to control our heating or lighting can be advantageous for the environment.

New companies and institutions will take the lead in the use of Big Data analytics, and only a few more traditional organisations will invest in controlling their data. Just as technology becomes more advanced, our society may become more vulnerable. Cyber criminals and governments alike can steal information relevant to them, take over our identities, slow down production and shut off our cities from gas, water and electricity. Transparency can help but cannot free us from our personal responsibilities in this new world.

Most cases detailing cyber crime in the financial sector depict short attacks on credit-card data or tax information. Forbes published 20 of the major data breaches of 2014[11] that show the amount of data gathered by hackers this way. Examples of more structural cyber crime with Big Data in the insurance sector are not yet available. As Deloitte puts it: 'We believe the number of long-term attacks may be silently growing as attackers quietly slip in undetected and establish a persistent, ongoing presence in critical IT environments.'[12] That said, insurers offering cyber-crime coverage need to be aware that they are handling very sensitive client data in order to underwrite risk. Indeed, sensitive information collected before underwriting cyber risk could put a policyholder's entire IT system at risk.[13]

The following case studies illustrate how data analytics can work to our advantage. The cases are based on real practices in Europe but have been rewritten to guarantee the anonymity of the companies and individuals involved. Here we can show how mass data can be transformed from smartcards to provide information that feeds decision-making and how tooling and the use of graphics can make the handling of data more efficient and help to signal unusual patterns. While examples such as these show how Big Data analytics has been used successfully to optimise customer experience or to trace fraud within the insurance industry, the methods used are also crucial for helping us to recognise changes in shopping behaviour or predicting the break down of a machine.

Case study 3.1: Big Data analytics and privacy

Europe enjoys a tight and thorough privacy regime. Effective law enforcement is in place, and the media are keen to expose high-profile organisations that appear slovenly with personal details or make themselves and their customers vulnerable to hacking. These factors make reputational damage hard to fight.

This case study follows the use of public transport in one of the bigger European urban agglomerations. For several years, they have used a chip card for payment, with several locations and organisations responsible for where you can buy and upload the card. Due to European law, there are several transport companies where you can pay using the chip card. One clearing house is responsible for collecting the money and paying the transport companies.

To optimise the privacy of travellers, the clearing house uses card numbers and deletes travel data on a weekly basis, all of which adheres to the relevant privacy requirements of authorities and customer organisations. The system is providing accurate data and is a satisfactory solution for all parties involved. However, transport organisations, customer groups and politicians now want to acquire more information from a system originally intended to facilitate payment procedures. In an effort to optimise routings and to ensure their investment more accurately reflects the needs of customers, the travel data has to be re-coded with random numbers to make it impossible to track the individual traveller while still making data analytics possible. It is an operation that is now required to analyse millions of card clicks per day, and to make calculations based on more than 1.5 terabytes of data.

In essence, what the stakeholders wish to establish, through Big Data analytics, is which are the busiest tracks, which are the most preferred routes, and how these can be shared between the various operators to ensure optimum travel conditions for their customers. In order to comply with privacy law, personal information must be disconnected from the card numbers. There can be no relation between the card number and a particular customer whatsoever. Anonymous card numbers must be combined with information about the starting point of a particular journey and the time taken to travel between various stations. Combining information gathered on the different cards moving from one point to another provides insight into the traffic between different points on the network. Comparing these insights with the available traffic or travel space of the available transport for each routing allows us to understand the capacity of each routing. Figure 3.1 depicts the larger stations as larger circles, and the lines provide statistics detailing the number of people travelling through these stations. In short, the thicker the lines, the more people there are taking these routes.

Case study 3.2: SynerScope tooling

A car-insurance company based in the Netherlands has implemented some efficiency drives. On the claim side expertise costs have been reduced. Small claims under €5,000 are handled using photographic evidence, without the need to send

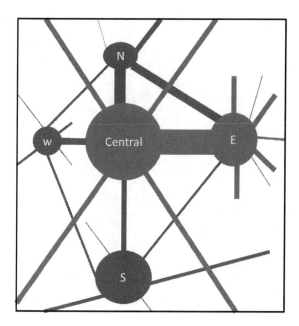

Figure 3.1 Travel data shown in graphic form.

Source: From Quant Base customer presentation, February 2015.

in an expert. However, after some time the number of claims just under €5,000 rises far above anticipated levels. While this result could be influenced by the opportunity for clients to save time, experts suspect fraud.

The question at this point is whether data analytic tooling can help detect questionable situations. This case was handled with expertise and tooling from SynerScope as shown below in Case study 3.3. Full context data, structured and unstructured, for customers and repair shops related to claims between €4,000 and €5,000 was ingested. By directly plotting the location of claimants, accidents and repair shops on a map, and in a connected interactive sequence view for distance, some cases not only feature extreme distances but also serve to identify geographic concentrations. In this area distances of over 100 km between the home address of claimants and their chosen repair shop present a question mark. However, the full context of the repair shop is needed to judge how awkward the situation is. As such, with one click SynerScope tooling is able to link large distance repairs to a specific repair shop, and with a single further click all other claimant home locations for repairs in the same repair shop over a 24-month period. Those new claimants are linked with one further click to other repair shops, to detect whether second or third repairs have taken place elsewhere. In a final drill down, this sub-group shows an uncommon level of the number of repairs per claimant, all well below the limit that would release adjuster attention.

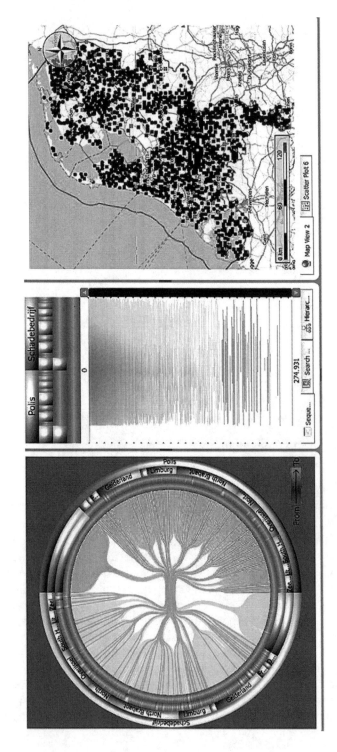

Figure 3.2 Presentation by SynerScope on repair shops and policyholders.

Source: Slide 4, SynerScope, December 2014.

This investigation provided evidence of fraud-ring activity causing damage of millions to the insurance carrier.

Case study 3.3: use of graphics

Graphics can be used to facilitate Big Data analytics. Indeed, visualisation makes looking for a needle in a haystack a much simpler proposition compared to some deeper calculations, which are hard to make using conventional database and rule-based systems.

In relation to the previous case study (Case study 3.2) Figure 3.2 provides an overview of the situation. The right of the circle in dark grey depicts the policyholders. The repair shops are shown on the left of the circle in light grey. Both are ranked by location and postcode. The map of the Netherlands on the right-hand side shows the area where the research took place, where the dots represent claims. The distance between the policyholder and the repair shop used by the policyholder (between 0 km and 275 km) is shown in the centre.

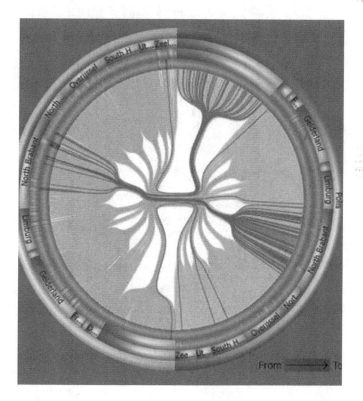

Figure 3.3 Circle graphic visualising connections between the registered location of policyholders and the location of repair shops.

Source: Slide 11, SynerScope, December 2014.

While coloured illustrations can of course provide a more detailed overview, Figure 3.3 provides a close up of the collected data in black, white and grey linking the registered location of policyholders to the location of repair shops. Exploring data at this deeper level reveals an interesting cluster of 20 repair shops. The black connection lines depict the policyholders who go to these repair shops. Ultimately, the graphic allows us to identify two groups, the first being the policyholders located within the same region or postal code as the repair shop, and the second the group of policyholders who live quite a distance from their selected repair shop.

The distance between policyholder and repair shop is expressed in Figure 3.4. As one would expect, most are within short range. However, for the purpose of this investigation, the interest lies in those policyholders situated a significant distance away from their selected repair shop. Because all information is connected, you can focus the research by clicking with the cursor on the lines you want to examine in greater detail.

Figure 3.4 Graphic showing distance to repair shop.

Source: Slide 1, SynerScope, December 2014.

Figure 3.5 Map view.

Source: Slide 12, SynerScope, December 2014.

The map of the Netherlands in Figure 3.5 shows the plots of selected policy-holders and their selected repair shops. This allows us to visualise distances and local concentration.

Notes

1 Loek Essers, IT World IDG news service, 19 December 2014, www.itworld.com/article/2861675/cyberattack-on-german-steel-factory-causes-massive-damage.html.
2 Maija Palmer, *Financial Times*, 27 January 2015, www.ft.com/cms/s/0/496359fa-851b-11e4-ab4e-00144feabdc0.html#axzz3lu07JJD6.
3 J. Höller, V. Tsiatsis, C. Mulligan, S. Karnouskos, S. Avesand and D. Boyle, *Machine-to-Machine to the Internet of Things: Introduction to a New Age of Intelligence*, Amsterdam: Academic Press, 2014.
4 Gartner report July 2013 quoted by Mark Milian, Bloomberg, 4 June 2014, www.bloomberg.com/news/2014-06-03/retailers-use-big-data-to-turn-you-into-a-big-spender.html.
5 Lily Kuo, Quartz, 12 November 2014, http://qz.com/295370/how-alibaba-is-using-bra-sizes-to-predict-online-shopping-habits/.

6   Interview Stephen Hawking, BBC, 2 December 2014, www.bbc.com/news/technology-30290540.

7   Stephen Hawking and others, open letter, Future of Life Institute, 12 January 2015, http://futureoflife.org/AI/open_letter.

8   Karin Scannell, *Financial Times*, 12 January 2015, www.ft.com/cms/s/0/8c1b46fa-9a7d-11e4-8426-00144feabdc0.html#axzz3oAyJn7EM.

9   Stephen (Catlin), 'Cyber risks too big to cover', *Asian Insurance Review*, 5 February 2015, http://on.ft.com/1C3miTR.

10 Ben Beeson quoted in *Financial Times*, 18 February 2015, www.ft.com/intl/cms/s/0/61880f7a-b3a7-11e4-a6c1-00144feab7de.html#axzz3o91SCWWK.

11 Bill Hardekopf, 'The Big Data breaches of 2014', Forbes, 13 January 2015, www.forbes.com/sites/moneybuilder/2015/01/13/the-big-data-breaches-of-2014/.

12 Global Cyber Executive Briefing Insurance case studies 2015 website, Deloitte, Belgium, www2.deloitte.com/be/en/pages/risk/articles/Global-Cyber-Briefing.html.

13 James Gibbons, 'The big issues with Big Data', Post, 29 May 2015, www.postonline.co.uk/post/blog-post/2408190/blog-the-big-issues-with-big-data.

4 Cyber risk and managing risk in the United States

Ruth Taplin

The nature of cyber risk in the United States

Cyber risk, both threat and attack, is both very much alive and increasing year on year in financial institutions in the United States (hereinafter US). The US is a different case than all other countries and regions covered in this book because cyber risk is on a larger scale, there is more of it and a good deal of the cyber attack is political and power based in nature. This is because the US is still the number-one country in the world in terms of size of economy, political power, individual wealth and technical innovation. This means that there are many governments, companies and individuals who are willing to use cyber attack to relieve the US of its innovative ideas, intellectual property, individual wealth and political power/ number-one status. This, therefore, is the context in which this chapter analyses cyber risk, both threat and attack, and managing such risks in the US.

Cyber attacking US financial institutions for political reasons

A report in 2014 on Bloomberg.com noted that the Federal Bureau of Investigation (FBI) has been investigating an incidence of Russian hackers attacking US financial institutions in what is suspected to be cyber attacks in retaliation for US-initiated economic sanctions against Russia for backing incursions into the Ukraine. Bloomberg stated there was a loss of a good deal of sensitive data with their security experts noting that only the professional and highly skilled could execute these attacks and not ordinary criminal hackers.

The *New York Times*, in following this report, stated that JPMorgan Chase, which is the largest bank in the US by assets, and four other financial institutions were subject to a coordinated attack that amassed huge amounts of data, mainly cheque and savings-account information. The cyber attack was not directly confirmed by JPMorgan Chase in keeping with the general under reporting of cyber attacks on financial institutions mentioned in the introductory chapter of this book. The *Wall Street Journal* confirmed through unnamed sources that a major breach of computer security had occurred.

The FBI has also been working indirectly with financial institutions through the increasing number of cyber attacks on the payment systems of retail stores in the US.

Target, a major US retailer, was subject to a pre-Christmas attack in 2013 in which 40 million credit and debit cards were compromised. The Target cyber attack received a good deal of publicity and forced banks to speed up their adoption of the microchip in credit and debit cards. Chip cards are deemed safer because, unlike magnetic strip cards that transfer a credit-card number when swiped, chip cards use a one-time code that moves between the chip and the retailer's register. Home Depot, the largest home improvement store in the US, experienced an even larger security breach that lasted for months and compromised the payment accounts, both credit and debit, of 56 million customers in the US and Canada.

Other US retailers have been affected by cyber attacks in relation to stealing customer payment information, including SUPERVALU and Sears Holdings' store KMart. The parent company Sears Holdings played down the hacking into their KMart customers' payment database. However, KMart did take a number of actions to manage the situation, working closely with law-enforcement agencies and banks. It removed malicious software from its systems, deployed software to protect customer information, offered temporary free credit-monitoring protection for customers shopping at KMart using credit and debit cards, and kept customers updated on its website. These protective measures were introduced quickly and efficiently to manage a cyber attack that could have caused the further decline of Sears stores, which have been struggling to keep their business relevant to customers.

Data breaches are enormously expensive and prolonged, especially in light of the fact that litigation is often the preferred way to resolve financial loss in the US. The Target data breach occurred in 2013 but the saga is still ongoing in 2015. This is because Target has been dealing with continuing litigation for financial loss and breaking of regulatory laws. Some of the costs that Target has had to incur, which in March 2015 amounted to US$252 million, from the 2013 breach includes financial compensation for civil damages, investigation of the breach, repairing compromised systems, complying with breach notification requirements, providing credit monitoring services for affected customers and legal fees arising from lawsuits and regulatory actions. As private litigation is not effective, most lawsuits are of a civil nature.[1] Other attendant costs can include loss of reputation, which is not only very costly in legal terms to try and defend but also needs to be included in any comprehensive insurance along with cyber risk.

Insurance

Comprehensive insurance is again a significant way to manage the financial losses in the US caused by cyber attack in relation to financial loss, business interruption, loss of data and reputation damage.

The US Congress has been debating the importance of cyber security legislation that addresses both the need to protect the federal government from the data-breach threat deriving from private companies that have been experiencing cyber attack and the implementation of a single federal standard for data-breach notification to supersede single-state legislation. Congressional lawmakers have been looking for guidance to produce a comprehensive, effective bill that deals with cyber security issues and are increasingly viewing the insurance industry as the best source for answers.[2]

In the case of Target, insurance played a major role in offsetting the losses incurred by Target Corporation from its 2013 security-data breach of US$61 million, offset by US$44 million in insurance payouts. Expenses incurred in financial year 2014 dating back to 2013 amounted to over US$191 million, which were offset by US$46 million in insurance proceeds.

By the end of 2014, total costs for the breach amounted to US$252 million, with receipt of US$90 million in insurance proceeds leaving Target accountable in 2013–14 for roughly US$162.00 million total net expenses.[3]

Businesses in the US are feeling so beleaguered by cyber attack, especially in relation to security-data breaches that are causing them great financial loss, business interruption and reputational loss that they are increasingly looking to bespoke cyber-risk insurance. A report from Marsh US in 2014, mentioned in Chapter 1 of this book, shows that increasing numbers of businesses are seeking financial protection through insurance coverage for data breach and business interruption. The number of Marsh-based clients buying standalone cyber-risk insurance increased 32 per cent from 2013 with the percentage of existing Marsh financial and professional liability clients rising by 16 per cent. The demand for standalone cyber-risk insurance is continuing to rise in 2015 for Marsh US clients.[4]

Cyber-risk regulation in the US

The US differs from many other countries not only in the amount of litigation that takes place in relation to cyber attacks and the enormous sums involved but also in relation to costs that need to be borne by businesses large and small because of the regulatory data-breach notification law. As Joel Lewis of Lloyd's noted:

> Cyber risk insurance has evolved in tandem both with technological and leg-islative developments. Whilst the technological risk factors are fairly simi-lar worldwide, the legislative environments have developed very differently. The first data breach notification law in the US was introduced in California in 2003, and by 2015 there were separate statutes in 47 different states, with a wide range of notification requirements, timescales and fines. The prolif-eration of such laws in the US, and in particular the substantial cost of meet-ing the notification obligations, has been a major factor in the development of and demand for cyber insurance products in the US – however the wide variation in requirements state to state has increased the complexity of under-writing, and the cost of managing notifications compliantly. There has been increasing momentum behind efforts to introduce federal legislation that would supersede the state laws and impose a uniform standard.
>
> In the UK the key relevant legislation has been the 1998 Data Protection Act, implementing the 1995 Data Protection Directive. Although the Directive brought a certain consistency of approach in Europe, it focussed

more on rights of access for data subjects, and did not impose data breach notification requirements or specify monetary penalties. The maximum penalty in the UK for breach of the Data Protection Act stands at £500,000. The pending EU proposals for a Data Protection Regulation and a Cyber Security Directive will prompt a paradigm shift in the European legislative environment, and are likely to be a powerful driver of demand for cyber insurance.[5]

The problem lies in the structure of US regulatory institutions that are devolved to create a checks and balances system. This means that such regulation can be carried out simultaneously on local, state and federal levels. At present regulation concerning a data-breach notification operates on a mainly state level as noted above, which means different regulation in each state and different fines. Given the complications of cyber attack and the potential for such great financial loss and the underreporting of cyber attacks by US banks, a federal law/bill is required to standardise notification requirements for all breaches of security-data information. Compliance can be costly, which means small and medium-sized enterprises (SMEs), in particular, will be burdened with data-breach notification costs they cannot afford. There is also increased cost for larger corporations whose business interests span many US states and that have to adhere to each state's data-breach notification regulatory law and fines.

This complexity and increased cost, which is unlikely to be absorbed fully by insurance policies, is the reason why the US Congress is taking so long to develop a comprehensive federally based regulatory law.

A cyber security law is being drafted by the Senate Intelligence Committee's most senior members Democrat Senator for California Dianne Feinstein and Republican Senator Richard Burr of North Carolina. It is believed that this legislation will be given bipartisan backing in 2015 because of the sharply increasing number of US companies falling victim to cyber attacks against their data stores, which is affecting millions of Americans.

A wider aim of this legislation is to encourage both government and companies to share information concerning breaches to help prevent future attacks. Information sharing is a very difficult area to agree on technically and legally because of issues of privacy and liability. In this chapter we will assess the possible success of employing a cyber-attack data-breach information-sharing system.

Another difficult area the new law will address is the extent companies can employ countermeasures. A Senate bill in 2014 attempted to deal with allowing companies to use countermeasures to prevent cyber attack on their own networks and related attacks on other company or government networks but only with written permission from the latter.

An example would be where a company could shut down its own network system to prevent a virus or malware from spreading but the difficulty arises if the virus or malware is also affecting another unrelated company network. The new draft bill deviates from the language of the previous attempt by forbidding a company to use countermeasures against another company's network by intentionally disabling or shutting it down without express permission from the other company. The draft law does not prohibit the US government from using countermeasures of its own.

Another aspect of the new draft bill covers retaliation for cyber attacks in which it is forbidden to make an attack back on the attacker. It is feared by lawmakers that without this proviso a chain of retaliatory hacks would ensue.

In 2014 lawmakers tried to put together a comprehensive cyber security law but failed in the Senate over privacy protection. What resulted was the House of Representatives passing its own cybersecurity bill entitled the Protecting Cyber Networks Act and the Senate Intelligence Committee proposing the Cybersecurity Information Sharing Act, yet to be voted on at the time of writing. President Obama in February 2015 hosted a summit in California to build more support and cooperation between government and industry sectors to resolve these issues so a comprehensive bill can be passed in Congress.[6]

Managing risk – a company-wide priority

At a recent Advisen conference in London on cyber risk, Eric Qualkenbush, a former member of the Central Intelligence Agency and a member of the board of directors of Black Ops Partners, made a valid point that insider threat as the source of cyber attack is often overlooked and that a company-wide approach needs to be taken against cyber threat/attack. He suggested an insider team comprising all major players such as lawyers, information technology (IT) technical staff, counter-intelligence experts, human-resource managers and those in finance and accounting could work together to find the weakest links in the company. This countermeasure could involve training and policy making that would target potential hackers based inside the company. The reasons why inside employees could perpetrate such cyber attacks are numerous including revenge, being disgruntled, financially motivated or politically motivated or because of a grudge. An insider team from different departments would have a greater chance of discovering from one perspective or another which employee could have a tendency to be a hacker. Such a strategy will be more difficult for an SME as they have fewer resources.[7] However, in my estimation, SMEs, having much smaller workforces than larger corporations, would be more familiar with their employees and it would be more difficult to disguise bad intentions and actions when working together in close proximities. The director of the Securities and Exchange Commission's (SEC) regional office in Chicago, David Glockner, emphasised that any security measure undertaken needs to be a meaningful one and more than a tick-box approach. Rather it should be a company-wide security measure that is part of the overall corporate governance framework. He stressed the importance of involvement of senior management and warned against relying solely on IT compliance.

These comments followed an SEC examination of all its registrants in relation to cyber-risk issues at advisor and broker-dealer practices. This is an ongoing review and did not give prescriptive guidance but drew out points that are certain to assist companies in the US with managing cyber risk. Some of the trends that the review uncovered were that less than a third of advisor firms had appointed a chief information security officer and that slightly more than half operate regular audits on their security policies.

Glockner noted that the SEC is not setting out to demand strict technical guidelines for companies to follow in relation to their cyber security but wanted companies to employ a reasonable set of procedures and policies to counter cyber attack. This is a wide brief but experts are beginning to agree that compliance with cyber security measures cannot be as simple as adhering to exercises. Each company is different and has its own culture so countermeasures need to be bespoke to each company. Cyber threat and attack, because of the nature of new technology, change rapidly therefore requiring any countermeasures to be equally fast changing and adaptable. The efficacy of any countermeasures in the final analysis rests with their effectiveness.[8]

Government slow to respond

Credit unions and banks are becoming so worried by what was termed at the recent Credit Union IT Security and Risk Management Tenth Summit as 'the decade of the breach' that they are asking the government why it is not doing enough. The Obama administration's launch of the National Cybersecurity Workforce Framework – a voluntary 'how-to guide' on enhancing cyber security – was deemed a good step in the right direction but Tom Schauer, CEO of the Seattle area-based TrustCC, criticised the Federal Financial Institutions Examination Council (FFIEC) for its failure to update its guidance on information security. During his presentation entitled 'CyberSecurity Framework: will the new guidance make the US more secure?' he lamented the fact that the guidance on information security was last updated in 2006.

The National Credit Union of America (NCUA) representative at the conference, Jerald Garner, stated that it is just a matter of when not if a major cyber attack will occur. He also noted that the complexity of cyber attacks is increasing and to manage this risk it is advisable that all boards of directors at financial institutions should have as a board member an information-security expert or information technologist.

Schauer agreed with Garner's assessment but still maintained that the FFIEC guidelines continue to be outdated and this was not the fault of the NCUA. Garner thought it was how the guidelines were interpreted rather than them being outdated that was the essential point. Schauer, however, argued that even with the NCUA overseeing the guidelines and credit unions proactively adopting the National Cybersecurity Workforce Framework, in certain aspects the financial industry is deadlocked with regard to cyber security. His concern seems to be that, while national cyber security offers a possible framework for defining and moving forward the industry security programme, there is a risk that the FFIEC could produce a framework that is wasteful and bureaucratic. As reflected in this book, Schauer and many of the presenters at this Credit Union conference believed that it was mainly retailers who would be the main target of security-data breaches. This has changed since the recent Carbanak malware incident in February 2014 in which over US$1 billion was stolen from 100 banks in 30 countries worldwide including the largest US bank JPMorgan Chase as mentioned in Chapter 1.

Schauer, whose company specialises in IT security, compliance risks and technology, stated that in managing this cyber risk credit unions should institute an enhanced cyber security network to brainstorm to find the best offensive measures to counter cyber attack. He said it was also imperative for executives to either hire a cyber security consultant or build an internal fraud-detection team in addition to adopting the National Cybersecurity Workforce Framework.[9]

Countermeasures in the US

While the countermeasure financial institutions in the US will find the most effective involves an interdisciplinary team internal to a company checking on all levels for both external and internal security-data breaches, there are others that derive from military and political organisations. As stated, US cyber risk to financial institutions is potentially the greatest in the world because of its status as the number-one economy with the largest political power. This alone invites have nots and competitors to divest the US of its wealth and political power. Additionally, the US is a relatively new country comprised of largely opportunistic migrants who left their home countries to settle in the land of opportunity. Trust in the US is low as compared to that, for example, in Japan where trust is high among Japanese who are bound by very traditional hegemonic rules set by society. US society, although seen to be one made up of all Americans, is sharply divided between, for example, the most populous white migrant groups of Germans and Irish, hispanics who feel that the US is very much an extension of Latin-based North and South America, and blacks who were brought to the US as slaves. Unwilling migrants form another distinct group. Although American, most refer back to their countries of origin, with Germans having settled in large numbers, for example, in Texas and Wisconsin, and re-creating in every US state, where they settled German-style beer halls or country retreats, still dancing to Lawrence Welk polkas. Trust is often invested in the country of origin of the migrants even after living in the US for generations. This lack of hegemony cannot provide a unified group of peoples who trust each other and present an American incorporated front against cyber attack as in Japan, which finds it easier to present a united front against cyber attack as shown in Chapter 8. Therefore, it may be that company-based solutions are best backed up by regulatory and military solutions.

Military solutions for managing risk

In the US, the Pentagon, the military defence branch of the US government, has tradtionally been the major innovator of high-technology solutions, which are spun out to the wider business community and populace from an original military application. GPS and a host of other inventions have emanated from the Pentagon, which were later adopted by civilians. The testing of these innovations has been as far flung as Australia's military base in Adelaide. Yet, Navy Admiral Michael S. Rogers testified on 4 March 2015 before the House Armed Services committee on cyber operations and improving the military's cyber security posture. He said in written testimony:

There is no Department of Defense [DoD] solution to our cybersecurity dilemmas. The global movement of threat activity in and through cyber-space blurs the US government's traditional understanding of how to address domestic and foreign military, criminal and intelligence activities.

Rogers also stated that the public and private sectors need each other's help:

The US government, the states and the private sector can't defend their infor-mation systems on their own against the most powerful cyber forces. We saw in the recent hack of Sony Pictures Entertainment that we have to be prepared to respond to cyber attacks with concerted actions across the whole of gov-ernment, using our nation's unique insights and complete range of capabili-ties in cooperation with the private sector.

Rogers noted that cyberspace is a very challenging environment that underlines its complexities and the need for a concerted effort to deal with it in tandem with the rest of government, business and the civilian population. He stated:

It is now part of virtually everything we in the US military do in all domains of the battle space and each of our lines of effort. There is hardly any mean-ingful distinction to be made now between events in cyberspace and events in the physical world, as they are so tightly linked.

He noted that Cybercom is expanding and operating at the same time, while per-forming a multitude of tasks across a diverse and complex mission set. In com-menting on progress of countermeasures to cyber attack he stated that new teams are guarding DoD networks and are prepared to help combatant commands deny freedom of maneuver to adversaries in cyberspace.

These steps forward are all occurring under Cybercom's Cyber Mission Force, which has been formed to turn strategy and plans into operational outcomes. The capability for Cybercom and its service cyber components is, Admiral Rogers further added, that '[w]e have a target of about 6,200 personnel in 133 teams, with the majority achieving at least initial operational capability by the end of fiscal year 2016'. Such insight is becoming increasingly urgent because every conflict in the world has a cyber dimension, and he added that the command sees patterns in cyber hostilities that indicate four main trends:

1   autocratic governments that view the open internet as a lethal threat to their regimes;
2   ongoing campaigns to steal intellectual property;
3   disruptions by a range of actors that range from denial-of-service attacks and network traffic manipulation to the use of destructive malware; and
4   states that develop capabilities and attain system access for potential hos-tilities, perhaps with the idea of enhancing deterrence or as a beachhead for future cyber sabotage.

Admiral Rogers said: 'We believe potential adversaries might be leaving cyber fingerprints on our critical infrastructure, partly to convey a message that our homeland is at risk if tensions ever escalate toward military conflict.'[10]

Managing two severe cyber attacks

In the US, as demonstrated by the examples given in Admiral Rogers' testimony, it is clear that leadership in dealing with cyber risk, threat and attack still comes from the military as it is often the first to be attacked and holds the relevant experience and resources. Two recent examples that the military's Cybercom dealt with in 2014 were that of Heartbleed and Shellshock.

The Heartbleed Bug is extremely serious and allows cyber attackers to steal often encrypted information, which is used to secure the internet for different applications such as email, websites and instant messaging. It also allows attackers to eavesdrop on communications, impersonate others and steal data from servers and users. Shellshock gives attackers the ability to run remote commands on a system. These serious flaws were left inadvertently in the software on which millions of computers and networks in many countries depend.

Admiral Rogers noted that responsible developers discovered both security holes and worked with trusted colleagues to quietly develop software patches that system administrators could use to gain an advantage on those who read the same vulnerability announcements and devised ways to identify and exploit unpatched computers.

Rogers stated: 'We at Cybercom and the National Security Agency [NSA] learned of Heartbleed and Shellshock at the same time that everyone else did.' The difference between Cybercom and civilian security is that military networks are tested for vulnerabilities thousands of times an hour and can catch vulnerabilities more quickly.

Rogers explained that '[b]y this point, our mission partners had devised ways to filter such probes before they touched our systems, [so] we were sheltered while we pushed out patches across DoD networks and monitored implementation'. This allowed administrators to start with the most vulnerable systems. He added further:

> Thanks to the efforts we have made in recent years, our responses . . . were comparatively quick, thorough and effective, and in both cases they helped inform corresponding efforts on the civilian side of the federal government. . . . We also know that other countries, including potential adversaries, struggled to cope with the Heartbleed and Shellshock vulnerabilities.[11]

Revising risk-management structures

Government-related agencies in the US are also beginning to take a risk management approach that, like the abovementioned military one, can be devolved to businesses such as financial institutions. They are working with representatives from government, industry and academia to update draft standards for cyber-physical systems (CPS) for cyber security and privacy. The National Institute of Standards and Technology (NIST) is reviewing its definitions of cyber security and the structure of risk management. As we argue in this book, no effective method can be fashioned to effectively manage cyber risk without a re-working of risk-management structures.

Victoria Pillitteri, who is leading the CPS cyber security group, stated: 'We have had an excellent ongoing discussion on our mailing list, both directly supporting the CPS framework and around general cybersecurity. I hope our community of interest continues with these discussions as we move forward.'

The new draft defines cyber security as a

[a] condition that results from the establishment and maintenance of protective measures that enable an enterprise to perform its mission or critical functions despite risks posed by threats to its use of information systems. Protective measures may involve a combination of deterrence, avoidance, prevention, detection, recovery, and correction that should form part of the enterprise's risk management approach.[12]

Additionally, the draft emphasises a holistic approach and defines privacy, safety and reliability within that framework when determining requirements for risk management.

The NIST working group draft does not propose one standard solution for all industry because of such great variation in sectors. NIST standards for the protection of critical infrastructure using traditional IT solutions are set within the context of '[b]uilding a "feedback loop" between deploying policy, monitoring events, analyzing for threats, and then responding (by notifying personnel or adjusting the policy) allows the CPS devices to defend themselves based on the events in their environment'. The draft changes NIST's focus in CPS from a cyber security 'tenets' and principles approach to a 'cross-property' risk-management approach. These discussions are to result in 2016 with the publication of a framework for CPS and directions for future actions on the internet of things devices.[13]

Change the password and biometrics

It has been argued that with cyber attack becoming more frequent the main line of defence should rest with the password, which is the entrance to the potential financial ill-gotten gains. The cyber security coordinator at the White House, Michael Daniel, stated at a security forum in 2014: 'I would love to kill the password dead as a primary security method because it's terrible.' To back up this statement is, as mentioned in this book a number of times, the fact that tens of millions of passwords have been stolen in breaches of major retailers and banks including Target, Home Depot and JPMorgan Chase. Password theft is a key element in identity theft, the biggest source of fraud complaints in the US.

Many IT companies have been supplying the current demand for biometrics as the alternative 'password', which can include fingerprints, iris scans, facial or voice recognition and other methods. Apple's introduction of its iPhones with Touch ID was one of the first biometric solutions, which was followed by Samsung with its own fingerprint scanner and Qualcomm's 3D fingerprint technology incorporated in the chips used in many mobile devices.

Apple's Touch ID is a fingerprint identity on the home button that is used to activate the phone, meaning that consumers do not need special training to use it and, importantly, is only stored on the device itself so there is no database to be hacked. E-commerce companies can use the phone's authentication for more secure transactions without passwords.

Microsoft announced in February 2015 that it will implement new authentication methods in Windows 10, which also include biometrics.

International Data Corp has stated that roughly 15 per cent of mobile devices will be accessed with biometrics in 2015, and the number will grow to 50 per cent by 2020.

Acuity Market Intelligence has projected that by 2020, global mobile biometric market revenues will reach US$33.3 billion, including biometrically enabled mobile devices, apps and software for payments.

Biometrics, however, is not without its critics. There are concerns that if an iris or a fingerprint is compromised it cannot be replaced so readily as a new credit card. There have already been successful efforts to falsify biometric solutions, with 'liveness' detection being developed to counter falsification.

James Lewis, a cyber security specialist at the Center for Strategic and International Studies in Washington, summed up the situation of pressure for a new identity-verification system being derived from the response to huge losses affecting the financial sector. He told Agence France-Presse: 'We don't know what the technology will be . . . [c]onsumers will decide what they like, and we will then see if the bad guys can figure out how to crack it.'[14]

Time to hack back?

At the February 2015 Davos Forum senior banking officials were reported to be lobbying for the right to strike back against hackers by finding their computers and disabling them. The bankers expressed their frustration at having their data stolen and their business disrupted from hackers in other countries.

Dennis Blair, the former Director of National Intelligence in the Obama administration, is now supporting electronic countermeasures, which are known in cyber security circles as strikeback or hacking back. He had in 2013 co-authored a report from the US Commission on the theft of American intellectual property that considered but did not actually authorise strikeback operations. Rather, the report suggested non-destructive alternatives, for example, such as electronically tagging stolen data. It did suggest that a re-think of the law forbidding strikeback should be considered. As law enforcers in Western countries do not have legal jurisdiction to prosecute hackers in other countries, they attempt to pass information to their counterparts in those countries. However, local police are often uncooperative. It is also illegal in most countries in the Western world to carry out vigilante justice.

There are less destructive forms of strikeback that may just involve probing the offending computer to find out what form of tool attackers are using for cyber attack, yet even that can be deemed illegal as trespass.

There is even the greater risk that a totally innocent set of computers, remotely controlled by cyber criminals, will be damaged as botnets – a collection of computers owned by innocent users that have been infected by malware – are often used. For example, cybercriminals frequently use compromised computers that are part of a botnet to launch their attacks, according to Bill Nelson, the executive director of Financial Services – Information Sharing and Analysis Center, a US industry forum for financial-services firms to privately share information about cyber threats.

It is against the law to hack into others' computers especially across borders but Bloomberg in December 2014 reported that bankers have been hiring contractors to disable hackers' computers that have been responsible for hacking into financial institutions computers. The watershed was a major attack on US banks by hackers believed to be based in Iran. According to Bloomberg, the FBI discovered that computers used in a cyber attack on the banking community had been disabled by a third party, and the agency had investigated banks to see if they had already engaged in strikeback activity on a cross-border basis. The banks under investigation were not found to be culpable.

John Pescatore, who worked in the Secret Service and the NSA before becoming a director of security research and training company the SANS Institute, stated that banks have been sensitive in particular to hacking across international borders. He stated further: 'They need to cross country boundaries to do it. That's what was really coming out of Davos, it's that boundary crossing issue where I think the larger financial institutions are saying: "we need some help".'

John Carson, the executive vice-president of BITS, the technology policy division of the US Financial Services Roundtable, an industry association for financial companies, noted that rather than engaging in such legally risky behaviour, banks that are attacked should share information about the attacks with the government to help prepare an industry-wide response. Carson warned that information sharing, while good for cyber security, may carry its own legal risks: 'Today if there is an attack, there's a reluctance to share that information because it could be used against that institution in a civil suit.'

In January 2015, the Cyber Intelligence Sharing and Protection Act (CISPA) was reintroduced in the House. The Act allows companies to share information about cyber threats and attacks with law-enforcement agencies without fear of legal reprisal.

In February 2015, Senator Tom Carper (D-Del) introduced the Cyber Threat Sharing Act of 2015, which is similar to CISPA. President Obama also signed an executive order supporting cyber security information sharing.

With this information entrusted to them, the US government might be the ideal partner to strikeback against cyber criminals. However, when dealing with such complex cross-border issues in which government is involved, the situation then becomes a political one rather than a legal one as other countries' legal jurisdictions vary to such a degree that one country's government support for hacking, as we will see below, is what another country cannot legally sanction.[15]

Managing cyber risk through politics

The US continues to be the number-one country in the world for producing innovative intellectual property rights. It is followed by Japan in terms of holding the greatest number of innovative patents, despite Japan no longer being the second-largest economy in the world. China is now the second-largest economy globally but does not produce anywhere near the same amount of high-quality patents as the US or Japan but has ambitions to be the world's number-one economy. The US is accordingly losing millions of dollars every year through intellectual property theft, and the intellectual property stolen is ever increasing in terms of number and seriousness.

Chinese government hacking

The FBI has been investigating a possible data breach of Register.com, a network that manages more than 1.4 million website addresses. The *Financial Times* reported that the cyber attack on US company Register.com included the theft of employee passwords and unauthorised access to its network over a year-long period that did not cause disruptions or theft of client data. It is believed by law-enforcement officials that this cyber hack was a step towards undermining major parts of internet infrastructure because the hacking gave hackers the ability to reroute traffic to other websites, access emails associated with the sites and steal data.

This latest cyber attack is another indication that Chinese state-sponsored cyber attacks are increasing. In 2014, the US Justice Department indicted five Chinese military personnel for hacking into a number of major US companies to steal trade secrets, which falls under intellectual property. This was an unprecedented ruling and is discussed further below.

Web.com, the parent company of Register.com, issued a statement in its February 2015 filings with the SEC that stated that cyber security risks run high and even when detected cannot be remedied in a timely manner.

As mentioned it is difficult for such US companies to develop security protocols and tools to monitor and curb hacking because of the dearth of federal standards, which are currently still being discussed in the US Senate.

As referred to in this book when discussing major health-insurance security breaches, in February 2015, the *Washington Post* reported that the Chinese government was linked to a hack of the major US health-insurance company Anthem, which involved the stealing of personal data, including the social security numbers of 80 million Anthem members and employees. In this security-data breach, a US cyber security firm concluded that the malware used was identical to the code used against a small US defence contractor and that the malware derived from China according to the FBI.[16]

From 2006 to 2014 an unprecedented indictment against a state actor occurred because of the hacking of a number of US companies by five Chinese military hackers who were subsequently indicted by a grand jury in the Western District of Pennsylvania in 2014 for computer hacking, economic espionage and other offences aimed at six US companies in metals, solar products and nuclear power.

Rather than a straightforward case of intellectual property rights theft, the Chinese hackers stole trade secrets that would be useful for Chinese competitors including the state-owned enterprises. They also stole sensitive data and emails in relation to trade disputes, which would provide competitors or adversaries in litigation insights into the strategies and weaknesses of the US companies in dispute.

The US Attorney-General at the time, Eric Holder, stated:

> This is a case alleging economic espionage by members of the Chinese military and represents the first ever charges against a state actor for this type of hacking, the range of trade secrets and other sensitive business information stolen in this case is significant and demands an aggressive response. Success in the global market place should be based solely on a company's ability to innovate and compete, not on a sponsor government's ability to spy and steal business secrets. This administration will not tolerate actions by any nation that seeks to illegally sabotage American companies and undermine the integrity of fair competition in the operation of the free market.

The FBI Director at the time, James B. Corney, noted:

> For too long, the Chinese government has blatantly sought to use cyber espionage to obtain economic advantage for its state-owned industries, the indictment announced today is an important step. But there are many more victims, and there is much more to be done. With our unique criminal and national security authorities, we will continue to use all legal tools at our disposal to counter cyber espionage from all sources.

'State actors engaged in cyber espionage for economic advantage are not immune from the law just because they hack under the shadow of their country's flag', said John Carlin, at the time Assistant Attorney General for National Security. 'Cyber theft is real theft and we will hold state sponsored cyber thieves accountable as we would any other transnational criminal organization that steals our goods and breaks our laws.'

'This 21st century burglary has to stop', said David Hickton, at the time US Attorney for the Western District of Pennsylvania. 'This prosecution vindicates hard working men and women in Western Pennsylvania and around the world who play by the rules and deserve a fair shot and a level playing field.'

Pittsburgh, Pennsylvania may seem a strange place to carry out an indictment but it is where Carnegie-Mellon's CERT is based, a public–private venture fighting cyber risk/threat. The five Chinese were officers in Unit 61398 of the Third Department of the Chinese People's Liberation Army, as is mentioned in Chapter 5 of this book, written by Motohiro Tsuchiya. Although an indictment is an accusation and a court of law presumes innocence until proved guilty, this is most likely the most serious confrontation with China over corporate, intellectual property secrets. The Chinese military hackers accused include the notorious cyber hackers known online as 'Ugly Gorilla' and 'Kandy Goo'.

The Chinese government's response was that economic and national security are one and the same. They also called the US government hypocritical as Edward Snowden's leaks showed the US spied on Huawei but it appeared it was being monitored to find out the countries buying Huawei's products.[17]

Cyber risk/attack within the framework of the quest for political power, competition, greed and mistrust is set to continue, with the latest race between the US and China to build the most supercomputers a sign of future relations. The US in February 2015 banned Intel and Nvidia from selling their processors to four Chinese supercomputer centres because the US government believes that the world's fastest computers, the Chinese-built Tianhe-2 and the seventeenth Tianhe-1A, are being used in nuclear tests and against US security and foreign policy.[18]

Conclusion

Financial institutions are not immune to this state-initiated and state-backed cyber hacking and attack. Negotiations have been ongoing between the Obama administration and Chinese officials concerning these issues but when economic growth, which is often based on cyber theft, and national security are viewed as one and the same, it is difficult to manage politically. It could be that information sharing and some form of strikeback through government law enforcement may be the only way to manage cyber risk in financial institutions and most especially in cross-border situations.

Notes

1 'Target data breach price tag: $252 million and counting' in *Cyber Risk Network News Byte* (26 February 2015) from original source *Mondaq Business Briefing*, Kevin McGinty, Advisen Ltd, www.privacyandsecuritymatters.com/2015/02/target-data-breach-price-tag-252-million-and-counting/?utm_source=Mondaq&utm_medium=syndication&utm_campaign=View-Original.
2 'Congress looks to insurance industry for cyber guidance' in the *Washington Post* 2015 as discussed by Erin Ayers in *Cyber Risk Network News Byte* (19 March 2015) Advisen Ltd, www.advisenltd.com/2015/03/19/congress-looks-to-insurance-industry-for-cyber-guidance/.
3 'Target data breach price tag: $252 million and counting'.
4 'Broader cyber insurance worries drive insurances purchases' in *Cyber Risk Network News Byte*, Erin Ayers (15 March 2015) Advisen Ltd, www.cyberrisknetwork.com/2015/03/15/broader-cyber-worries-drive-cyber-insurance-purchases/.

5 Joel Lewis of Lloyd's of London, written for this book and loosely related to his presentation at the Association of Business Insurance conference on 5 May 2015 on cyber risk.
6 'Draft of Senate cyber bill tackles retaliation rules' in *Cyber Risk News Bytes* (19 February 2015), Advisen Ltd. Source Damian Paletta for *Dow Jones News Service*, www.wsj.com/articles/draft-of-senate-cyber-bill-tackles-retaliation-rules-1424382920.
7 With permission from Advisen Ltd, Cyber Risk Insights Conference held in London, UK, 10 February 2015.
8 'SEC warns firm leaders on cyber security policies' in *Cyber Risk News Bytes* (8 June 2015) from *Financial Planning* Kenneth Corbin (online) (3 June 2015), www.financial-planning.com/news/regulatory_compliance/sec-warns-firm-leaders-on-cybersecurity-policies-2692162-1.html.
9 'Some have referred to 2014 as "The Year of the Breach," but we could be headed for "The Decade of the Breach," if all the stakeholders, including financial institutions and their regulators, don't speed up their efforts to head off mounting security threats.' 'Industry, regulators can't afford to drag their heels on cybersecurity', *The Credit Union Journal* (online) (24 February 2015), www.cujournal.com/news/technology/industry-regulators-cant-afford-to-drag-their-heels-on-cybersecurity-1024010-1.html.
10 'Cybercom chief: cyber threat blurs roles, relationships', Cheryl Pellerin on DoD News from *Defense Documents and Publications* (6 March 2015), www.defense.gov/News-Article-View/Article/604225.
11 Ibid.
12 'Counterintelligence awareness glossary', Center for Development of Security Excellence (n.d.), www.cdse.edu/documents/toolkits-fsos/ci-definitions.pdf, p. 5.
13 Joshua Higgins, 'NIST defines cybersecurity for cyber-physical systems' (19 February 2015), http://dev.insidecybersecurity.com/daily-news/nist-defines-cybersecurity-cyber-physical-systems-outlines-risk-management.
14 'As hacking grows, biometric security gains momentum', Agence France-Presse World News (3/7/15), https://twitter.com/afp/status/574214635307556864.
15 'Should we hack the hackers', *Guardian* (online) (9 March 2015), www.theguardian.com/technology/2015/mar/09/cybercrime-should-we-hack-the-hackers.
16 'FBI looking into Chinese military involvement in cyber hack of US company', *UPI Top Stories* (18 March2015), www.upi.com/Top_News/World-News/2015/03/18/FBI-looking-into-Chinese-military-involvement-in-cyber-hack-of-US-company/2531426688682/.
17 For further details of this case and the source of the above information, see *Reuters Online News* (19 May 2015) (also see Appendix for details of this case).
18 'US blocks Intel from supplying chips for Chinese supercomputers', Jeffrey Burt, *eWeek.com*, QuinStreet Inc. (11 April 2015), www.eweek.com/servers/us-blocks-intel-from-supplying-chips-for-chinese-supercomputers.html.

Appendix: Huawei case details

Summary of the indictment

Defendants: Wang Dong, Sun Kailiang, Wen Xinyu, Huang Zhenyu and Gu Chunhui, who were officers in Unit 61398 of the Third Department of the

Chinese People's Liberation Army. The indictment alleges that Wang, Sun and Wen, among others known and unknown to the grand jury, hacked or attempted to hack into US entities named in the indictment, while Huang and Gu supported their conspiracy by, among other things, managing infrastructure (e.g. domain accounts) used for hacking.

Victims: Westinghouse Electric Co. (Westinghouse), US subsidiaries of Solar World AG (SolarWorld), United States Steel Corp. (US Steel), Allegheny Technologies Inc. (ATI), the United Steel, Paper and Forestry, Rubber, Manufacturing, Energy, Allied Industrial and Service Workers International Union (known as USW) and Alcoa Inc.

Time period: 2006–14.

Crimes: Thirty-one counts as follows (all defendants are charged on all counts).

Table 4.1 Summary of the indictment

Count(s)	Charge	Statute	Maximum penalty
1	Conspiring to commit computer fraud and abuse	18 U.S.C. § 1030(b)	10 years
2–9	Accessing (or attempting to access) a protected computer without authorisation to obtain information for the purpose of commercial advantage and private financial gain	18 U.S.C. §§ 1030(a)(2) (C), 1030(c)(2)(B) (i)–(iii), and 2	5 years (each count)
10–23	Transmitting a program, information, code or command with the intent to cause damage to protected computers	18 U.S.C. §§ 1030(a) (5)(A), 1030(c)(4)(B) and 2	10 years (each count)
24–9	Aggravated identity theft	18 U.S.C. §§ 1028A(a) (1), (b), (c)(4) and 2	2 years (mandatory consecutive)
30	Economic espionage	18 U.S.C. §§ 1831(a)(2), (a)(4) and 2	15 years
31	Trade-secret theft	18 U.S.C. §§ 1832(a)(2), (a)(4) and 2	10 years

Table 4.2 Summary of defendants' conduct alleged in the indictment

Defendant	Victim	Criminal conduct
Sun	Westinghouse	In 2010, while Westinghouse was building four AP1000 power plants in China and negotiating other terms of the construction with a Chinese state-owned enterprise (SOE) (SOE-1), including technology transfers, Sun stole confidential and proprietary technical and design specifications for pipes, pipe supports and pipe routing within the AP1000 plant buildings. Additionally, in 2010 and 2011, while Westinghouse was exploring other business ventures with SOE-1, Sun stole sensitive, non-public and deliberative emails belonging to senior decision-makers responsible for Westinghouse's business relationship with SOE-1.
Wen	SolarWorld	In 2012, at about the same time the Commerce Department found that Chinese solar product manufacturers had 'dumped' products into US markets at prices below fair value, Wen and at least one other, unidentified co-conspirator stole thousands of files including information about SolarWorld's cash flow, manufacturing metrics, production line information, costs, and privileged attorney-client communications relating to ongoing trade litigation, among other things. Such information would have enabled a Chinese competitor to target SolarWorld's business operations aggressively from a variety of angles.
Wang and Sun	US Steel	In 2010, US Steel was participating in trade cases with Chinese steel companies, including one particular SOE (SOE-2). Shortly before the scheduled release of a preliminary determination in one such litigation, Sun sent spearphishing emails to US Steel employees, some of whom were in a division associated with the litigation. Some of these emails resulted in the installation of malware on US Steel computers. Three days later, Wang stole hostnames and descriptions of US Steel computers (including those that controlled physical access to company facilities and mobile device access to company networks). Wang thereafter took steps to identify and exploit vulnerable servers on that list.
Wen	ATI	In 2012, ATI was engaged in a joint venture with SOE-2, competed with SOE-2 and was involved in a trade dispute with SOE-2. In April of that year, Wen gained access to ATI's network and stole network credentials for virtually every ATI employee.

Wen	USW	In 2012, USW was involved in public disputes over Chinese trade practices in at least two industries. At or about the time USW issued public statements regarding those trade disputes and related legislative proposals, Wen stole emails from senior USW employees containing sensitive, non-public and deliberative information about USW strategies, including strategies related to pending trade disputes. USW's computers continued to beacon to the conspiracy's infrastructure until at least early 2013.
Sun	Alcoa	About three weeks after Alcoa announced a partnership with a Chinese SOE (SOE-3) in February 2008, Sun sent a spearphishing email to Alcoa. Thereafter, in or about June 2008, unidentified individuals stole thousands of email messages and attachments from Alcoa's computers, including internal discussions concerning that transaction.
Huang		Huang facilitated hacking activities by registering and managing domain accounts that his co-conspirators used to hack into US entities. Additionally, between 2006 and at least 2009, Unit 61398 assigned Huang to perform programming work for SOE-2, including the creation of a 'secret' database designed to hold corporate 'intelligence' about the iron and steel industries, including information about American companies.
Gu		Gu managed domain accounts used to facilitate hacking activities against American entities and also tested spearphishing emails in furtherance of the conspiracy.

5 Cyber security of financial sectors in Japan, South Korea and China

Motohiro Tsuchiya

Introduction

Japanese financial sectors faced huge organisational reforms called the 'financial big bang' from 1996 through 2002. Large and deep market reorganisations were seen and many financial companies were consolidated into a few groups. They were forced to enter global competition, and great protective measures and regulation called the 'convoy system' were removed. Needs for cost cutting and the penetration of internet services made financial companies reduce the number of offline branches and accelerate the rollout of telephone banking and internet banking services. However, such cyber services have raised risks of cyber threat, crimes and attacks.

The same types of rapid changes are taking place in the Republic of Korea (ROK – South Korea) and the People's Republic of China (PRC – China). In 1997 the Asian financial crisis left huge damage to the South Korean economy. International pressures by the International Monetary Fund and others forced South Korea to start structural reforms of the financial sectors. Transparency of financial transactions was a key target to dispense with the bad parts of the *chaebol* (conglomerate)-based economy. One of the proposed solutions was adoption of the internet. After the Asian financial crisis South Korea became one of the most advanced broadband adopters in the world. Such dependency on the internet, however, raised cyber risks. In fact, South Korea has received a lot of small and large cyber threats and attacks since then.

China has been increasingly asked to open up its market especially after its entry to the World Trade Organization in 2001. Needless to say, Chinese economic policy and financial policy are under the strong control of the Chinese Communist Party. However, the size of the Chinese market leads to the larger influence of China in the world market and the Chinese government is not allowed to have free hand over economic and financial policies in the Chinese economy. China recovered from the 1997 Asian financial crisis by using all measures at its disposal, but structural problems such as the recent 'shadow banks' expose its underdeveloped side. China is notorious for originating cyber attacks around the world. However, after an internal inspection of China, domestic cyber incidents are rapidly increasing and they are quite serious in nature. As economic and financial development expands, so too is the rising number of cyber risks.

This chapter outlines cyber risks of the financial sectors in these three countries while mostly focusing on Japan. The next section looks at the general situation of cyber attacks in East Asia. The third section deals with cyber risks in financial sectors and governmental institutional responses, which continue to be the most important actors in East Asia.

Cyber attacks in East Asia

Rise in numbers of internet users and cyber attacks

The main reason why East Asia is one of the most active cyber battlegrounds is that it is the most dynamically developing area of the internet. Figure 5.1 shows the trends of internet populations in Japan, South Korea and China. This indicates that Japan and South Korea reached saturated conditions in the late 2000s, but China is still growing. At the end of 2013, Japan's internet penetration rate was 82.8 per cent and Korea's was 82.1 per cent, while China's was just 45.8 per cent. There continues to be much capacity for growth in China. Such increases in the internet population have made cyberspace a new domain for cyber risk and crime.

In February 2013 the *New York Times* reported that a 12-storey building in the northeastern part of Shanghai was the site from which cyber attacks emanated against the United States and other countries. The article stated that Unit 61398 of the Chinese People's Liberation Army (PLA) was housed in the building and that the unit was organising large-scale and sophisticated cyber operations based on a report by Mandiant, an American private security company. The area where the building was sited is well known to native Shanghai residents as a military district. Apartments housing military families surround the building.

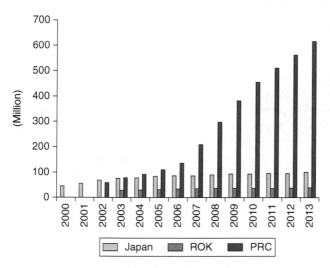

Figure 5.1 Trends of internet population growth in Japan, South Korea and China.

Sources: Japanese Ministry of Internal Affairs and Communications, Korea Internet & Security Agency and China Internet Network Information Center.

However, this news was not so new. The name of the Unit 61398 was mentioned in another report, 'The Chinese People's Liberation Army signals intelligence and cyber reconnaissance infrastructure', by Project 2049 Institute in 2011, two years before the Mandiant report. If this is not new, why did the *New York Times* report this in February 2013? It is probably because the time was right for the US government to be able to confirm it, albeit informally. In 2011, the US government did not respond to the Project 2049 Institute report. However, two years later, there was no harm or obstacle in reporting this to the public and it was no longer worth protecting it as a valuable information asset. It also coincided with the executive branch of the US government's request for an increase in budget from Congress for cyber security. The news was a good impetus to seek further funding. Directly after the report, President Barack Obama made a State of Union address and signed an executive order for cyber security. It became a kind of political show to highlight the importance of cyber security in political arenas.

On 20 March 2013, the ROK witnessed cyber attacks against broadcasting stations and banks. Back-office systems of broadcasters were forced to stop and automated teller machines (ATMs) of banks became inoperable. However, these attacks were odd. Broadcasters were attacked, but their broadcasting systems themselves still remained live. This meant that they could broadcast that they were being attacked, which incorporates both threat and attack. The attackers seemed to not break broadcasting systems in order to have the attack advertised on the news. Attacks against ATMs also signal that the attackers wished to make a point that they could attack South Korea through cyberspace if they so wished. If the attackers genuinely wished to disrupt the South Korean economy and to cause damage to its military forces, other strategic targets could have been selected. It was reported that the Democratic People's Republic of Korea (DPRK – North Korea) launched these attacks. The DPRK is reported to have thousands of cyber warriors inside its military forces.

Distributed Denial of Service (DDoS)

There are several types of methods of cyber attacks. The first is DDoS attacks. This is a rather classic type of cyber attack and we have seen many examples in the world. One of the most notorious examples was in Estonia in 2007. Estonia shares a border with Russia and is one of the three Baltic States that were occupied by the Soviet Union during the Second World War. Estonia's capital city is Tallinn. A big bronze statue was situated in a park in the central part of the city. The statue was to remember past Soviet heroes, but the Estonian government tried to move it to a suburban cemetery for fallen heroes after following the necessary procedures including contacting bereaved families of the heroes. Right after this news was reported in Russia, DDoS attacks broke out against Estonia.

DDoS attacks utilise zombie personal computers (PCs), which are infected with computer viruses and distributed throughout the world. Zombie PC networks are called 'botnets' as mentioned in Chapter 2. After commands from attackers, these botnets begin accessing targeted computer servers. The servers receive an enormous amount of access from many computers in the world. The access comes from all over the world and appears to be legitimate. It is very difficult to distinguish malicious access zombie PCs from normal access. Finally these servers are forced to shut down due to overcapacity.

Estonia is one of the most advanced information societies in the world, because as a former satellite country of the Soviet Union it was entrusted with many of its people trained to operate the Russian space programme. People use very little cash in their daily lives. They use digital cash in the form of smart cards or mobile phones. The DDoS attacks brought down many necessary servers in Estonian society for several days. This was the first case in which a country lost social functions through cyber attack. It was reported that a Russian patriot group did organise these attacks, but the involvement of the Russian government was not confirmed.

Similar DDoS attacks were found in many countries after this case. One of the most shocking DDoS attacks were the ones against the US and the ROK in July 2009. It occurred on July 4th, American Independence Day. Websites of the Department of Defense, the Department of Treasury and other governmental and commercial organisations were hit simultaneously by infected computers from global sites. Owners of such infected computers had no idea of what their computers were doing. Those affected websites were forced to shut down or became very slow to respond to access attempts.

Three days later the same types of attacks were seen in the ROK. Further investigation revealed that the same attacker launched the attacks against the two countries. It was also reported that the DPRK was responsible. Japan was not a victim, but was shocked by the fact that eight servers in Japan were used to attack the two countries. South Korean police contacted Japanese police and identified eight servers, but the owners of the servers were oblivious. They were unaware their servers were involved in the attacks. Someone had penetrated their servers and embedded malicious codes in them.

However, this shocking fact was not widely discussed in Japan. What was happening in July and August 2009? It was the final phase of Prime Minister Taro Aso's administration. Aso's Liberal Democratic Party had lost the national election in August, and Yukio Hatoyama of the Democratic Party of Japan became the new prime minister. The Japanese government was too preoccupied to address the July DDoS attacks in the US and the ROK.

In December that year, five months after the attacks, Hirofumi Hirano, Chief Cabinet Secretary of the Hatoyama administration, mentioned in a press conference that 'the government is assuming that Japan can be a target of similar attacks. Cyber attacks are issues of national security and crisis management.' It then took five months for the government to establish the 'Information Security Strategy for Protecting the Nation' in May 2010.[1]

In September of that year, a Chinese fishing boat crashed into a Japanese Coast Guard's patrol boat and the captain of the Chinese fishing boat was arrested by the Japanese Coast Guard. After this incident large-scale street demonstrations against Japan began in many cities in China and they spilled over onto the internet. Messages such as 'Attack Japan Online!' were posted on bulletin boards.

One of them listed Japanese government websites and private-sector targets including famous cartoonists as possible targets of DDoS attacks. The list was very long and targets were almost indiscriminate. However, the Japanese government could read such online postings in Japan, and after the 2010 Strategy the government became so well-prepared that subsequent damage from such attacks was kept to a minimum. DDoS attacks cause annoyance to victims, but they are not lethal.

Advanced Persistent Threats (APTs)

In light of possibilities to be used against financial sectors, the second type of cyber attack is called APTs. Email is a decisively attractive application for internet users. Many APTs use email as a starting point. On 11 March 2011 Japan was hit by big earthquakes and tsunamis. Many people lost their lives and northeast Japan was in a state of confusion. Twenty days later, many Japanese government officials received email messages entitled 'Yesterday's Radiation Levels'. Fukushima Daiichi nuclear power plant was in serious trouble due to a radiation leak. Everyone in Japan was so worried about it that most government officials opened email attachment files without any doubts. Those files contained customised computer viruses and attackers penetrated government networks. 'Customised' means that viruses were created to fit into the targets' systems and environments. As they were not commodity-type viruses, anti-virus software could not detect them initially. Such software is adding newly found viruses on a daily basis, but it requires some time to be updated. Undetected periods of a few days offer a window of opportunity for attackers. They use advanced persistent methods to get into target computers and networks. Once they can enter into computers, they make the best use of available information. For example, they send disguised emails to the targets' friends, partners or higher valuable targets to enter into more computers and networks.

In September 2011, *Yomiuri Shinbun*, one of the most popular newspapers in Japan, reported on its front page that Mitsubishi Heavy Industries (MHI) had been a target of APTs. Before attacks against MHI, an industry association was the first victim. The association did not pay attention to cyber security risks at all, as it believed it did not hold confidential or high-value information. One of the employees of the association was compromised and this employee's email account was manipulated remotely. Disguised email messages were sent to MHI and other Japanese military contractors. One or more of MHI's employees opened disguised emails and attachments from the association because they looked real.

Political leaders at the National Diet (Parliament) of Japan were distressed by this news, as MHI had high-tech information from American military contractors for joint production of weapons and such. Loss of this type of high-tech information might have ruined the Japan–US relationship. However, later investigations revealed email passwords of all National Diet members were stolen and their email messages were being read by attackers. Kaspersky Lab called the attacker group 'Icefog' and reported that the group was attacking not only Japanese but also South Korean military contractors.[2] They were probably cyber mercenaries.

Analysis of the computer viruses found signs that their creators must be native Chinese users, but the attacks needed native Japanese and Korean speakers as well. As the attacks were carried out very quickly, it is probable that the group was hired for its professional skills.

APTs do not usually cause physical damage or loss of lives. They are rather cyber-espionage activities to steal confidential information or intellectual property rights. However, some attackers intend to destroy data too. In 2012 Aramco, an oil company in Saudi Arabia, lost data in 30,000 of their computers. As stated above, South Korean broadcasters' computers lost data and bank ATMs ceased to work in March 2013. The methods used in the two countries were quite similar. Attackers were more interested in disrupting targets businesses rather than stealing data. This is known as business disruption as explained in Chapter 1 of this book.

US–China summit talks

During the 2008 US presidential election campaign, Democratic candidate Barack Obama made the best use of the internet. His campaign team utilised Twitter, Facebook, YouTube and other methods as well as online donations. He and his team knew the power of the internet. In contrast, it was said that President George W. Bush was not very interested in the internet. However, the preparation of the Operation Olympic Games started during the Bush administration. It was targeting a nuclear facility in Iran. Before its official operation code name was leaked, it had been called 'Stuxnet'.[3] When President-elect Obama met President Bush before the administration change, they talked about the continuation of the operation and agreed on it.

Shortly after his inauguration President Obama ordered his staff to conduct a review on cyber security. He received a '60-days review report', which was formally entitled 'Cyberspace policy review: assuring a trusted and resilient information and communications infrastructure', in two months. Then, in June 2009, an order to establish the United States Cyber Command (USCYBERCOM) under the United States Strategic Command was issued. Three-star general Keith Alexander was promoted to a four-star general and became the first commander of the USCYBERCOM while continuing his directorship at the National Security Agency (NSA), a powerful signals-intelligence agency under the Department of Defense.[4]

Is there a threat of a looming cyber war? In October 2012 Secretary of Defense Leon E. Panetta warned:

> The collective result of these kinds of attacks could be a cyber Pearl Harbor; an attack that would cause physical destruction and the loss of life. In fact, it would paralyze and shock the nation and create a new, profound sense of vulnerability.[5]

A cyber Pearl Harbor could be more than DDoS attacks or APTs. How can we respond to these risks and threats?

In June 2013 the United States and China held a summit talk in California. One of the topics discussed between President Obama and President Xi Jinping was cyber security. However, they did not speak about a 'cyber war'. Instead, they talked about economic theft of American intellectual property rights. After the summit talks, Tom Donilon, national security advisor, held a press briefing and stated: 'What we're talking about here are efforts by entities in China to, through cyber attacks, engage in the theft of public and private property – intellectual property and other property in the United States.'[6] It implied that the Chinese PLA and government sectors were assisting Chinese companies to obtain valuable technology, business and other information through cyber attacks or cyber espionage.

This cyber security discussion was disturbed by Edward Snowden's revelation of NSA top-secret documents. Snowden was a former contract worker for NSA in Hawaii, but he flew to Hong Kong and contacted media reporters to give them documents, which he downloaded at an NSA facility. Right before both presidents met, the *Guardian* released breaking news that NSA was collecting on a massive scale communications data from Verizon, one of the largest American telephone operators.[7] China stiffened its stance on cyber security issues and did not agree on any points with the US. After Snowden's revelations, China claimed that it was a victim of US cyber attacks.

However, without Snowden's revelations, it was highly probable that China could not reach an agreement with the US. For China, cyber security was a domestic issue as well as an international issue. People outside China tend to think that the Chinese government is highly strategic and the government coordinates everything including cyber attacks. It is not necessarily true. If you look at the internal workings of China, domestic cyber security issues are very serious. Chinese black-hat hackers attack each other and government systems are sometimes targets of cyber attacks and cyber espionage. Economically valuable information is traded on the black market and employees steal corporate information to get a better job in a different company.

Chinese business people at the National People's Congress are demanding the government to take stricter and more effective responses to cyber risks and threats. It is almost impossible to stop and eliminate cyber incidents inside and outside China.[8] It is probable that China is experiencing cyber attacks and espionage from foreign players. Therefore, it is partly true that China is a victim of cyber attacks. For the Chinese, maintaining honour and face is considered as very important. President Xi cannot make a promise that he could not keep.

Cyber risks in financial sectors and governmental responses

Finance as a critical infrastructure

The financial sector is recognised as one of the most critical infrastructures in many countries. In Japan's case, critical infrastructures include: (1) telecommunications; (2) finance; (3) airlines; (4) railways; (5) electricity; (6) gas; (7) government services (including local municipalities); (8) medical services; (9) water supply; and (10) logistics. In May 2014, the Japanese government added:

(11) chemical plants; (12) credit services; and (13) oil (Table 5.1). Protection of critical infrastructure in Japan has been defined and discussed in government action plans published in December 2005, February 2009 and May 2014.

The financial sector includes four subsectors: banking; life insurance; non-life insurance; and securities. Anticipated system failures in these subsectors are stoppage of: (1) paying out of deposits, financial transactions and loan businesses; (2) accounting clearance; (3) information services regarding electronic records and fund settlements; (4) paying out of insurance monies; (5) buying and selling of securities; (6) money transfers of corporate bonds and securities; and (7) transactions of financial instruments.[9] Whether it is due to a cyber attack or not, affected financial institutions must report any actions such as service stoppage or delay to the government based on business laws such as the Banking Act or the Securities and Exchange Act.

Cyber risks in financial sectors

Financial transactions are increasingly dependent on computers and networks. There used to be financial centers such as Wall Street in New York or Kabutocho in Tokyo. Physical location was important for businesses as well as direct human interaction. However, computers now process most financial transactions, and space for human activities is becoming reduced. Many transactions are automated by computer programs and are completed in milliseconds, or sometimes in microseconds.[10] If there is a system error in such competitive market environments, that

Table 5.1 Critical infrastructure sectors in Japan

Sectors	Presiding ministry
Finance	Financial Services Agency
Telecommunications	Ministry of Internal Affairs and Communications
Government services (including local municipalities)	
Medical services	Ministry of Health, Labour and Welfare
Water supply	
Electricity	Ministry of Economy, Trade and Industry
Gas	
Chemical	
Credit	
Oil	
Airlines	Ministry of Land, Infrastructure and Transport
Railways	
Logistics	

Source: ISPC, 'The Third Action Plan for Information Security Preparedness of Critical Infrastructures', www.nisc.go.jp/active/infra/pdf/infra_rt3.pdf, 19 May 2014 (in Japanese).

business has to accept huge losses. Even if there is no direct loss, investors will shun that company. If a stock exchange has such a system error, its reputation will be lost and market confidence will be lost too.

American stock exchanges, which are believed to be ahead of other foreign exchanges, are experiencing many system failures lately.[11] On 22 August 2013, NASDAQ, which deals with Apple and other high-tech companies, was forced to stop exchanges of all securities for three hours. Two days before this, the market was in trouble because of a mistake made by Goldman Sachs' automated transaction system. Prices of some issues declined to new lows quickly. It was said that software was not catching up with upgraded ultra-fast transaction methods.

In November 2005 a program mistake forced the Tokyo Stock Exchange (TSE) to temporarily stop transactions of all issues.[12] In January 2006, overflow of transactions again caused the stoppage of all issue transactions. Repeated system failures demonstrated the limit of TSE's systems.

TSE's troubles continued in July 2008. It stopped transactions of all derivatives. In February 2012 a problem with an information distribution system caused the stoppage of 241 issues in the morning. Again in August the TSE stopped all derivative transactions.

Not only in the securities subsector, but also in the banking subsector there has been a series of system failures. On 16 December 2011, the Financial Services Agency (FSA) of Japan issued an order to stop business transactions of Citibank, a Japanese company under US Citigroup.[13] The primary reason was that the bank did not explain the risks of investment trust funds and foreign-currency trading to its customers, but the FSA worried about defects of business management and frequent system failures.

On 10 January 2012, Shinsei Bank announced that it failed to complete 35,000 transactions such as wire transfers by individual customers to other banks.[14] Its system failure took place during the hours 8.30 am to 11 am on that day. The bank realised the failure and switched to a back-up system, but some of the transactions were delayed.

On 22 April 2014, Sumitomo Mitsui Banking Corporation found system failures in some of their ATMs throughout Japan. The number of affected ATMs was 429 of around 6,000 ATMs in total. The bank was conducting a maintenance operation during the previous night for the ATM system. That also caused problems.[15]

On 30 April 2014, the Bank of Tokyo-Mitsubishi UFJ announced that it found system failure in a service and failed to complete transactions. Among a scheduled 64,000 transactions, 23,000 transactions were left uncompleted in time. The total amount was around three billion Japanese yen.

Illegal money transfers exploiting internet banking systems are increasing.[16] According to the Japanese Bankers Association there were 1,257 cases during January and November 2014. The total amount was around 1.86 billion Japanese yen. This number surpassed the number during the 12 months in 2013 (661 cases and 810 million yen). In 2014 the number of corporate victims increased more rapidly, though the number of individuals is still increasing. Methods of illegal transfers are changing. In the past, fake sites were set up and users were taken to those sites to have their identities and passwords stolen. In recent cases, more computer viruses are used to steal such information.

It is believed that a one-time password solution is more secure. Sumitomo Mitsui Banking Corporation, however, found a new type of virus to steal one-time passwords in May 2014. As of January 2015, most of Japanese internet banking systems show warnings for possible scams.

According to the National Police Agency of Japan, about 90 per cent of holders of banking accounts receiving illegal money transfers were held by Chinese nationals in 2011 with 214 accounts of 235 owned under names of Chinese nationals.[17] That number was reduced to 69.5 per cent in the first half of 2014, while 26.0 per cent was owned by Japanese nationals, 2.7 per cent was other nationals and 1.8 per cent was corporate accounts.[18]

According to the Japanese Bankers Association, only one bank was a victim in fiscal year 2012, but 34 banks were victims in fiscal year 2013. The affected amount was 182 million yen.[19]

There were no reports of banks being targeted by DDoS or other major cyber attacks in Japan. However, South Korean banks have been hit several times. Among them, the case of 20 March 2013, as mentioned above briefly, is well known. On that day, banking systems as well as broadcasting systems were forced to stop by computer viruses. Shinhan Bank needed two hours to restore its ATM system. The ROK government established its cyber-crisis management headquarters jointly from government, private-sector and military personnel. Around 32,000 computers were affected in the targeted banks and broadcasting stations. However, their transaction data were not modified or destroyed. No money was stolen. This was a kind of show attack. Later investigations by the South Korean government strongly implied that North Korea was responsible for the attack.

Chinese financial systems were until recently rather closed and regulations and infrastructures were different from advanced economies. Chinese financial markets are gradually becoming open and deregulated. However, rapid changes create distortions in the market such as 'shadow banking' systems with a great deal of bad debts.

There have been also many cyber incidents inside China. Many representatives to the National People's Congress submitted proposals to request better cyber security management by the government. It means that China is getting cyber attacks from outside and there are also many domestic cyber attacks. These are daily occurrences and are becoming increasingly serious. In November 2014, the CNCERT (National Computer Network Emergency Response Technical Team) surveillance system found 320 falsified government websites and 106 government websites with embedded backdoors.

The most well-known cyber incident in the Chinese financial sector took place on 16 August 2013. Everbright Securities, one of the largest securities companies, made a large number of mistaken orders in the market on that day. These mistaken orders to buy a lot of stocks were issued at 11.05 am and the Shanghai Composite Index rose by more than 5 per cent compared with the previous day.

Shanghai Stock Exchange stopped Everbright Securities business in the afternoon. The company stated later that its arbitrage trading system, which was used by a strategic investment section, had experienced problems.

After realising the mistaken orders, Everbright Securities made a short sale of stock-price index futures to compensate for the loss without announcing its mistaken orders. On 30 August the China Securities Regulatory Commission found it was an insider transaction and fined the company 500 million Chinese yuan.[20] Four persons who were responsible for the transactions were fined and excluded from the securities business forever.

The actual loss on the books of Everbright Securities was 194 million yuan, and this number was less than previously estimated. However, the Chinese government authority realised there had been problems with financial computer systems. The president of the company resigned. This incident showed that system risks might affect corporate governance, even if they are not by cyber attacks.

Responses by the Japanese government

How does the Japanese government respond to these growing cyber incidents and system failures? On 16 September 2014 the Cyber Crime Unit of the Tokyo Metropolitan Police Department froze 52 accounts in four banks, which were seemingly opened to receive illegal transactions by theft of one-time passwords for internet banking services.[21] Of the 52 accounts, 32 accounts were actually used for 38 cases of illegal transfers amounting to 20 million yen. Of the 38 cases, money had been withdrawn in 19 cases, but it was able to stop the other 19 cases.

These cyber crimes can be responded to after a victim reports it to the police. However, many companies do not wish to make reports because they worry about stock prices or their reputations. The financial sector in particular conceals them. Therefore, there appears to be many hidden, unreported cyber incidents in the financial markets. The Japanese government set up CEPTOAR (Capability for Engineering of Protection, Technical Operation, Analysis and Response) councils to share information among sectors without announcing incidents in the public domain.

It is the FSA that oversees the financial sector in Japan. Until 1998 the Ministry of Finance oversaw the sector, but ministries and agencies were reorganised after several scandals in the government sectors. In January 2001, there was another re-shuffle of the ministries and agencies. The FSA was set up as one of the extra-ministerial bureaus of the Cabinet Office.

In Japan's case, as stated above, the financial sector includes four subsectors: banking; life insurance; non-life insurance; and securities. The FSA has guidelines for each of the four subsectors (Table 5.2).

Here we can see the banking subsector. 'Comprehensive oversight guidelines for major banks and others' was revised in December 2014. In this document, cyber attacks are included in the category of 'system risks', which was defined as 'risks that financial institutions might be harmed by stoppage or malfunction of computer systems or system failures and risks that financial institutions might experience loss by the illegal operation of computers'.[22]

Table 5.2 Major government guidelines covering financial sectors in Japan

Subsectors	Services	Major guidelines
Banking	Deposit, lending, and money order	Comprehensive oversight guidelines for major banks and others
	Financial clearance	Comprehensive oversight guidelines for clearance and money transfer agencies
	Electronic records and others	Business guidelines third volume: financial corporations (12 electronic asset records agencies)
Life insurance	Payment of insurance moneys and others	Comprehensive oversight guidelines for insurance companies
Non-life insurance	Payment of insurance moneys and others	Comprehensive oversight guidelines for insurance companies
Securities	Buying and selling, mediation and clearance of securities and others	Comprehensive oversight guidelines for financial instruments business operator and others
	Establishment of financial instruments business markets	Cabinet Office order for financial instruments businesses article 112, item 7
	Money transfer business	Comprehensive oversight guidelines for clearance and money transfer agencies
	Business of assumption of obligation in financial instruments	Comprehensive oversight guidelines for clearance and money transfer agencies

Source: ISPC, 'The third action plan for information security preparedness of critical infrastructures', www.nisc.go.jp/active/infra/pdf/infra_rt3.pdf, 19 May 2014 (in Japanese).

According to the guidelines, in cases that financial institutions recognise any system failures, they have to notify the FSA immediately and send a report later on. Furthermore, if they recognise any warnings of cyber attacks or if they detect any signs of such attacks and believe they might be harmed, they have to notify the FSA. In the case in which the FSA recognises any serious problems, the FSA can issue a business-improvement order based on article 26 of the Banking Act. These mandates are the same as in 'Comprehensive oversight guidelines for financial instruments business operator and others'[23] covering the securities subsector as well.

In 'Comprehensive oversight guidelines for insurance companies,'[24] there is no mention of cyber attacks and system risks. However, again, the FSA can demand a report from the securities companies and issue a business-improvement order if necessary.

Year 2016/2020 problems

The worst security incidents in Japan are related to Mizuho Bank. This bank was established by merging three different banks (Dai-ichi Kangyo Bank, Fuji Bank and Industrial Bank of Japan) under Mizuho Financial Group, which was formed after the 'financial big bang' in the 1990s. This merger created huge system risks. Because these three banks were using totally different transaction systems, it was very difficult to merge them. The first big system failure came in April 2002 right after the merger. After receiving harsh criticism from the public, who had believed in the infallibility of banks, Mizuho Bank invested a great deal in new systems.

However, the second big system failure came on 15 March 2011, right after the Tohoku Region Pacific Coast Earthquake on 11 March. The earthquakes and tsunamis caused huge human and non-human losses in the northeastern part of Japan. People started sending wire transfers for donations to assigned bank accounts. The size of money transfers went beyond the capacity of Mizuho Bank. Customers could not withdraw cash from ATMs and 1.16 million wire transfers were delayed. The system failures went on for a week and this was the worst case of failure in the Japanese financial sector. People rarely use personal cheques in Japan and cash is not used for salary payments. They are dependent on bank wire transfers. As payments of utility services were also affected in this incident, a lot of consumers were in dire straits. Financial clearance is one of the core businesses of banks and it was lost. On 28 March, the FSA notified an on-the-spot inspection at Mizuho Bank. It is quite rare that such inspections are done in a major financial institution. Mizuho Bank lost trust among its customers.

On 28 April, Mizuho Bank submitted an investigation report to the FSA. The FSA analysed that not only machine problems but also human errors in the recovery process enlarged failures and damages. On 13 May, Mizuho Bank President Takashi Tsukamoto apologised publicly in a press conference. He also said the bank lost two billion yen worth of fees from customers, because the collection of fees was cancelled due to the transaction delays. The bank paid additional costs of 700 million yen and spent five billion yen for system upgrades. During the closure of ATMs, there were 4,000 illegal cash withdrawals at temporary tellers, and the damage amounted to around 400 million yen.

On 31 May, the FSA formally issued a business-improvement order, which requested Mizuho Bank to clarify management responsibilities and Mizuho Financial Group, a holding company, to revise system strategies and personnel systems. In response to the order, Mizuho Bank and Mizuho Financial Group submitted business-improvement plans to the FSA on 29 June. Mizuho Bank included a full-scale check of system risks and the creation of a new contingency plan by October 2011. Mizuho Financial Group promised the creation of a new system strategy by March 2012 and announced the intention of a merger of the two banks (Mizuho Bank and Mizuho Corporate Bank) under the group to integrate their businesses.

After the Mizuho Bank incident, the FSA strengthened supervision of banks to prevent future large-scale system failures. The agency investigated about 700 banks, credit banks and credit unions all over Japan. Further thorough investigations were organised for problematic institutions until the summer of 2012.[25]

In July 2013, Mizuho Financial Group officially announced the merger of Mizuho Bank and Mizuho Corporate Bank and the integration of their computer systems into one. Initial plans outlined that the merger would be completed by spring of 2016, but a one-year delay was announced in February 2012 to ensure the best integration.

However, the system-solution industry in Japan is facing problems for the years 2016 and 2020. Many large-scale system upgrades are expected in 2016 including: (1) the Mizuho Bank merger; (2) central and local government system upgrades to establish 'My Number' system for a common number system to integrate social security and tax systems' (3) derivative trade system upgrades of the Japan Exchange Group; and (4) Japan Post's system upgrades for initial public offering. There is serious manpower shortage in the system-solution industry. Furthermore, Tokyo will host the Olympic Games in 2020. Large-scale infrastructure investments have started already to prepare for the Olympics. Personnel and other costs are rapidly rising. With the rapid rise of cyber attacks and threats, the Japanese financial sector must prepare for a very hard time.

Shock of new Chinese rules

In late 2014 the Chinese government started considering new rules to prevent terrorism. The government's main goal was to deter future attacks from domestic and foreign terrorists. As part of the new rules, the government asked Chinese financial companies to use domestic software for financial transactions. If they use foreign software, vendors of such software must provide source codes and set up so-called backdoors for the Chinese government.[26]

This is the next phase of the series of US–China cyber conflicts after the Huawei and ZTE spy allegations, the summit talk in California, the Snowden revelations and the indictment of five PLA officers by the Federal Bureau of Investigation in addition to a number of analysis reports by US private security companies revealing Chinese cyber operations and attacks.

The Obama administration claimed that the Chinese new rules were a new trade barrier for American software companies selling products in China and American commercial companies operating in China. Intellectual property rights of American companies can be lost after handing source codes of software to the Chinese government, and financial transactions of not only Chinese but also foreign companies can be monitored by Chinese authorities.

Under the new rules foreign companies have to choose their business options: exit or obey. The Chinese government insisted that this policy change was not for an economic purpose, but for a national security purpose. However, it was speculated that the government was trying to promote domestic demand and raise competitiveness of Chinese companies. For any government, financial sectors are among the most critical infrastructure. To protect the sector from any risk is a high priority in cyber security.

Conclusion

The National Diet of Japan passed the Cyber Security Basic Act in early November 2014. A 'basic act' usually sets mid-term and long-term policy directions. The 2014 Cyber Security Basic Act was designed to fulfil policy goals set by the 2013 Cyber Security Strategy. One of them was to strengthen the roles and functions of the NISC. NISC used to be an acronym of the National Information Security Center, but the Cyber Security Basic Act changed it to the National Center of Incident Readiness and Strategy for Cybersecurity. The Information Security Policy Council (ISPC) was also reorganised as the Cyber Security Strategy Headquarters (CSSH). Both the NISC and the CSSH gained more authority than before. Japan is stepping up readiness for cyber security.

Cyber security these days includes defence, offence and exploitation. Exploitation means unusual ways of using technologies and architectures beyond original intentions. Military commands access enemy systems to look for vulnerabilities, dig security holes, penetrate systems and implant cyber weapons for future operations. Low-intensity cyber conflicts are taking place even in peacetime. Japan is receiving more attacks in cyberspace than in the other four operational domains and needs to invest more to defend social systems and infrastructures.

Financial services are competing in milliseconds or microseconds globally. Computer and network systems are playing core roles in their businesses. The protection of software, hardware and total infrastructure is critical for all financial institutions today.

Notes

1 Motohiro Tsuchiya, 'Cybersecurity in East Asia: Japan and the 2009 attacks on South Korea and the United States', in Kim Andreasson, ed., *Cybersecurity: Public Sector Threats and Responses*, Boca Raton, FL: CRC Press, 2012, pp. 55–76.
2 Kaspersky Lab, 'Kaspersky Lab exposes "Icefog": a new cyber-espionage campaign focusing on supply chain attacks', www.kaspersky.com/about/news/virus/2013/ Kaspersky_Lab_exposes_Icefog_a_new_cyber-espionage_campaign_focusing_on_ supply_chain_attacks, 26 September 2013.
3 David E. Sanger, *Confront and Conceal: Obama's Secret Wars and Surprising Use of American Power*, New York: Crown Publishers, 2012.
4 Robert M. Gates, *Duty: Memoirs of a Secretary at War*, New York: Alfred A. Knopf, 2014.
5 Leon E. Panetta, 'Remarks by Secretary Panetta on cybersecurity to the business executives for national security, New York City', US Department of Defense, http://archive. defense.gov/transcripts/transcript.aspx?transcriptid=5136 (archived), 11 October 2012.
6 Tom Donilon, 'Press briefing by national security advisor Tom Donilon', The White House Office of the Press Secretary, www.whitehouse.gov/the-press-office/2013/06/08/ press-briefing-national-security-advisor-tom-donilon, 8 June 2013.
7 Glenn Greenwald, 'NSA collecting phone records of millions of Verizon customers daily', The *Guardian*, www.theguardian.com/world/2013/jun/06/nsa-phone-records-verizon-court-order, 5 June 2013.
8 The 21st Century Public Policy Institute, 'Status of cyber attacks and defense against them', www.21ppi.org/pdf/thesis/130611.pdf, May 2013 (in Japanese).
9 ISPC, 'The third action plan for information security preparedness of critical infrastructures', www.nisc.go.jp/active/infra/pdf/infra_rt3.pdf, 19 May 2014 (in Japanese).
10 Michael Lewis, *Flash Boys*, New York: W.W. Norton & Company, 2014.
11 *Nihon Keizai Shinbun*, 24 August 2013 (in Japanese).
12 *Nihon Keizai Shinbun*, 5 March 2013 (in Japanese).

13 *Nihon Keizai Shinbun*, 16 December 2011 (in Japanese).
14 *Nihon Keizai Shinbun*, 10 January 2012 (in Japanese).
15 *Nihon Keizai Shinbun*, 22 April 2014 (in Japanese).
16 *Nihon Keizai Shinbun*, 27 December 2014 (in Japanese).
17 *Nihon Keizai Shinbun*, 15 December 2011 (in Japanese).
18 National Police Agency, 'Status of illegal money transfer in the first half of year 2014', www.npa.go.jp/cyber/pdf/H260904_banking.pdf, 4 September 2014 (in Japanese).
19 *Nihon Keizai Shinbun*, 23 May 2014 (in Japanese).
20 *Nihon Keizai Shinbun*, 30 August 2013 (in Japanese).
21 *Nihon Keizai Shinbun*, 16 September 2014 (in Japanese).
22 FSA, 'Comprehensive oversight guidelines for major banks and others', www.fsa.go.jp/common/law/guide/city/index.html, December 2014 (in Japanese).
23 FSA, 'Comprehensive oversight guidelines for financial instruments business operator and others', www.fsa.go.jp/common/law/guide/kinyushohin/, September 2014 (in Japanese).
24 FSA, 'Comprehensive oversight guidelines for insurance companies', www.fsa.go.jp/common/law/guide/ins/03c.html, November 2014 (in Japanese).
25 *Nihon Keizai Shinbun*, 21 March 2012 (in Japanese).
26 Paul Mozur, 'New rules in China upset Western tech companies', *New York Times*, http://nyti.ms/1BoangA, 29 January 2015.

6 Real-world evidence and Big Data in medicine

Is there a financial and legal risk linked to cyber crime?

Marcin Czech

The vast majority of us human beings possess medical records. We usually start this collection with a birth certificate, issued as our first document. With a few exceptions of developing countries, this is usually followed by infant-screening programme results, first blood tests, ultrasound examinations and others.

Approaching 50, I have a bigger collection of medical documentation, especially the more recent information. Being relatively healthy, I have documents concerning blood tests, urinary tests, a couple of USG tests, two, maybe three CT scans, taken after sport injuries, one MRI, ECGs, Holter examinations, stress test results, a few hospital discharges, slightly more doctors' opinions, and eye examinations (I wear glasses). All of them are nicely stored in a thick, white, old-fashioned paper bag, safely placed on a shelf in my home library. But are these sensitive documents really private (excluding healthcare professionals, who have access to them for obvious reasons) and are they really safe?

In the contemporary world, almost all healthcare records are digitised and (protected) electronic health information is exchanged on the internet.

Medical records are full of our most sensitive personal details including not only medical history per se, but also insurance records, social security numbers, home addresses, family details, credit-card information, list of medications and their costs. All that mass of information makes this area very attractive for hackers, and cyber attacks on healthcare providers are escalating.

Ninety-four per cent of medical institutions in the United States claim their organisations have been victims of a cyber attack, according to the Ponemon Institute.[1] What is more, phishing and malware attacks will intensify in 2015, as cyber criminals assess this 'market' as more attractive than other industries including commercial entities.[2]

Let us first analyse what medical data are collected, how they are defined and divided and what purposes they may serve. There is a huge diversity of types of data in the medical and related domains; they can be also perceived through their source, sample population, advantages and disadvantages for different purposes. All these aspects are especially important in the healthcare sector, where the value of relevant information should not be underestimated. The issue of data-protection mechanisms and regulations deserves also the highest priority, which it is not always given globally.

Big Data can be defined as extremely large data sets that may be analysed computationally to reveal patterns, trends and associations, especially relating to human behaviour and interactions.[3] It is a blanket term for any collection of data sets too complex and diverse to process using traditional processing applications.

Big Data can be characterised by three Vs: Volume, Velocity and Variety.[4] Volume refers to the recent increase in the amount of data collected and exploited, often existing at software platforms. Increased data allow for better analyses and prediction based on more complex models. The health and healthcare-related content is generated from numerous patient care points of contact, diagnostic and medical devices, and web-based health communities. The main sources of health Big Data are not only the most recent ones, genomics-driven Big Data covering genotyping, gene expression, sequencing, but also more traditional ones such as electronic medical records, medical-charts reviews, disease registries, surveillance systems, pharmacy prescription, claim databases/administrative data, insurance records and patient feedback and responses.[5]

Volume creates certain challenges to the information technology (IT) structure and function including storage (e.g. raw sequencing data from a single person is approximately four terabytes), querying and processing. Even simple data on demographics, medical services, medications and outcomes, including patient-reported ones collected over a long period of time, pose a challenge while extracting them. On top of that there are well-defined, by state law and/or internal regulations, requirements for building a privacy-preserving and trustworthy health infrastructure as well as for conducting ethical research in this complex domain.[6]

Many institutions already possess large amounts of archived data but have limitations in effectively processing them (especially as a publicly available source of information). The German Institute for Quality and Efficiency in Healthcare or the Polish National Health Fund may serve as examples.

Velocity concerns rapid changes and the pace with which new data are created and added to existing sets. The value of data from this point of view depends on the speed of a feedback loop. Only if it is effective can a dynamic character of data serve the decision-making process properly. Velocity is important in sales and marketing data processed by the pharmaceutical industry.

Variety reflects the diverse nature and character of stored information. This feature creates a challenge to data merging and processing. Rarely can data from different sources be directly used in one application. Analyses often require one data type from one data source to be mapped to the correct data type of another data source. Looking from this point of view, the data sets can be structured such as well-defined patient-level data sets; semi-structured such as those collected with the use of questionnaires, e.g. patient-reported outcomes; or unstructured such as the ones collected from blogs or mobile instruments. The variety can range from randomised controlled trials, through observational studies to quality-of-life assessments or tweets.

In health economics the term Big Data is often used interchangeably with real-world data (RWD). The latter is defined as any data that go beyond what is normally collected in the phase III clinical trials programme; they are not interventional, but provide a measure in understanding healthcare data collected under real-life practice circumstances. They comprise the same sources as previously described, namely: electronic medical records, (payers'/insurers') claims data, national surveys, disease-specific registries, surveillance systems, online communities, data on prescription patterns, marketing, sales and distribution, and (human) genome data. If we treat these groups as a primary data source, one can also distinguish secondary sources based on processed/analysed/researched data. Observational studies frequently use retrospective data from administrative databases or electronic medical records. In contrast, cohort study is a longitudinal study where a group of persons with the same characteristics/exposure is followed in time until an outcome of interest occurs. In a pragmatic trial, conducted in clinical practice, effectiveness rather than efficacy is assessed, and in patient-reported outcomes, information is provided by patients themselves.

Among main stakeholders using Big Data in medicine and healthcare one can list: regulatory agencies, (state) payers, (state) insurance companies, healthcare providers, health-technology agencies, clinicians, patients, manufacturers and consultants.

For the regulatory agencies such as the European Medicine Agency (EMA) or the Food and Drug Administration in the United States, Big Data are a natural source of long-term information on safety and interactions of a registered drug collected in a practical, clinical setting. Disease-specific registries or sentinel initiatives widespread across the globe can serve as good examples. In epidemiology, sentinel surveillance is a reporting system based on selected institutions or people who provide regular, complete reports on one or more diseases occurring ideally in a defined attachment. It also provides additional data on cases.[7] New EMA pharmacovigilance legislation has been in effect since July 2012 with an objective to strengthen the legal basis to require post-authorisation studies for efficacy and safety at the time of authorisation or post-authorisation. It reflects an increased emphasis on post-launch safety, with a lifecycle approach to benefit–risk assessment.[8]

RWD give payers an increased understanding of how a marketed medicine is performing outside of controlled clinical trials. Based on them they are able to make more informed, conscious decisions regarding granting or withdrawing reimbursement. In addition they can identify patients' subgroups, uncover safety concerns and monitor utilisation, look at relative or comparative benefits, assess an economic value, especially in high-cost therapeutic areas, and last but not least, collect reliable data on mortality and morbidity.

Among healthcare professionals, medical doctors in particular, an interest in RWD utilisation is growing as they give insight into a product's use in a real-life clinical practice with a more diverse patient population. According to the recent research, 87 per cent of oncologists are considering RWD on product effectiveness and safety most or all of the time when prescribing treatments. This group of doctors is also prioritising quality of life (94 per cent) and patient affordability of the product (65 per cent) when they prescribe medications.[9] It has to be mentioned, however, that the majority of healthcare practitioners make their treatment decisions based on individual experience and preferences rather than evidence that stems from Big Data sets.

Patients also care whether added benefit of a treatment can be achieved outside of controlled trials in routine clinical use. They also express more and more interest in quality-of-life assessments.

In the case of the pharmaceutical industry, RWD plays a role in the formulation of strategies both internally supporting decisions for investment, product development and commercialisation, and externally allowing for engagement with a wide range of stakeholders. Using registries may help with collecting and providing data on drugs' efficiency, effectiveness and safety, it assures treatment adherence and persistence, and it allows for gaining and defending best market access, including risk-sharing. Businesswise, the Big Data can change drug-development paradigms with an aim to stop increases in product-development costs, target drugs where treatment offers payers the greatest value, allow best return on investment, and give greater understanding of diseases and treatments.[10]

Collecting and processing personal data, often in a Big Data format, is at the core of the insurance business. Insurers have a platform where they collect clients' data over long periods of time including claims, types of agreements, risks and so forth. From the potential savings and risk-mitigation perspective, insurance companies use data to assess the probable maximum loss of catastrophic events as well as to detect the potential for fraudulent claims. From a revenue growth point of view, they use Big Data to adequately price new insurance offerings. With Big Data technologies, insurance companies are able to analyse information at the level of an insured person and consider a single insurance claim. This increased in-depth analysis has the potential to improve the quality and accuracy of risk models and market predictions.[11] Another issue is personal data protection, which can be a target of cyber attacks. A special document – the Code of Practice on Data Protection for the Insurance Sector – has been created along with other documents in order to mitigate this risk.[12] The document, approved by the Data Protection Commissioner, was created on the basis of the Data Protection Act, the European Commission document, last updated in October 2014.[13] The Code of Practice on Data Protection for the Insurance Sector sets out the requirements of the Data Protection Acts, how personal information is processed by the insurance sector and how insurance companies must comply with the legislation when collecting, handling and storing personal data. In the document, there are eight rules of data protection, according to which a data controller must: obtain and process the information fairly; keep it only for one or more specified and lawful purpose, process it only in ways compatible with the purposes for which it was given to you initially; keep it safe and secure; keep it accurate and up to date; ensure that it is adequate, relevant and not excessive; retain it no longer than is necessary for the specified purpose or purposes; and give a copy of his/her personal data to any individual, on request.[14]

Healthcare providers store all medical information regarding patients in a Big Data format allowing fast access if needed. There is a recent trend of using many databases to get most of the value out of data stored there. Such sources are called meta-databases and merge information coming from different, often physically remote places. Among other initiatives, BRIDGE provides a unique searchable and comprehensive compendium of information on population healthcare databases worldwide, allowing the healthcare professional to obtain profiles on various population data sets on a single website. The database profiles are updated with the most current data and verified by the respective database managers or representatives. Updated database profiles replace older versions to avoid duplicate reporting. The subscribers can perform robust and advanced searches for a wide range of database profiles using the easy-to-use search page.

The search results are displayed based on a relevancy-ranking system that allows the profiles with the most closely matched search terms to appear first. The users obtain detailed information on pharmacoepidemiologic and other population data sources for use in epidemiology, health-services research, healthcare economics and as models for designing healthcare systems and data resources worldwide.[15]

In Europe there is a specialised resource database (meta-database) – the European Network of Centres for Pharmacoepidemiology and Pharmacovigilance (ENCePP) – established in 2006 by the European Medicines Agency. The resource database is an electronic index of available European Union (EU) research organisations, networks and data sources in the field of pharmacoepidemiology and pharmacovigilance, and is a key component of the ENCePP web portal serving also other purposes. The resource database serves as a hub for both researchers and study sponsors seeking to identify organisations and data sets for conducting specific pharmacoepidemiology and pharmacovigilance studies in Europe. The database comprises the ENCePP inventory and the EU data sources registry. Both the inventory and the registry are fully searchable and allow the identification of centres and data sets by country, type and other relevant criteria.[16]

Database mapping seems to be key in effective use of Big Data. No matter if it is a scientific research or a decision-making support, the process should be divided into phases. First, a well-defined question should be formulated; second, a proper search question/study design has to be defined followed by data preparation (based on existing data assets) in a report format (assuring the best quality). In this phase a patient population is characterised, treatment options/patterns initially assessed, outcome measures chosen, and resource use/costs information selected. The third step is devoted to data analysis and interpretation of the search/research results. The last phase is reserved for a decision-making process per se and/or practical applications/implementation. A systematic approach (often with a use of meta-databases) and gap analysis increase quality of medical Big Data mapping.

When analysing the Big Data sets, it is important to consider transparency, reporting, outcomes and exposure measurements, and missing values. Although there are still debates on how to research, define and interpret RWD, first standards have been developed in this domain.[17] They address the main challenges regarding internal validity, types of biases, confounding factors, study design and other aspects versus increasing need of comparative effectiveness research as a basis of medical decision making. A general recommendation of the Good Research Practices for Comparative Effectiveness Research Task Force is that for comparative effectiveness research, an observational study must approximate a randomised study to minimise a selection bias associated by definition with Big Data processing. A detailed statistical analysis plan should complement the study protocol; ex ante definition of treatment, outcomes and covariates should be formulated. Prior definition of clinical meaningful differences, detailed specification of statistical methods to address bias, sensitivity analyses and missing values are also key elements here.

There are many sources of bias in Big Data research/analysis. The first one is a classification bias in the measurement of exposure and outcomes, e.g. if patients under medication have a higher probability to visit a GP more frequently. A discussion of the direction of potential sources of misclassification should be applied.[18]

The second type of bias concerns missing values. Missing data are commonly encountered in RWD, mainly registries. Frequently there are missing values for one or more variables across different observations and sometimes observations may be completely missing for an important variable. There are some methods to address these problems. An extra category of missing data can be created (for categorical variables). All observations with incomplete data for at least one analysis variable can be deleted. A missing value can be replaced by the overall mean of the variable in the sample; alternatively the last observed value in the longitudinal study can be carried forward. It is also possible to use a regression model based on the observed data, which can be used to estimate unobserved values for each individual.

Confounding is also a relevant source of bias, by indication or by disease severity. Statistical methods can be used to adjust for confounder variables: stratification, multiple regression, propensity score matching, instrumental variable approach, machine learning.[19]

A multiple regression provides an estimate of the treatment effect after simultaneously adjusting for a large number of covariates in the model. Propensity score matching creates similar pairs of treated and untreated individuals and ensures sufficient overlap between groups. The use of instrumental variables is the only way to account for imbalances in unobserved variables, but finding appropriate instrumental variables is difficult in practice.

Among others (Guidelines for Good Pharmaco-epidemiologic Practice, 2005; AHRQ Guide for Conducting Comparative Effectiveness Reviews, 2007; ISPOR Comparative Effectiveness Research Methods, 2009; AHRQ Registries for Evaluating Patient Outcomes, 2010), a STROBE checklist was created to guide reporting of these kinds of studies.[20]

There are many examples of different Big Data assets in medicine. Claim data are often used. They are usually complete within the range of collected information, with unified, standardised coding systems, including disease identification (ICD-9, ICD-10). As they were created for reimbursement/refunding purposes, they cover only beneficiaries. Diagnoses, treatment patterns, resource utilisation and costs can be easily traced based on this type of RWD. The UK's National Health Service system can serve as an example here.[21]

Electronic medical records can serve the same purpose in terms of the scope, in addition providing information on clinical effectiveness. They contain symptoms description, lifestyle habits, laboratory tests, diagnostic tests and past histories. This source usually covers outpatient services only; data on treatment compliance/adherence, even about prescribed drug purchases, are usually missing. There are numerous examples of studies performed on this basis in many medical specialties.[22]

National surveys are databases that capture clinical and lifestyle data on individuals with a disease description and risk factors. They use standard measures and are usually representative for a general population. Many examples of this approach can be found, concerning different medical specialties, in Central Europe, for instance, due to high incidence and prevalence of cardiovascular diseases, in cardiology.[23]

Online communities and social media can also be a good source of Big Data in medicine, recently of growing importance. There are obvious limitations while approaching and analysing this type of data. They are subject to a selection bias (usually negative events only are discussed), they are entirely patient-reported (not confirmed by healthcare professionals) and fragmented, with no follow-up. For example, Twitter is a communication platform that can be used to conduct health science research, but a full understanding of its use remains unclear.[24]

Disease-specific registries are probably the most frequently used assets of RWD. Patient, clinical or disease registries may be used for many purposes including an evaluation of patient outcomes. They are designed prospectively, to fulfil specific purposes or answer specific questions rather than being data driven. They can also be geographically based, designed for public health reporting e.g. national cancer registries[25] and without tracking outcomes such as vaccine registries.[26] They capture (all) patients with a given disease or type of treatment, they are usually run by healthcare professionals and a lot of supplementary information such as laboratory tests or co-morbidities is included. They are longitudinal, so patients are traced over a certain period. Sometimes a follow-up is difficult, when they 'leave' the registry (often due to unknown reasons). There are many examples, both in communicable[27] and non-communicable disease areas.[28]

The need for monitoring of infectious diseases started the era of surveillance systems. Now they are databases that capture data on infectious diseases but also birth defects[29] and others. They are often population-based, detailed and run by healthcare professionals.

Recently growing interest is attracted by data captured from medical devices operating online or storing the data on the internet. Telemedicine[30] is one of the fastest growing domains in healthcare. The idea of smart homes, telemonitoring,[31] implanted sensors[32] and telerehabilitation[33] becomes everyday life in the most developed countries. A lot of these programs/devices are very effective.[34] In a recent literature review[35] medical publications from the last five years on telemedicine in the elderly (above 65 years old) were searched. Only people suffering from cardiovascular diseases or experiencing falls were included. The impact of

Table 6.1 The impact of telemedicine solutions

	Number of publications		
Influence on:	Increased	Decreased	Unchanged
Treatment cost	2	4	4
Hospitalisations	0	5	4
Quality of life	9	0	2

Source: Czech, M. and Szczepanik, K., 2015, unpublished research.

telemedicine solutions on quality-of-life improvement, costs of treatment and the number of hospitalisations was assessed. Out of the initially selected 468 studies, 286 were excluded as not being original (meta-analyses, reports, reviews) and 169 due to lack of correlation with quality-of-life improvement, costs of treatment or hospitalisations. Thirteen publications were analysed in detail including patient characteristics and efficacy/effectiveness measures in disease groups. The impact of telemedicine solutions on quality-of-life improvement, costs of treatment and number of hospitalisations is presented in Table 6.1.

Different Big Data assets in medicine are unequally suitable for extraction of concrete information; by their characteristics they have strengths and weaknesses in certain aspects. The most important are summarised in Table 6.2.

Table 6.2 Different Big Data assets and their characteristics in selected aspects

	Claims data	Electronic medical records	National surveys	Social media	Registries	Surveillance systems	Medical devices/ telemedicine
Clinical data	—	++	++	–/+	++	++	+
Quality-of-life data	—	–/+	+	–/+	+	–	+/–
Resources use	++	+	+	–	+	–/+	–/+
Costs	++	+	+	–	+/–	–	–
Coding	++	++	+	–	++	+	–
Standardised structure	+	++	+	–	+	–/+	+
External validity	–	+	++	–	–	–	+/–
Prospective/ longitudinal	+/–	++	–	+	+/–	–	+
Follow-up	–	–/+	–	–	–	+	–/+

Notes
— very weak; – weak; + strong; ++ very strong.
Source: Czech, M. and Szczepanik, K., 2015, unpublished research.

Weaknesses of different data assets can be compensated by linking data derived from different sources. What is important is that the databases from outside healthcare systems can also be combined. Mortality data, social security data on absenteeism and disability can be linked with medical Big Data. Linking data sources allows for construction of large data sets. It can be done under one condition: a client/patient/citizen identifier (usually a personal identification number) needs to be consistent all across data sources. The United States and Scandinavia are the most advanced in this kind of research. There is an increasing number of this kind of initiatives in different parts of Europe and sometimes they serve as a source of validation or criticism of different approaches.[36]

In health economics, in modelling in particular, traditionally different data inputs are required. Usually clinical (efficacy, safety, tolerability, adherence, compliance), epidemiological (incidence, prevalence, natural disease history, treatment pathways), and resource use related to treatment and diagnosis as well as costs inputs are needed. They rely not only on Big Data input sources but also create (large) secondary data sets of pharmacoeconomic evidence (Figure 6.1).

An objective of pharmacoeconomic evaluation is to find the most rational way of drug management or, in broader terms, healthcare management. Taking this approach into consideration, it is a supportive tool in a decision-making process. This process should be planned, executed and controlled based on reliable information and within a certain timeframe. Decisions are made by healthcare professionals as well as administrators under defined constraints and with certain objectives. For these reasons, pharmacoeconomic evaluation should be reliable, repeatable, transparent and trustworthy. Meeting these conditions is only possible

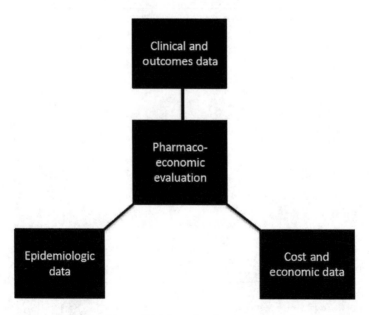

Figure 6.1 Types of input (Big) Data for pharmacoeconomic evaluation.

when well-established and verified methodology is used. In full pharmacoeconomic analysis at least two alternative technologies should be compared in terms of their costs and outcomes. Usually it is performed in the form of marginal analysis, which measures whether expenses incurred for the more expensive alternative treatment justify additional benefits.

Health Technology Assessment (HTA) is a multidisciplinary process that summarises information about medical, social, economic and ethical issues related to the use of a health technology in a systematic, transparent, unbiased and robust manner. Its aim is to inform about safe, effective health policies that are patient-focused and seek to achieve best value.[37] The scope of HTA is broad and it is aimed at decision-makers' needs. Recently, there are more and more cases when input data are derived from Big Data assets of different kinds and origins.

There are many country-level initiatives concerning Big Data. A recent American one related to health Big Data analytics is the National Science Foundation (NSF) Smart Health and Wellbeing programme, which seeks to address fundamental technical and scientific issues that would support a much-needed transformation of healthcare from reactive and hospital-centred to preventive, proactive, evidence-based, person-centred and focused on wellbeing rather than disease control. The research topics include sensor technology, networking, information and machine learning technology, modelling cognitive processes, system and process modelling, and social and economic issues.[38]

There is a long list of real and potential issues with medical Big Data collection, storage, processing, access and sharing. They are of a technical nature, from their volume, through data mining, to integration challenges when trying to link data from many sources. Establishing standards on how to assure quality, analyse and present the data is also crucial. The issues regarding data ownership and sharing can also create many problems from the organisational point of view. There is a scarcity in the talent pool as there are few people with significant skills and experience in dealing with the uniqueness of such large data sets. Last but not least Big Data protection is key both from users' and regulators' standpoints.

Beyond a shadow of doubt the volume of medical Big Data stored worldwide will increase, and we will have to learn how to effectively utilise them not only focusing on benefits for different stakeholders but also mitigating potential and real dangers associated with them, which involves both cyber risk and cyber crime.

Computer crime, or cyber crime, refers to any crime that involves a computer and a network.[39] Nowadays practically all medical instruments, databases and applications are connected to the internet, becoming a target for cyber criminals. And no organisation is immune to this kind of threat. According to a recently published report,[40] when we take a malicious internet protocol (IP) traffic as a measure of cyber risk, practically all healthcare organisations are affected:

- healthcare providers – 72.0 per cent of malicious traffic;
- healthcare business associates – 9.9 per cent of malicious traffic;
- health plans – 6.1 per cent of malicious traffic;
- pharmaceutical – 2.9 per cent of malicious traffic.

The reason healthcare providers are so strongly impacted is that the research group was very diverse, including, on one hand, small companies, and, on the other hand, large teaching hospitals with various entities and security-system organisations. The most probable reason why the pharmaceutical industry is relatively well protected is that this kind of business organisation has a long history of data protection, both imposed by the regulations and for purely business reasons. Traditionally the level of compliance with business-sensitive data protection in these kinds of organisations is high. Big Data security throughout all stages of a product lifecycle is key. Corporate secrets are protected practically from invention and in the early stages of a product's development. Producers seek to secure pre-clinical and clinical trials data to create and maintain a competitive advantage. Innovative industry operations are closely linked to intellectual property and patents' protection. Data-exclusivity periods linked to new products' licensing allows for return on investment, which is substantial, and rising. It is estimated that more than approximately 1.2 billion euros was spent on research and development of a new chemical or biological entity in 2012, compared to 199 million in 1979.[41] To compensate for this investment, and also against the risk associated with decreasing chances of market success with a new product, it is vital to protect such data by law. In the exclusivity period competitors have no or limited access to research and development data and have no right to place a generic equivalent on the market. Trials' results are only available for regulatory (registering) agencies and in a form of scientific articles in a public domain.

Rare data are stored in corporate databases protected by sophisticated IT systems. The objective is to secure data while at rest and while in transit. A certain method's utilisation is dictated by the operating systems, transport protocols or other applications. Various measures are in use. For example, discretionary access-controls are means of restricting access to objects based on the identity of subjects or groups to which they belong where the designation of the permission set is at the discretion of the information owner. All the restriction measures are typically provided by an operating system. A database management system is a set of computer programs that controls the creation, maintenance and use of a database. The implementation of encryption also increases a guarantee of information confidentiality, integrity and authenticity. It is the process of transforming information using an algorithm to make it unreadable to anyone except those possessing special knowledge. When transferring data, a Secure Shell technology can be used. It is defined by a network protocol that allows data to be exchanged using a secure channel between two networked devices.

There is special training provided to involved personnel; detailed procedures and regular internal and external audits are in place. Companies' employees take part in dedicated training courses, both online and traditional ones, in order to become familiar with main threats, corporate regulations and standard operating procedures. The operational efficacy is verified by specialised departments internally as well as by externally contracted organisations. If data are shared or made public, this is always done anonymously so the individual patients' information is not accessible. In the near future there will be not only new solutions but also potential and real challenges to Big Data protection in research and development processes. At the early stage of new chemical entities' development, by leveraging the diversity of available molecular and clinical data, predictive modelling of biological processes and drugs will become significantly widespread. Patients' enrolment in clinical studies, traditionally realised through doctors' visits, will use social media and internet platforms, where a group of people interested in a certain condition are gathered. The inclusion criteria will take significantly more factors such as genetic information into account. It will be a chance to decrease the recently rising costs of trials due to their limited size and specificity. Thanks to faster data processing and improved communication capabilities, clinical trials will be monitored in real time to rapidly identify safety or operational issues. The pace of research and development process seems to be key for a successful business case and return on investment associated with a new chemical entity. In order to speed up the research and development process and reduce the risk of promising drugs falling by the wayside late in development, companies want to be able to get an understanding of which drug works in a particular patient group. The current drug-development model uses placebo-controlled clinical trials in restricted groups of patients, within an idealised setting that doesn't reflect the complications of many real-world treatment cases. This divergence carries risks that approved products won't deliver expected outcomes, something that can be controlled through the incorporation of real-world evidence.[42] Drugs' safety is another area of potential and real concern. An adverse drug event (ADE) refers to any injury occurring at the time a drug is used, whether or not it is identified as a cause of the injury. An adverse drug reaction (ADR) is a special type of ADE in which a causative relationship can be shown. The study of ADRs is the concern of the field known as pharmacovigilance.[43] Manufacturers build a competitive advantage on safety not only in their submissions but also after regulatory approval, once the drug is already on the market. Safety monitoring becomes more sophisticated in order to track safety signals concerning rare adverse events. These signals can be detected from a wide range of sources such as patient enquiries on websites and search engines. Bayesian analytical methods, which can identify adverse events from incoming data, could highlight rare or ambiguous safety signals with greater accuracy and speed. The American Food and Drug Administration has invested in the evaluation of electronic health records through the Sentinel Initiative linking and analysing data from multiple sources, recently securing access to data comprising more than 120 million patients nationwide.[44] The data stored there have the highest level of protection typical of American state-owned institutions.

There is also one more type of Big Data carefully protected from the 'external world'. These are pure business data including business intelligence, marketing, co-operating entities or customers' data. The latter seem to be crucial as they usually concern healthcare professionals. Information of this kind, also including financial agreements, is stored and processed due to business ethics, compliance and law requirements. Preventive actions, including proper systems development, procedures, training and audits, are aimed at data safety here. Again, discretionary access-controls, a database management system and encryptions are commonly used. Despite all these preventive actions, there are many reasons why the medical Big Data are under threat according to the cited report:[45]

- The sheer volume of IP addresses detected in their targeted sample can be extrapolated to assume that there are, in fact, millions of compromised healthcare organisations, applications, devices and systems sending malicious packets from around the globe.
- Current security practices and strategies around endpoints in general, but especially attackers are bypassing perimeter protections en-masse and do not need to use stealth techniques to do so.
- The networks are not only vulnerable to breaches, but also available to be used for attacks such as phishing and fraudulent activities launched against other networks and victims.
- Personal health care information and organization intellectual property, as well as medical billing and payment organizations, are all increasingly at risk of data theft and fraud. Poorly protected medical endpoints, including personal health devices, become gateways, exposing consumers' personal computers and information to prowling cybercriminals.
- Today, compliance does not equal security. Organizations may think they're compliant, but they are not secure.
- The costs of failed compliance or compromises are increasing. These costs go far beyond the regulatory fines, the burden of notification to victims or immediate remediation costs—there are legal risks from class-action lawsuits incurred following a breach, potential fallout in stock prices and the intangible costs of brand damage when word gets out about the company's missteps.

In practical terms there are many devices and applications emitting malevolent traffic including security that healthcare organisations most rely on to protect them, along with non-traditional medical endpoints. According to a report[46] the most frequently affected medical endpoints are presented below (Figure 6.2).

The extremely complex character of Big Data in medicine requires stringent legal regulations with an objective to protect sensitive information and predict future cyber threats in this area, from external attacks via the internet and from internal violations resulting from malice or simple carelessness.

In the United States the Health Insurance Portability and Accountability Act (HIPAA) and the Institutional Review Board created the legal framework for requirements for building a privacy-preserving and trustworthy health infrastructure and conducting ethical health-related research.[47] The security rules specifically address individually identifiable health information that is transmitted or maintained in an electronic format. Security systems should be applied to the entire technical infrastructure and implemented into the institutional work culture.

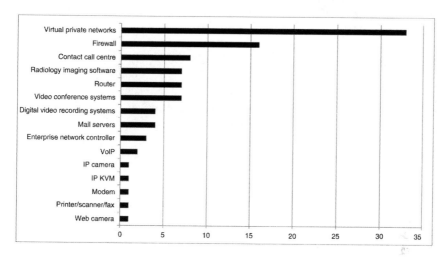

Figure 6.2 Devices emitting malicious traffic (per cent).

Source: NORS–Sans Health Care Cyberthreat Report, 2014.

Security refers to all of the policies, procedures, tools and techniques used to assure privacy and confidentiality. HIPAA requires all covered entities that transmit or maintain electronic health information to perform, and document, a risk assessment for security and develop a security plan to address major areas of concern. The majority of jurisdictions possess security legislation across the globe with similar kind of regulations.

Healthcare organisations of all kinds are obliged to implement the solutions assuring security. The efforts are made around the world by governments and standard-setting organisations in order to maintain the privacy and integrity of electronic records, not only the computer-based safeguards, but also the internal systems and procedures.

Some healthcare stakeholders plan to strengthen their defences. They will focus in particular on:[48]

- encryption and mobile device security;
- two-factor authentication;
- security risk analysis;
- advanced email gateway software;
- incident response management;
- expansion of IT security staff; and
- data loss prevention (DLP) tools.

The security programme management is one of the key initiatives. It usually includes:[49]

1   Strategizing and Planning, which includes defining target state, identifying and prioritizing security requirements, based on business objectives, the threat and risk environment, and compliance requirements; establish[ing] accountability for security; developing a security programme aligned with business needs.

2   Developing Governance meaning establishing effective governance processes and forums; developing an optimal process for making decisions and assigning decision rights; identifying and engaging stakeholders; defining decision-making authority and flow.

3   Driving Change Management aimed at setting up a system for communicating and socializing new ideas and strategies via multiple channels, getting buy-in from stakeholders at all levels, assessing progress, and driving stakeholder commitment to the change.

4   Executing, so optimally operating the initiative in accordance with business goals; updating and driving new elements of the initiative in response to changing business requirements and threat scenarios.

5   Measuring and Improving in order to know how the initiative has affected business outcomes; driv[ing] improvements through process changes and upgrades.

In fact all the security strategies, measures and tools aiming at medical Big Data assets protection are similar to the ones used in other management areas.

With a new organisational structure and function, healthcare institutions now gather and openly exchange healthcare information between regulators, insurers, doctors, pharmacists and patients. However, because of this, the threat of cyber risk and cyber crime will increase. The time to act was yesterday. Organisations must become aware of the many attack surfaces in their organisations and follow best practices for configuring systems and monitoring them for abuse.[50]

My white paper bag with personal health information, although definitely not containing Big Data, can be fully operated offline and, for this reason, seems to be the safest place for storing my medical records.

Notes

1   Ponemon Institute, 2014, www.healthcareitnews.com/news/healthcare-data-breaches-trend-upward-come-potential-7b-price-tag, accessed 4 January 2015.

2   JohnMoore,2014,iHealthBeat,www.ihealthbeat.org/insight/2014/health-care-industry-to-see-phishing-malware-attacks-intensify-in-2015, accessed 4 January 2015.

3   *Oxford English Dictionary*, 2014, Oxford: Oxford University Press.

4   Dumbill, E., 2012, 'Volume, velocity, variety: what you need to know about Big Data', www.forbes.com/sites/oreillymedia/2012/01/19/volume-velocity-variety-what-you-need-to-know-about-big-data/, accessed 2 October 2015. Miller, K., 2012, 'Big data analytics in biomedical research', *Biomedical Computation Review*, www.bcr.org/content/big-data-analytics-biomedical-research, accessed 2 October 2015.

5   Miller, 2012, 'Big data analytics in biomedical research'.

6 Gelfand, A., 2011/2012, 'Privacy and biomedical research: building a trust infrastructure—an exploration of data-driven and process-driven approaches to data privacy', *Biomedical Computation Review*, http://biomedicalcomputationreview.org/content/privacy-and-biomedical-research-building-trust-infrastructure, accessed 2 August 2012.

7 Porta, Miquel, 2008, *A Dictionary of Epidemiology*, Oxford: Oxford University Press.

8 Towse, A. and Garau, M., 2014, *Futurescapes: Expectations in Europe for Relative Effectiveness Evidence for Drugs in 2020*. White paper. Office of Health Economics, www.futuremedicine.com/doi/pdf/10.2217/cer.15.7, accessed 4 January 2015.

9 IPSOS, 2014, www.ipsos-na.com/download/pr.aspx?id=12651, accessed 4 January 2015. Cattell, Jamie, Chilukuri, Sastry and Levy, Michael, 2013, 'How Big Data can revolutionize pharmaceutical R&D, www.mckinsey.com/insights/health_systems_and_services/how_big_data_can_revolutionize_pharmaceutical_r_and_d, accessed 24 January 2015.

10 Towse and Garau, 2014, *Futurescapes*.

11 Mathiprakasam, Murthy, 2014, 'Big Data helps insurance companies create a more protected world', http://blogs.informatica.com/perspectives/2014/12/11/big-data-helps-insurance-companies-create-a-more-protected-world/#fbid=m8yMQ5qzKOg, accessed 26 January 2015.

12 Code of Practice on Data Protection for the Insurance Sector, www.insuranceireland.eu/media/documents/20130626_Code_of_Practice_Final.pdf, accessed 26 January 2015.

13 Data Protection Act 1988 Revised, 2015, www.lawreform.ie/_fileupload/RevisedActs/WithAnnotations/EN_ACT_1988_0025.PDF, accessed 14 April 2015.

14 Code of Practice on Data Protection for the Insurance Sector.

15 BRIDGE, www.bridgetodata.org, accessed 4 January 2015.

16 ENCePP, www.encepp.eu/encepp/resourcesDatabase.jsp, accessed 4 January 2015.

17 Berger, M.L. et al., 2009, 'Good research practices for comparative effectiveness research: defining, reporting and interpreting nonrandomized studies of treatment effects using secondary data sources: the ISPOR good research practices for retrospective database analysis task force report – part I', *Value in Health* 12(8):1044–52, www.ispor.org/taskforces/documents/rdparti.pdf, accessed 2 October 2015.

18 Cox, E. et al., 2009, 'Good research practices for comparative effectiveness research: approaches to mitigate bias and confounding in the design of nonrandomized studies of treatment effects using secondary data sources: the International Society for Pharmacoeconomics and Outcomes Research good research practices for retrospective database analysis task force report – part II', *Value in Health* 12(8):1053–61, www.ispor.org/taskforces/documents/RDPartII.pdf, accessed 2 October 2015.

19 Neal, Radford M., 2014, 'Statistical methods for machine learning and data mining', www.utstat.utoronto.ca/~radford/sta414/week1.pdf, accessed 2 October 2015.

20 Berger et al., 2009, 'Good research practices for comparative effectiveness research'.

21 National Health Service, 2014, www.england.nhs.uk/wp-content/uploads/2014/07/nhs-comm-board-ann-rep-1314.pdf, accessed 5 January 2015.

22 Sachdeva, S. et al., 2014, 'Analysis of clinical parameters and cardiac magnetic resonance imaging as predictors of outcome in pediatric myocarditis'. *American Journal of Cardiology*, www.ajconline.org/article/S0002-9149(14)02170-5/fulltext, accessed 2 October 2015.

23 Czech, M. et al., 2013, 'Costs of Heart Failure in Poland in 2011. Polish programme assessing diagnostic procedures, treatment and costs in patients with heart failure in

randomly selected outpatient clinics and hospitals at different levels of care – POLKARD', *Kardiologia Polska* 71(3): 22–32.

24 Finfgeld-Connett, D., 2014, 'Twitter and health science research', *Western Journal of Nursing Research*, http://wjn.sagepub.com/content/37/10/1269.abstract, accessed 2 October 2015.

25 National Cancer Registry (Krajowy Rejestr Nowotworow), 2014, http://onkologia.org.pl/, accessed 5 January 2015.

26 NYC Health, https://a816-healthpsi.nyc.gov/cir/provider-client/servlet/PC, accessed 5 January 2015.

27 Philippine HIV and AIDS Registry, 2014, www.doh.gov.ph/, accessed 5 January 2014.

28 Acute Coronary Syndrome Registry (Rejestr Ostrych Zespolow Wiencowych), 2014, http://www.rejestrozw.republika.pl/, accessed 5 January 2014.

29 Texas Department of State Health Services, 2015, www.dshs.state.tx.us/birthdefects/, accessed 5 January 2014.

30 Craig, J. and Patterson, V., 2005, 'Introduction to the practice of telemedicine', *Journal of Telemedicine and Telecare* 11: 3–9.

31 Bhimaraj, A., 2013, 'Remote monitoring of heart failure patients', *Methodist DeBakey Cardiovascular Journal* 9(1): 26–31.

32 Hughes, L. et al., 2012, 'A review of protocol implementations and energy efficient cross-layer design for wireless body area networks', *Sensors*, 12(11): 14730–73, www.mdpi.com/1424-8220/12/11/14730, accessed 2 October 2015.

33 Jelcic, N. et al., 2014, 'Feasibility and efficacy of cognitive telerehabilitation in early Alzheimer's disease: a pilot study', *Journal of Clinical Interventions in Aging* 9: 1605–11.

34 Nouchi, R., Taki, Y. And Takeuchi, H., 2012, 'Brain training game improves executive functions and processing speed in the elderly: a randomized controlled trial', *Plos One*, 7(1), http://journals.plos.org/plosone/article?id=10.1371/journal.pone.0029676, accessed 2 October 2015.

35 Czech, M. and Szczepanik, K., 2015, unpublished research.

36 Franek, E. et al., 2013, 'Mortality after surgery in Europe', *Lancet* 381(9864): 369–70, www.thelancet.com/journals/lancet/article/PIIS0140-6736(13)60161-0/fulltext, accessed 2 October 2015.

37 Garrido, M.V., 2006, 'Health technology assessment and health policy-making in Europe', European Observatory on Health Systems and Policies, www.euro.who.int/__data/assets/pdf_file/0003/90426/E91922.pdf, accessed 12 October 2015.

38 NSF, 2015, www.nsf.gov/funding/pgm_summ.jsp?pims_id=503556, accessed 6 January 2014.

39 Moore, R., 2005, *Cyber Crime: Investigating High-technology Computer Crime.* Cleveland, MI: Anderson Publishing.

40 Norse–Sans Health Care Cyberthreat Report, 2014, http://pages.norse-corp.com/rs/norse/images/Norse-SANS-Healthcare-Cyberthreat-Report2014.pdf, accessed 5 January 2014.

41 EFPIA, www.efpia.eu/facts-figures, accessed 24 January 2015.

42 Elvidge, S. and Disley, T. 2015, 'Real world evidence and digital healthcare: the next frontier', Eye for Pharma, http://social.eyeforpharma.com/market-access/real-world-evidence-maximize-benefits-healthcare, accessed 2 October 2015.

43 'Guideline for good clinical practice', International Conference on Harmonisation of Technical Requirements for Registration of Pharmaceuticals for Human Use, http://private.ich.org/LOB/media/MEDIA482.pdf, accessed 24 January 2015.

44 Cattell et al., 2013, 'How Big Data can revolutionize pharmaceutical R&D'.
45 Norse–Sans Health Care Cyberthreat Report, 2014.
46 Ibid.
47 Gelfand, 2011/2012, 'Privacy and biomedical research: building a trust infrastructure'.
48 iHealtBeat,2015,www.ihealthbeat.org/insight/2014/health-care-industry-to-see-phishing-malware-attacks-intensify-in-2015, accessed 4 January 2015.
49 Gartner, 2015, www.gartner.com/doc/2611017?ref=ddisp, accessed 5 January 2015.
50 Norse–Sans Health Care Cyberthreat Report, 2014.

7 Cyber risk and data protection in Polish financial sectors

Malgorzata Skorzewska-Amberg

Introduction

Many of our most vital activities have been moved into cyberspace, making the society of today increasingly dependent on information and communication systems, including the internet. More than 42 per cent of the world's population uses the internet[1] (mid-year 2014). The profits from cyber crime exceeded the profits from drug trafficking already at the turn of the twenty-first century. Today, these profits are now reaching the level of income from illegal and legal trade in arms,[2] which clearly shows what a gargantuan threat the criminal use of information and communication technologies (ICTs) constitutes and how crucial it is that legislation is adopted in order to be able to meet the challenges of the emergence of new ICTs.

Freedom and security of the individual constitute the most basic rights protected by criminal law with regard to cyberspace. These common rights are understood, for example, as the right to protection of privacy of the individual; the right of the individual to be able to trust in information and communication systems, documents and data stored in such systems; freedom to decide and to act on entitled rights; free and exclusive disposal of possessed information; and freedom to decide on the scope and nature of data to be disclosed. Protection given by criminal law also concerns the safety of the credibility of trade and the authenticity of documents etc.

Polish criminal law aims to protect the integrity of and access to information stored and processed in data communication networks and the integrity and security of computer systems. The broad subjective right to dispose of such information[3] is also protected by law, in particular through the constitutionally guaranteed right to privacy and secrecy of communication.[4]

Criminal law also protects property, defined in civil-law terms as ownership and other property rights.[5] Actions taken in cyberspace are often directly targeted against property – spoofing (including phishing) can be mentioned as an example of such actions.

The range of infringements in the internet is extremely wide and multifaceted and related to many different domains. It is increasingly difficult to define and demarcate individual forms of violation carried out with the use of information technology (IT). These are often interconnected as a consequence of, or rather the cause for, another specific violation. Today viruses, previously created as malicious software with the sole aim to destroy data, are often used for the purpose of gaining control over transmitted data. Various forms of fraud, including computer fraud, are often linked to the breaking of security measures (e.g. copying the credit-card magnetic stripe connected with obtaining the card's PIN code with the use of a camera mounted on the automated teller machine – ATM).

Methods used in computer abuse have been changing and will continue to change along with further technological development of computer systems and networks. Types of unauthorised interference with computer systems are increasingly sophisticated and complex. It is, of course, feasible to identify different types of abuse in computer systems and computer networks as well as the entire cyberspace but, in a situation where practically every computer user can gain access to the network sooner or later, such distinctions are increasingly less important.

Computer networks are the target of numerous and multifaceted attacks. Very often the cyber attackers try to gain higher-level permission to access than that to which they are entitled. Typically, such actions are often only a prelude for capture, modification or destruction of data.

Some of the cyber attacks rely on obtaining concrete and vital information (e.g. sniffers, Trojans), the goal of others is to destroy data (e.g. most viruses) or to hinder the operations of a computer system or network (e.g. flooding and pinging[6]), while others (spoofing) aim to impersonate someone else.

Spoofing is tampering with network services and protocols in order to hide the attacker's identity and is an example of computer-network fraud. There are many different forms of spoofing, e.g. *internet protocol (IP) spoofing*[7] consisting of sending messages (IP datagrams) with a changed IP of the sender in order to make it difficult or impossible to disclose the real source of information; *data spoofing* modifies data between hosts in a communication session; *email spoofing* is when unauthorised electronic mail is sent in the name of other persons; *web spoofing*[8] is pretending to be an internet service provider. It is today increasingly difficult to distinguish different forms of spoofing. *Email spoofing* often takes the form of *phishing*, which consists primarily of sending messages in the name of a trusted sender (e.g. auction sites, social web portals, financial institutions), while providing links to concocted internet sites. Attacks called *pharming* consist of redirecting[9] the user to a concocted website (often difficult to distinguish from the authentic one), while making it possible to extract confidential information. With the use of various *spoofing* methods, it is possible to gain unauthorised network access to such confidential information as login, passwords, credit-card numbers and personal data.

Although Polish criminal law, in most cases, meets the challenges of cyber risk, both threat and attack, some issues remain and require new regulations or adaptation of the existing rules.

The aim of this chapter is to present these challenges to Polish criminal law, identify the areas that seem to require changes and propose possible solutions.

Data integrity protection

Polish criminal law protects access to information against its unauthorised usage. Article 267 of the Penal Code, in § 1, imposes penalties on the illegal opening of a sealed document, unlawful connecting to telecommunication networks or breaching or bypassing electronic, magnetic or other special protection of the information, in § 2 violation of the integrity of an information system, and in § 3 unauthorised installing, handling and tapping, visual or any other device, software or technology.

Article 268 § 1 of the Penal Code imposes penalties on the unauthorised destroying, damaging, removing or altering the recording of the relevant information or in other ways foiling or obstructing an authorised person's access to the content of such information. The liability of the perpetrator is enhanced in case the action is linked to the computer information carrier (Article 268 § 2 of the Penal Code) or causes considerable economic loss (Article 268 § 3 of the Penal Code).

Integrity protection of strictly digital information, including that not recorded on the physical carrier and also that in a given moment is only located in an information system or in a computer's memory, is stipulated by Article 268a of the Penal Code.

Article 268a § 1 of the Penal Code ('Whoever, without being authorised to do so, destroys, damages, removes, alters or impedes the access to IT data . . .') suggests that only the access to such data is protected and not the integrity of the data themselves. Therefore, the scope of criminalisation introduced by that regulation is not clear. It seems advisable to expand the protection afforded by Article 268a § 1 of the Penal Code to the protection of the information itself and not only the access to information. Where in the case of Article 267 § 1 of the Penal Code the criminalisation of acquiring the access to information is adequate (as it is not important whether the perpetrator reads the content of information or not, getting an opportunity to do so in respect of secured information is what matters), in the case of Article 268a § 1 of the Penal Code it seems that actions performed such as 'destroying, damaging, removing, altering' should refer to the data themselves, while 'impeding' should refer to the access of such data. There are also doubts as to keeping Article 268 § 2 of the Penal Code, which refers to the matter provided under Article 268a but is a less far-reaching provision, as it limits penalisation to a record of significant information and does not differ from Article 268a either by the sanction or the method of prosecution. The phrase 'Whoever, without being authorised to do so, destroys, damages, deletes or alters IT data, or prevents or impedes the access to the same . . .' in Article 268a § 1 would not leave any room for doubts as to the subject matter of legal protection governed by it. Article 268 § 2 of the Penal Code should be deleted, while considering that the content of the same was absorbed by Article 268a § 1.

Article 269 of the Penal Code enhances criminal liability for destruction, removing, damaging or altering IT data of particular importance for national defence, public safety, functioning of governmental administration, other state authority organs or state or local government institutions, as well as for disturbing or alternatively rendering impossible automatic processing and transmission of such information.[10]

Seriously disturbing the functioning of a computer system or a data communication network through unauthorised violation of its integrity or transmission of IT data is criminalised in Article 269a of the Penal Code. An example of such actions can be the introduction of viruses into a system – not so much aiming at the destruction of data, but to a great extent slowing down the computer system. Another example is a DDoS (Distributed Denial of Service) attack.

In turn, Article 269b § 1 of the Penal Code imposes penalties on the manufacture, disposal or the sharing with others of any devices or computer software adapted to commit enumerated offences. Punishment also includes those activities in respect of computer passwords, access codes or other data enabling illicit access to information stored in a computer system or a data communication network. The lack of a precise definition of what kind of information stored in the computer system or IT network should be protected results in a provision that can impose penalties on any behaviour that accesses any information in the data communication network (e.g. links to webpages). The simple addition to the provision content may completely change its application in practice – in accordance, moreover, with the likely intention of the legislator. Instead of 'access to information stored on a computer system or a data communication network', it should therefore be 'access to secured information stored on a computer system or a data communication network'.

Property protection

Fraud and computer fraud

In the Polish Penal Code, the legislator distinguished two types of fraud: 'normal' – defined in Article 286 § 1 of the Penal Code, and 'computer fraud' – defined in Article 287 § 1 of the Penal Code. Fraud, in the light of Article 286 § 1 of the Penal Code, is understood as bringing another person to an unfavourable disposition of one's own or someone else's property by misleading this person or making use of any mistake, as well as taking advantage of this person's inability to assess properly the actions taken. Misleading describes behaviour intended to cause a false perception of reality, e.g. concealment of defects in purchased goods, exploitation of an error, a lack of correction, clarification or determination of the actual state of affairs. Taking advantage of a person's inability to assess properly the actions taken means persuading this person to dispose of the property in question, at the moment when they are not in a position to be able to properly assess the significance and consequences of their actions.[11] Such inability may be permanent or temporary, or even momentary. However, this is not relevant from the point of view of a criminal perpetrator who takes advantage of such a situation.

The criteria of the act prohibited in Article 286 of the Penal Code are fulfilled only if the actions of the offender are made in order to achieve material benefit by deception or exploitation of an error or an inability to properly understand actions taken and thus lead another person to an unfavorable disposition of the property. The Supreme Court, in the judgment of 30 August 2000 (V KKN 267/00,

OSNKW 2000, vols 9–10, item 85), indicates that the constituent elements of the offence, described in Article 286 § 1 of the Penal Code, will be met if the perpetrator, 'acting in the manner described in this chapter, leads the other person to dispose of the property in a way that is detrimental to the interests of this person or other wronged person or persons', while stressing that 'the damage to the property is not a necessary condition to accept that there has taken place what is understood as unfavourable disposition'. The legal literature is dominated by the view that unfavourable disposition of property, described in Article 286 of the Penal Code, includes any property decisions and

> every act of such action, to which the disposing person was legally authorised, casually associated with misleading of the disposing person, adverse to the interests of a victim, i.e. directly causing harm to him or her, or threatening the adverse consequences to those interests.[12]

Additionally, the regulation of Article 286 of the Penal Code

> does not appear that identity between the person making the disposition of the property and the wronged person is necessary. The criteria of a fraud require only the identity of the entity with respect to deceive, exploit error or inability to properly understand the action taken and the disposition of the property.[13]

An example of violation of the provision may be email spoofing. If an email contains, for example, a sale offer, it may lead to unfavourable property disposition, even by financial payment to the fraudster.

The criminality condition of the act, described in Article 286 of the Penal Code, is directed towards the person or body who is able to commit a mistake, or be in a condition excluding a correct understanding of the actions taken. The problem arises when material benefit obtained by the offender, or the harm caused by the offender's deed, results from the data-processing system. In such cases, the machine cannot be blamed, for the mode of its action is obviously determined by the human who controls it. From the point of view of the issues discussed here, two cases are of particular interest: first, error on the part of the person compiling the software involved; second, human activity with the intention to cause damage or to make profit. Such activity can consist of altering the software, introducing incorrect data or manipulating the result of the processing.

A malfunctioning software causing, for example, the adding of sum fractions to bank accounts in connection with financial transactions does not have to be aimed at violating the law. Such software should not be introduced before the end of its testing period, hence making sure that such mistakes and irregularities will not take place. If the operation of such software nonetheless results in an unintentional change of property of a wronged person, then liability shall be applied – but not for fraud as the action was not taken in order to obtain financial benefit by misleading or making use of any mistake. However, activity intended to obtain financial benefit or to cause damage to another person by affecting data processing or violation of digital information is an activity that shall be liable under criminal law as a fraud.

Criminal liability for computer fraud is described in Article 287 of the Penal Code. This provision defines a new type of criminal offence, as fraud committed with the use of devices for automatic processing, storing or transferring of data includes no element of the offender misleading another person or making use of his or her mistake. To exhaust the criteria of an offence, only the technological influence on data processing is essential. The activity of the offender acting in order to obtain financial benefit or to cause damage to another person is not aimed explicitly at the harmed person.[14] At the same time, cases

> where automated data collection, processing and transmission technologies are used to mislead another person in order to get financial gain, will not constitute a computer fraud but meet the criteria of a classical fraud as in this case a digital device is only a means through which the perpetrator influences the decision-making process of the person he/she deceives.[15]

Not only the activity consisting of changing (or erasing) data stored in a computer system, modifying or interfering with the data-processing software operation or changing the information as a result of processing, but also mechanical inter-ference in the data-processing devices or connecting to a system of data trans-mission, meets the criteria of the offence described in Article 287 of the Penal Code. Change, deletion and entry of data, i.e. modification of information on the data carrier, also meet the criteria of the offence described in Article 287 § 1 of the Penal Code. Such modifications can be made both on the actual data-storage device and in the data communication networks. The offence may involve, for example, redirection of bank transfers or modification of financial applica-tions resulting in adding bank interest to the account of an unauthorised person. Another example of computer fraud, prosecuted by Article 287 of the Penal Code, is so called *carding*, i.e. activity involving the use of legal tenders from a credit card whose number has been stolen, for example, while carrying out financial transactions on the internet.

An essential question in this regard refers to the specification of the subject of protection described in Article 287 of the Penal Code, particularly with respect to new types of fraud, which are distinguished by ICTs (e.g. phishing or pharming). Placing computer fraud in the chapter referring to offences against property indi-cates that the aim of Article 287 of the Penal Code is the protection of property.

According to Article 44 of the Civil Code, property is the ownership or other proprietary rights (both real rights other than property and proprietary rights result-ing from the relations between property and persons), so Article 287 of the Penal Code protects the property, i.e. all the proprietary rights confirmed by the record in the system storing, processing or automatically transmitting the data or the records on the computer data carrier, or property that refers to such record.[16] Thus if IT data are not connected with proprietary rights, violation of their integrity is not subject to the provisions of property protection but is subject to the provisions described in the chapter referring to the offence against protection of the information.

An effect of phishing or pharming may be the disclosure of information that allows access to the secured information (e.g. network access data) or infection of the computer, which results in a violation of the integrity of the information or data communications system (e.g. viruses, worms etc.), or the acquisition of a remote control of the device (e.g. computer zombies). Yet another result may be an acquisition of information that may enable identity theft.

If an effect of the perpetrator's actions is a violation of the integrity of the data or information and communication system, and these data are not related to property rights, then the violation of their integrity is not subject to the provisions on the protection of property, but to the provisions of the chapter on crimes against protection of information, where activity of the offender does not have to be intended to obtain material benefit or cause damage to another person.[17]

Definition of the character of computer fraud defined in Article § 1 of the Penal Code as a material (consequential) or formal (non-consequential) offence raises controversy in the doctrine. According to the first notion, on the one hand, computer fraud has been qualified as an 'offence with no result' since the result in the form of obtaining financial benefit or causing damage to another person does not belong to its statutory constituent elements.[18] On the other hand, it is argued that the fact of affecting the data processing alone is the result of the offence, which occurs at the moment of affecting the automatic processing, storing or transmitting of the data or at the moment of making changes, deletion or entering new information on the data-storage device.[19]

The result is defined in the doctrine as 'a change in the outside world which may be of a different character and which can be distinguished from the actual behaviour'.[20] Thus affecting the processing of information or changing the information on the data carrier is not a result of the offence, but only an activity indispensable to meeting the criteria of the offence. Despite a few ambiguities, computer fraud is a formal offence because committing the offence does not depend on the production of the result, i.e. obtaining financial benefit by the offender or causing damage to another person. Producing such a result is outside the scope of the criteria stipulated in Article 287 of the Penal Code.

Another type of computer fraud (so-called phone fraud), criminalised in Article 285 § 1 of the Penal Code, is an activity where an offender activates pulse signals at someone else's expense by connecting a device to the telephone, whereas joining the telecommunication network involves 'every technical activity as a result of which the offender has the possibility to use someone else's telecommunication connection'.[21] Permanent or temporary connection 'means obtaining access to telecommunication network in any possible way',[22] whereby to meet the criteria of the offence stipulated in Article 285 of the Penal Code 'it is not necessary for the offender to obtain for himself (on any other person) a paid service of the telecommunication company'.[23]

The provision does not define the way of 'activating the pulse signals'. Thus sending text messages may mean activation of the pulse signals.[24] The notion of a pulse signal is still being used although telecommunication companies used to talk about 'call units', which determine the length of a call. In today's era of widely used digital technology, it would be appropriate to precisely define the disposition of Article 285 § 1 of the Penal Code, e.g. by substituting the wording 'activating pulse signals at someone else's expense' with 'someone, who connects to the telecommunication device, making the call at someone else's expense'.

Article 294 of the Penal Code tightens the responsibility for fraud (Article 286 § 1 of the Penal Code), computer fraud (Article 287 § 1 of the Penal Code) and phone fraud (Article 285 § 1 of the Penal Code), committed in relation to a property of significant value (Article 294 § 1 of the Penal Code) or in relation to goods of special importance to the culture (Article 294 § 1 of the Penal Code).

Fraud is prosecuted on complaint when it is committed to the detriment of a person defined in the Article 115 § 11 of the Penal Code (spouse, ascendant, descendant, sibling, relative in the same line or degree, the adopted person and his or her spouse, as well as a person staying in cohabitation), otherwise it is an indictable offence.

Theft

The liability issues associated with unauthorised access and data modification are also regulated to some extent by the provisions concerning protection of property. This sphere is particularly affected by the criminal law regulations related to copyright protection.

Articles 16 and 17 of the Act on Copyright and Related Rights of 4 February 1994 (consolidated text: Journal of Laws of 2006, no. 90, item 631, as amended) protect the right of authors to the exclusive and free disposal of their work and their right to receive financial remuneration.

Any interference in a computer program is a violation of the rights of its creators to maintain the integrity of their work. It is not permitted *inter alia* to permanently or temporarily multiply a computer program or a part thereof, by any means and in any form, without the consent of its author. Above all, an unauthorised person may not, in any way, distribute a computer program or a copy thereof (Article 74). Article 77[1] of the Act prohibits the use of technical means, including computer programs, whose goal is to 'facilitate the unauthorised removal or circumvention of technical protection measures'. The authorised person has the right to demand of the user of a computer program to destroy such measures remaining in his or her possession.

Illegal copying and distribution of software is a violation of the copyright law, in particular the right to dispose of the work and to derive income from its distribution. Articles 116 and 117 of the Act provide criminal penalties for the unauthorised distribution, reproduction or multiplication of another person's work, in order to distribute, and Article 118 the criminal liability of any person for handling stolen work's carrier. Criminal liability for the manufacturing and trade of devices or their components intended for 'unauthorised removal or bypassing of effective technological protection measures before playing, recording or multiplications of works or objects of related rights', was introduced in Article 118[1] of the Act. Sharing and dissemination of the software, enabling illicit use of copyright protected works (e.g. computer programs, films and audio files) is an ever-growing problem. Article 118[1] allows the prosecution and punishment for such an activity. Making available any information about methods of breaking such protection measures is also treated as an accessory and is punishable as such.

The subject of the criminal provisions contained in the Act on Copyright is primarily copyright or related rights, while the right of ownership or other property rights relating to the computer program are the subject of protection under Article 278 § 2 of the Penal Code. Article 278 § 2 of the Penal Code provides criminal liability of a person, who obtains somebody else's computer program without the consent of that person, in order to obtain financial gain. It is doubtful whether the benefit, which is the objective of an offender, refers to the program acquisition by the perpetrator, who does not have to bear the cost of purchasing the program, or if it refers to the income that the perpetrator intends to achieve, e.g. by multiplicating and selling a program. It is consistent with the interpretation of financial benefit, which also includes the avoidance of loss in the property. The view that a statement of purpose would be superfluous[25] seems to prevail, since the achievement of financial benefit would be tantamount to obtaining the program without consent. According to another view, already the using of a copied computer program can be seen as the achievement of financial benefits.[26]

Article 278 § 2 of the Penal Code makes it possible to prosecute crimes of taking possession of computer software in an unauthorised way (including making a copy of the software), even if the carrier on which such software is recorded and the primary version of the software remains in the possession of the authorised user. Program theft involving an unauthorised copying of the program, i.e. taking possession of it without transferring of the ownership of the original program and its carrier, as well as theft of the program with a carrier, should be punished. Theft of computer software along with the carrier on which it is recorded involves a concurrence of regulations – the perpetrator will be held liable both under Article 278 § 2 of the Penal Code for acquisition of computer software and for taking someone else's movable property – a carrier (Article 278 § 1 of the Penal Code). The area penalised for the act provided under the aforesaid regulation is broader than the one provided under Article 117 of the copyright law. If a single act infringes the interests of both the user and the author, it is subject to a cumulative liability.

The strict criminal liability is provided under Article 279 § 1 of the Penal Code for the 'theft' of a computer program made through hacking into a system in which the program is used or stored.

In accordance with Article 293 § 1 of the Penal Code, the provisions on fencing (Articles 291 and 292 of the Penal Code) shall be applied *mutatis mutandis* to the computer program.

The subject matter of the theft provided under Article 278 of the Penal Code is someone else's movable property. Civil law defines property as a tangible item. However, from a civil point of view property could also consist of documents providing the existence of a right and of securities. *Sui generis*, money is property as well. Also penal law (Article 115 § 9 of the Penal Code) defines as property money or other means of payment as well as documents entitling to a sum of money. For example, a payment card is such a document. The payment card is included in a broader set of documents provided under Article 115 § 14 of the Penal Code and it meets the definition of a specific document referred to as movable property in Article 115 § 9 of the Penal Code. Having regard to a specific subject matter of an action performed, Article 278 § 5 of the Penal Code classifies theft of an ATM card separately. In its resolution of 21 October 2003 (I KZP 33/03, OSKW 2003, vols 11–12, item 96), the Supreme Court indicated that the purpose of separately defining the crime of card theft, and thus making it impossible to classify such an act as an offence, was to enhance the legal protection of such subject matter. Taking a card for the purpose of appropriation meets the criteria of a crime. A perpetrator who withdraws the money commits another theft.

Article 288 of the Penal Code protects the ownership and the possession of property against destruction, damage or the making of the property unusable. Preventing the use of computer hardware by the authorised person by changing his or her access codes (in exceptional cases also due to unauthorised modification of digital data stored in the computer system) meets the criteria of a crime defined in the provision in question.

The Penal Code uses the term 'movable property', which in some circumstances can cause unnecessary narrowing of the responsibility on the part of the offender. It would be worth considering restoring the term 'property' rather than using the rather civilistic expression 'movable property' to describe the executive subject of the crimes against property. In certain circumstances not only computer hardware but also digitally stored data could be treated as objects to which the provision relates. If the concept of property is to be treated in the same way as in the Penal Codes from 1932 and 1969, then also a document of material value should be considered as a property. That would, in certain cases, also allow digital data breaches to be prosecuted as theft, e.g. if the infringement applies to the publication of an ordered text intended to be published. Data stored on the magnetic strips of credit cards would in such cases also be clearly defined as a property.

It should also be worth taking into consideration a standardisation of the terminology used in the Penal Code, Act of 19 August 2011 on Payment Services (consolidated text Journal of Laws of 2014, item 873, as amended) and Act of 29 August 1997 – the Banking Law (consolidated text Journal of Laws of 2002, no. 72, item 665, as amended). Article 278 § 5 of the Penal Code relies on the specific concept of an ATM card, while the Act on Payment Services and the Banking Law use the term 'payment card' and define it as a card that authorises cash withdrawals or allows placement of a payment order, i.e. a statement containing an instruction for a payment transaction. Such harmonisation could be effected by amending Article 278 § 5 of the Penal Code by way of replacing the term 'ATM card' with the more general expression 'payment card'.

Identity theft

Identity theft is a form of usurpation of another person's identity – the impersonation of another person by assuming another person's identity – usually with the aim to cause harm or to gain unfair advantage. Identity theft occurs when someone uses information identifying another person (e.g. the name and the surname of another person), without the consent of this person and in order to cause harm. The term *identity theft* has been in use for quite a long time, though it should be noted that the expression is not fully adequate. Indeed, it is difficult to talk about identity as something it is possible to steal.

Identity theft can mean *inter alia* impersonating another person with the purpose to commit an offence, impersonating another person in order to obtain credit, goods or services, impersonating another person to use their identity in everyday life, etc.

Identity theft, and more specifically impersonating another person, was introduced to the Polish Penal Code by the Law of 25 February 2011 amending the Penal Code (Journal of Laws of 2011, no. 72, item 381). Article 190a § 2 of the Penal Code imposes penalties with regard to an offender who is pretending to be another person, or uses an image or other personal information of this person, in order to cause personal or financial harm.

Article 6.2 of the Data Protection Act of 29 August 1997 (consolidated text Journal of Laws of 2014, item 1182), defines personal data as any information relating to an identified or identifiable natural person. Therefore, 'personal data are any information relating to an identified or possible to identify person, and not only such information, which are used to identify a person'.[27] However, it is not always clear if, for example, information about digital profiles (such as username or login and password) can always be considered as personal data.

Under Article 190a § 2 of the Penal Code the offence is a directional crime, carried out solely for the purpose of causing property damage or personal harm, while unauthorised collection of data that can be used to steal somebody's identity or to impersonate another person is not criminalised. It would be worth considering, in particular in the information society where each tiny piece of information can constitute a potential commodity, whether such unauthorised retrieval of data (not necessarily in order to cause the harm) should be criminalised.

Another important issue is to identify the person to whom the perpetrator causes injury by his or her actions. Article 190a § 2 of the Penal Code clearly indicates that the activity is criminalised only if the perpetrator carries it out in order to cause harm to the person being impersonated.

It seems that the liability of an identity thief may be excessively limited in this way, e.g. when the perpetrator accepts that the person whose identity he/she steals from will suffer injury, although the purpose of his or her activity is to cause injury to a completely different person. It appears therefore to be well founded to consider the deletion of the definition of the person injured by the perpetrator and make punishment of the perpetrator dependent only on the causing of injury (to the person whose data were used or to a third party).

There is no doubt that Article 190a § 2 of the Penal Code criminalises such behaviour of the offender only if it concerns existing persons. The data of fictitious persons are not to be considered as personal data within the meaning of the Data Protection Act.

However, it would be worthwhile to consider the criminalisation of impersonating someone else for the sole purpose of hiding one's identity (without the element of harm caused to a person whose identity is being used) including the creation of a fictional identity, in order to cause harm to another person, especially since the problem of creating fictitious identities (digital profiles in particular) in order to harm another person is expected to continue to increase.

Computer forgery

Computer forgery can be applied to both forgery of a traditional document, carried out with the use of computer hardware and software (e.g. counterfeiting of official forms with the use of a scanner and software for processing graphic documents), as well as forgery of a document created, stored or transmitted in electronic form (e.g. changes in electronic trade books).

The aim of the legal document protection is not only to protect information as such, but also, above all, to provide documents with credibility, and thus confidence, in legal transactions.

In accordance with Article 115 § 14 of the Penal Code, a document is every object or any other carrier of recorded information to which a specified right is attached or, due to its content, certifies a right, a legal relationship or legally relevant circumstances.

Besides, the definition of a document is also included in Article 2.3 of the Act on Protection of Classified Information of 5 August 2010 (Journal of Laws, no. 182, item 1228, as amended), which provides that recorded classified information is also to be considered a document.

On the one hand, the Act on Electronic Signature of 18 September 2001 (consolidated text: Journal of Laws of 2013, item 262, as amended) in Article 5.2 considers the data in electronic form bearing a secure electronic signature verified by a valid qualified certificate to be equivalent in the terms of legal effects to the documents bearing handwritten signatures, if separate provisions do not state otherwise.[28]

On the other hand, the Act on Informatisation of Operations of Entities Executing Public Tasks of 17 February 2005 (consolidated text: Journal of Laws of 2014, item 1114) uses the term 'electronic document' – as a set of data constituting a separate meaningful whole, organised within a defined internal structure and recorded on an IT data carrier. The IT data carrier is a material or a device used to record, store and read data in digital or analogue format (Article 3). Those terms harmonise the terminology for the purpose of informatisation and, in accordance with Article 61 of the Act, if any questions concerning interpretation of terms used in other acts arise (e.g. electronic data carrier, electronic information carrier, IT data, electronic data), they should be accepted as valid definitions to replace any other terms used.

In accordance with the decision of the Supreme Court of 7 September 2000 (file ref. no.: I KZP 25/00 of 2000, vol. 11, item 23) a property that 'does not, of itself, evidence a right, legal relationship or legally relevant circumstances' cannot be considered as a document.

A definition of a document, contained in Article 115 § 14 of the Penal Code seems not to prejudge that the document carrier is a physical object. Since, within the meaning of the Penal Code, the substance of a document is determined solely by whether a specific right is attached to the same or whether it includes a legally relevant content,[29] a recorded intangible information carrier should be considered as a document as well. It is clear that a document must be submitted in a physically available format. It is therefore considered that the new wording of the provision broadens the scope of the document's protection in the criminal law, including both tangible and intangible carriers of the collected, processed or transmitted IT data. In the literature, however, you can also find the view that 'all documents are purely material', because the 'recorded carrier' is a document, and the definition of a computer carrier of information indicates that it is a carrier on which the content was recorded in the manner specified for the appropriate carrier.[30]

Provisions relating to offences against the credibility of documents protect the certainty of legal transactions. Such certainty is based on trusting the content of the document in question. Due to the content contained therein, the document is proof of the law, but to act as such the recorded information carrier, both tangible and intangible, must appear in a visible form.

Legally protected interests connected with a document may be compromised by physical falsification – Article 270 § 1 of the Penal Code: 'whoever, in order to use it as authentic, forges or alters a document or uses such forged or altered document'[31] or intellectual falsification of such document: direct – Article 271, or indirect – Article 273 of the Penal Code.

Article 270 § 1 of the Penal Code provides for two forms of document falsification – forgery and alternation. As the *Polish Language Dictionary* has it,[32] 'to forge' means 'to imitate with intent to use as the original, to counterfeit; to make a copy with intent to use it illegally', and 'to alter' – 'to re-make, change the shape, form of something to make it fit for a new purpose'. The Supreme Court, in the judgment of 27 November 2000 (III KKN 233/98), ruled that 'a document is forged when it does not come from the person in the name of whom it has been prepared and it is altered when an unauthorised person makes changes to an authentic document'. Similarly, in the judgment of 5 September 2000 (II KKN 569/97), the Supreme Court ruled:

> The crime provided under Article 265 of the Penal Code of 1969 (identical to the one under Article 270 the Penal Code of 1997) may be committed in two ways. One is making a letter to appear as a document to create an impression that the content of the same comes from the issuer mentioned therein, while in fact this is not the case (forgery). The other is changing the content of an existing authentic document by the perpetrator (alternation).

The criteria of the act prohibited under Article 270 § 1 of the Penal Code are met not only by the forgery of an entire document but also by the alternation or forgery of any part of the same, e.g. a signature or a date. In the decision of 8 April 2002, the Supreme Court (IV KKN 421/98) stressed, that 'alternation of the document, within the meaning of . . . Article 270 § 1 of the Penal Code, may also lies in writing something in addition, without the consent of the victim'. It is worth emphasising that, in accordance with Article 270 § 2 of the Penal Code,

> the perpetrator must act to the detriment of the signatory, which does not mean that injury must actually occur. A sufficient condition is that such injury may be caused. This is not just financial injury, although it will probably be most frequent in practice, but also moral injury.[33]

A person who prepares the offence referred to in Article 270 § 1 and 2 of the Penal Code is also a subject to criminal sanction.

Despite some claims in the literature that electronic documents may cause unclear qualification of an act of manipulating the content of the said documents (in particular alternation of the same), some concerns may be raised as to whether manipulating the content of a digital document meets the criteria of an act prohibited under Article 270 § 1 of the Penal Code or whether such activity should be treated as a computer fraud prosecuted under Article 287 § 1 of the Penal Code. The problem of such differentiation arises as the falsification of electronic documents is not identified in the Penal Code.[34] It seems that the alteration of a content of an electronic document, i.e. giving it a different content than the original one, should always be treated, in accordance with Article 115 § 14 of the Penal Code, as document forgery, therefore an offence referred to in Article 270 § 1 of the Penal Code. A situation in which an electronic record is modified for financial gain or to cause injury to a person should be considered as a concurrence of regulations. Such position was confirmed by the Court of Appeal in Lublin in the judgment of 30 March 2000 (II Aka 41/00):

> In the case where the offender forged or altered a document, and then made use of it . . . to bring another person to the unfavorable disposition of property, it must be concluded that he is guilty of two offenses: forgery of a document (Article 270 § 1 of the Penal Code) and fraud (Article 286 § 1 of the Penal Code).

Article 270 § 2 of the Penal Code provides for a crime of unauthorised filling in a form signed by someone else, against the will of the signatory and to the detriment of the same, and a crime of unauthorised use of a form. Penalisation is not dependent on actual injury. The crime is committed when actions that make up the filling in of a form are taken up, provided that the issuer of a form is injured by the sole filling in of such form. If not, the crime is committed when circumstances that may cause injury to the issuer arise.[35]

Different views refer also to the interpretation of a form. Two views formed on the basis of Article 194 of the Penal Code of 1932 remain valid also for a form as a subject matter of an action performed in the crime provided under Article 270 § 2 of the Penal Code. On the one hand, according to Leon Peiper, besides a promissory note form and a check form, a blank sheet of paper is a form as well. On the other hand, in the opinion of Juliusz Makarewicz, a form is a paper with a specific shape and look, designated to make legally binding representations.[36] The first view is supported by the majority of the doctrine. The phrase 'signed form of a specified document' used in Article 270 § 2 of the Penal Code indicates that, within the meaning of the said regulation, a form is each item signed by a person, which – considering specified formal or actual circumstances – may constitute a document.[37]

The introduction of an electronic signature eliminates the possibility of unauthorised additions to the document bearing such a signature (including the filling of a form bearing someone else's signature), as an electronic signature in fact depends on each character of a signed message, and thus will be different for different messages, though always identifying the signatory.

The crime under Article 271 § 1 of the Penal Code consists of giving false testimony regarding circumstances with legal significance by a person authorised to issue a document (intellectual falsification of a document). Article 271 § 3 provides for the type qualified based on the purpose of the perpetrator.

According to the judgment of the Court of Appeal in Cracow of 25 November 1999 (II Aka 173/99, KZS 199/12/24):

> The testimony under Article 271 of the Penal Code is only documents 'issued' to the public, designated to prove circumstances testified therein without a need to support the same with other evidence, which are presumed to be true and enjoy public confidence. They do not include documents prepared by public officials for internal use of the office (memoranda, etc.) or documents governing obligations between natural or legal persons (agreements, representations, etc.).[38]

Procurement of a false testimony by misleading an authorised person is a crime prosecuted under Article 272 of the Penal Code. That crime, like the one under Article 271 of the Penal Code, is committed when the document with a false testimony is placed on the market, and the use of such document – while using its legal significance – is a crime provided under Article 273 of the Penal Code.

Legal interest associated with the document may also be adversely affected by the destruction or damage of the document, or other similar action against the document. Article 276 kk prescribes criminal sanctions against a person who destroys, damages, hides, eliminates or makes a document unusable, while not possessing the rights to exercise exclusive control over the document. Destruction of a document could take the form of destroying the carrier of the document or destroying the data information recorded on the carrier.[39] Hiding the document's storage place meets the criteria of concealing the document, while preventing an access to the document e.g. by locking it in an armoured closet, meets the criteria of removal of the document.[40] The Supreme Court, in the judgment of 23 May 2002 (V KKN 404/99, OSNKW 2002, vols 9–10, item 72) indicates that a person may be accused of the crime provided under Article 276 of the Penal Code, consisting of concealing a document specified therein, only when it is indicated that he/she himself/herself took an action to conceal a document, to which he/she had no exclusive right of disposition, from a person authorised to dispose of the same, i.e. the document was put in a place such person is not aware of or has no or difficult access to. . . .

Thus preventing or hindering the access to the document referred to in Article 276 of the Penal Code also meets the criteria of concealing of the document. Concealing the document within the meaning of Article 276 of the Penal Code may also be, in the light of the judgment of the Supreme Court of 9 August 2000 (V KKN 208/00, OSNKW 2000, vols 9–10, item 84), 'the denial of possession of a document, keeping the possession of the document and failure to give the document, in spite of the request, to the entitled person'.

It can therefore be assumed that blocking access to an electronic document, e.g. by changing access codes, can also be treated as a concealment of the document in question.

Criminal liability of Articles 270–3 and 276 of the Penal Code occurs when the perpetrator acts intentionally, while Article 271 of the Penal Code describes an offence that can be committed by a specific person only (a public official or other person authorised to issue a document).

Document falsification may also take a form of creating false evidence in proceedings before public authorities, which entails legal consequences. For example, a person who falsifies evidence and directs a prosecution for a crime against a specified person is held liable under Article 235 of the Penal Code, in addition to liability under Article 270 of the Penal Code.

Article 310 § 1 of the Penal Code provides for penal sanctions *inter alia* for forging or altering money or other means of payment and documents entitling to a sum of money. In accordance with the doctrine, this regulation also protects plastic money and electronic money, among others, as both aforesaid types of money 'are accepted as means of payment in trade and used to discharge payment obligations'[41] and thus, 'they may appear as designations of "other means of payment" referred to under Article 310 § 1 of the Penal Code'.[42]

Electronic money is defined under Article 2.21a of the Act on Payment Services as a monetary value kept in an electronic (including magnetic) format, issued – with an obligation to redeem the same – for the purpose of payment transactions and accepted by entities other than the sole issuer of such electronic money. Besides, the same Act defines a payment instrument as a personalised device or a set of procedures agreed upon by the user and the provider, used by the user to place a payment order[43] (Article 2.10) and a payment card as a card that authorises cash withdrawals or allows the placement of a payment order (Article 2.15a, as well as a debit card – Article 2.15aa, and a credit card – Article 2.15ab).

The concept of 'other means of payment' used in the Article 310 § 1 of the Penal Code enables the extension of the protection afforded by the provision in question to the payment instruments, payment cards, as well as to electronic money. This is extremely important in situations in which financial transactions are carried out by means of electronic communication, as well as in relation to the frequent replacement of tangible carriers of securities by digital carriers.

Preparing for the offence of Article 310 § 1 of the Penal Code, e.g. through the creation or distribution of programs that can generate credit-card numbers, is punishable under Article 310 § 4 of the Penal Code.

Cyber crimes – from a practical point of view

The problem of cyber crime is still fairly recent. Its development is closely related to the dissemination of the internet (and it must not be forgotten that the internet on today's scale is a phenomenon that, roughly speaking, emerged only two decades ago), and the appearance and development of the global information society of today.

A large majority of modern people's daily activities, associated with all sorts of correspondence, acquisition and transfer of information and current financial affairs, is being carried out through an IT network – with the use of a computer, tablet, smartphone or phone. Consequently, crime (including organised crime) is quickly adapting to the widespread advanced technologies, using ICT systems to commit crime on a global scale. Automated networks are used even to commit economic espionage fraud in relation to financial transactions, to attack companies and force extortion.

Many criminal activities are carried out in a very simple way. One of the simplest examples of spoofing (email spoofing and more specific phishing) is sending letters allegedly coming from reputable senders, e.g. banks or other financial or payment institutions. Such letters, frequently referring to alleged attempts of unauthorised access, contain a request to change personal data, offering a link to a page where such change should be made. Of course, the page is controlled by the offender.

The email shown in Figure 7.1 contains a link redirecting the recipient to a fake webpage (looking almost exactly like the real one) and enabling him or her to log into an Apple account. While logging into the account the credentials of the victim are disclosed to the criminals. Other information in the email (FAQ link) refers to Apple's real webpages. Only the sender's address – in this case info@ukidapple. uk – does not look like an authentic Apple address (generally the address should contain the company's domain name such as apple.com, itunes.com).

Pharming is another variant of spoofing, becoming more and more common. Pharming is an attack that redirects a user (even after entering the correct web address) to a fake website – often extremely difficult to distinguish from the genuine one.

IT systems, in particular those supporting the financial sector, are generally well protected, therefore the criminals primarily aim at individual users of financial services, including e-banking systems and payment cards.

One of the most common operations in Poland of this kind is skimming. Skimming means copying data from the magnetic stripe of a payment card. Such copying is done mostly with the use of a special device (a skimmer), mounted on the inlet of an

Figure 7.1 An example of phishing.

Source: An email received by the author.

ATM. Copied data are used to produce a duplicate card. The PIN needed to confirm transactions is most often obtained through a miniature camera mounted above the ATM keyboard or through a false keyboard applied on the top of the real one.

The vast majority of payment cards in Poland carry a built-in chip. Information on the chip is stored on the magnetic strip of the card. The chip card initiates the EMV module.[44] Duplicate cards based on the scanned magnetic stripe contains information about the chip, but since a duplicate card does not contain an exact chip (for which information is stored on the magnetic strip), devices supporting an EMV module will not authorise the required transaction. This is the reason why the vast majority of transactions made with the use of skimmed cards are performed in countries where EMV is not very common. For example, cards skimmed in Poland have been used in Bulgaria, Indonesia and South America.[45]

A particular case of skimming in Poland was the subject of a final court settlement in late 2013. A group, acting from September to November 2011, installed skimmers on ATMs and was able to record any keystrokes on the ATM keyboards when entering a PIN. This gave access to the PIN-code sequence and the identity of the individual cards. The perpetrators were then able to forge magnetic cards (legally speaking – other means of payment) and break the security of a total of 297 Bulgarian ATMs in November 2011, using the copied cards to withdraw considerable sums from the accounts of the owners of the original cards.

The District Court in Olsztyn, in its judgment of 18 December 2012 (II K 218/12), found the described actions as a crime of Article 267 § 3 of the Penal Code (fraud), Article 310 § 1 of the Penal Code (forgery of means of payment) and Article 287 § 1 of the Penal Code (computer fraud), and sentenced the perpetrators to imprisonment and fines. The Court of Appeal, in Białystok (judgment of 12 March 2013, II AKa 23/13), upheld the sentence in full.

Security measures for cards and ATMs resulted in a clear reduction of skimming cases, but the scale of crime is still very high. Only in December 2014 and just in the area of Warsaw alone a few dozen cases of skimming have been disclosed.[46]

Another widespread method of criminal activity is obtaining data in order to carry out 'card not present' transactions (e.g. internet payments), using card numbers, card verification codes (CVCs) and the name of the card owner. It should be noted that in some countries only the card number and name of the owner embossed on the card are necessary to remit the card payment.

Skimming and phishing are prevalent and troublesome crimes, but crimes with the use of malware are much more serious. The most widespread type of malware in Poland in 2013[47] were Trojans created in order to carry out theft from e-banking customers.

The large majority of attacks carried out in Poland is directed against Polish citizens and Polish companies, but the Polish internet has become at the same time a popular platform for attacks carried out on a global scale, e.g..pl domains[48] are used by exploit kits, which in turn are part of larger cyber-crime campaigns.

Criminals usually try to get as much information as they can, normally more than they are entitled to. They often focus on information vulnerable from a security perspective, e.g. access codes, or try to change the content of electronic transmissions. Malware and botnets are the most commonly used for this type of action.

A botnet is a group of computers infected with malware. The malware is hidden from the computer user. The bootmaster (the owner of a botnet) remotely controls the computers included in the botnet with the use of a managing server or a group of servers (command and control). The bootmaster, thanks to the command and control server, is able to, for example, distribute malware remotely and perform other attacks with the use of botnets.[49] It is estimated that between 170,000 to 300,000 infected computers are in use in Poland.[50]

The innovative tools and new methods of extortion and theft of funds from bank accounts are more and more common in Poland. That includes new malware (such as PowerZeus, vmZeuS, Citadela, VBKlip), infections of mobile devices (E-Security, Antivirus), attacks on routers and domain name servers (DNSs), and allegedly erroneous transfers.

Bank Trojans (e.g. Zeus, PowerZeus) are one of the most serious categories of malware found in Poland. Such software may allow unauthorised wire transfers from a person's account. In most cases the malware in question can modify bank websites (webinject function) available on the infected computer. Such modification takes place after the deprotection of the webpage (the secure socket layer is already removed), but before the displaying of the website content to the user.[51]

The simple application VBKlip is another example of popular malware. When the key combination CTRL + C (copy) and CTRL + V (paste) is used, the VBKlip searches in the clipboard for character strings matching the account number and exchanges it with a number indicated by the cyber criminals. This application has proven to be very effective and difficult to detect and results in the sending of all transfers made from the infected machine to a designated (substituted) account.[52]

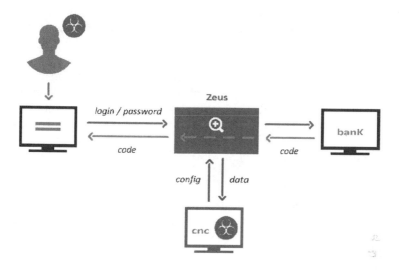

Figure 7.2 Banking Trojans' workflow.

Source: www.cert.pl. Original source with permission www.cert.pl/PDF/Raport_CP_2013.pdf.

E-Security malware and its mutations are based on a fairly simple solution. A message appears on the smartphone alerting that an E-Security certificate should be installed in order to enhance its security. The installation enables the criminals to take control over the phone. When E-Security ceases to be effective, its mutation appears. It is based on a false antivirus program, which allegedly can prevent cases similar to E-Security. When the program is installed, it makes it possible to take control of the phone, allowing the fraudsters to obtain, for example, texted access and approval codes.[53]

Another method of obtaining unauthorised funds from banking services is an attack with a trusted recipient. In late 2013, customers of several banks in Poland were attacked (malware based on the mutation associated with the installation of a distributed free antivirus application). After each successful login to the transaction system, the data identifying the bank – the customer's login and password, as well as the balance of his or her account – were sent to the server of the criminals. Later, the customer was falsely informed that the bank had changed the account number format and there was a need to confirm the operation and to define a new account number as a trusted recipient (no secondary authorisation code would be required in future transactions). The new account number is active after a few days and a failure to perform the requested operation would result in the impossibility of accepting transfers to an existing account. A new recipient addition form is obviously filled with data transmitted from the server of the criminals (in different formats, depending on the particular bank). The operation is approved by a texted single code. Once the operation is completed the message is sent to the server of the criminals, who are able to log into the victims' accounts, without the necessity of entering any codes, and carry out transfers to the newly defined recipient.[54]

A concrete example of such criminal activities by an organised group, operating in Poland from October 2004 to January 2005, caused the owners of bank accounts held by a certain bank financial damage and tried to harm the owners of these bank accounts. Funds allocated to the victims' bank accounts were transferred to accounts specifically set up for this purpose by a substituted person. Such transfers were possible after an unauthorised change of IT data records, consisting of electronic records of financial transactions on the accounts of victims conducted by the bank. The unauthorised change of the IT records was made possible with the use of information obtained without permission by breaking the electronic protection (passwords and access codes to the accounts of victims). In some cases, the transaction failed because of the challenge and the suspension of transactions by the bank. The District Court in Jelenia Góra in the judgment of 13 December 2013 (III K 151/11) considered a violation of *inter alia* Article 267 § 1 of the Penal Code (unauthorised access to information) and Article 287 § 1 of the Penal Code (computer fraud). The judgment of the District Court was upheld by the Court of Appeal in Wrocław in its judgment of 1 October 2014 (II AKa 144/14).

Ransomware and DDoS attacks are different types of threat, but are quickly developing.

Ransomware attacks are so far mostly infecting computers with malware (worms, exploit kits etc.), causing the computer to lock. A message is displayed on the computer screen informing that suspicious activity of the computer was detected by the police and that there is a need to pay a fine to have the lock removed. Removing the lock is not too difficult with the right software, but many people pay the required 'ransom', which usually is not too prohibitive.[55]

DDoS attacks are designed to impede or prevent the operation of the service. Frequently visited sites, such as common auction sites (in Poland the most popular auction site allegro.pl fell victim to such an attack) and banks are the most frequent targets. The requirement to stop the attack is to pay the criminals a certain amount of money.[56]

The structure and the nature of the threats are changing along with the technology development and an increasing participation of the society in ICT networks. The first group of attacks includes those that can be treated as pure vandalism; the second group of attacks aimed at identity or financial information theft. The third group includes attacks performed in a highly specialised way, complex and staged, targeted at specific companies (so-called Advanced Persistent Threat – APT).[57] Criminals are increasingly skilled at hiding the malware, making it an effective operation of standard security systems (especially antivirus software or classic firewalls), difficult or even impossible to detect.

At the same time, the basic principle of protection against any attack remains the same, the data are safe to the extent to which the weakest point in the security chain is protected. An important aspect – if not the most important – is to educate and train users of IT networks. The next step in building an effective protection to apply not only traditional security, but also to introduce systems that operate only in relation to the data that have been passed through conventional systems (i.e. a new generation of security solutions).[58] This is especially important in the case of institutions that are in particular danger of APT attacks. The importance of cooperation between operators should also not be ignored. Cooperation between the local, regional and global network operators is also crucial – especially in dealing with DDoS attacks. The larger the operator, the higher the bandwidth of its network, which makes it easier for the operator to control a sudden increase of network traffic (typical for DDoS attacks). It is also possible, if the reaction is swift, to stop the attack before it develops and disseminates.[59]

Conclusions

The technological revolution is moving a large part of human activity to the virtual sphere and consequently making the global society strongly dependent on ICT systems. At the same time this activity in the virtual sphere can cause the same consequences in the physical sphere.

Development and dissemination of computer networks, as well as their globalisation, impacted on the lookout for solutions allowing not only communication, but above all data transmission at a distance. An obvious next step was to develop ways of carrying out various financial transactions with the use of the computer networks. E-banking, e-shopping, e-government, all these new digital forms of organising our daily life opened up new possibilities and largely enhanced the productivity, efficiency and administrative speed, while at the same time creating huge challenges for legislation, forcing an entirely new approach to the law itself.

Legal standards, presumably, should regulate certain social behaviours – on the one hand, they should stabilise the existing social order, on the other, give impetus to change. The primary function of the law is, however, the determination of certain values that should be specifically protected.

Widespread use of global data communication networks led to an unprecedented development of society, including the development of science – through unlimited time and space to exchange information, trade and services and through the development of e-banking and e-signature, culture and the arts – by audiovisual digital transmission. Scarcely any area of modern society is left untouched by the digital revolution. It cannot be forgotten, however, that getting a powerful tool to support development, paradoxically, also exposes us to many new dangers. Fraud, theft, blackmail and defamation are threats that have been known for centuries, but never before has the area of criminal activity been open in an almost unlimited way – there are no boundaries, no distance and no time to limit these unwanted activities.

It ought to be stressed that technological development often causes legislative problems resulting from an insufficient understanding of the technological language by the language of law. The primary problem that had to be faced in this respect is the necessity of a different perception of the protected good. Two examples may be cited under Polish criminal law – Articles 267 and 269 of the Penal Code, both concerning the protection of digital information.

Article 267 of the Penal Code, in a previous appearance and apart from the protection of communication secrecy ('whoever acquires information not destined for him/her, by opening a sealed letter, or connecting to a cable that transmits information'), also ensured the protection of information against unauthorised access ('whoever, without being authorised to do so, acquires information not destined for him/her . . . by breaching electronic, magnetic or other special protection of the same'). Only the information was protected, hence in cases when access to a system was gained without visibly obtaining any information (e.g. the offender obtained information in a completely different network, in another country or in a manner that does not necessarily link losing of information in one system with an unauthorised entry to another system), the perpetrator could avoid the responsibility for his or her actions. Doubts also arose whether activities such as bypassing security or taking advantage of software gaps were equivalent to protection breaking. Amendments introduced at the end of 2008[60] shift the protection from information to access to information, which makes it possible to prosecute gaining access to information, even without coming in possession of its content. It appears though that the legislator should in this place also have considered the criminalisation of any preparatory acts enabling such violation.

In turn, Article 269b § 1 imposes penalties on the manufacture, the disposal or the sharing with others any devices or computer software adapted to commit enumerated offences. Punishment also includes those activities in respect of computer passwords, access codes or other data enabling illicit access to information stored in a computer system or an IT network. The legislator's intention was to indicate the illicitness of action intended to breach the information integrity. However, the lack of a precise definition of what kind of information stored in a computer system or in a network should be protected resulted in a provision that can impose penalties on any behaviour that accesses any information in an ICT network (e.g. links to webpages).

Of course, in normal circumstances access to an IT network will not impose any penalties, but it weakens the impact of the law. This example can be an illustration of the Cartesian opposition to the rational drafting of the law and to its creation by practice. However, Hans Kelsen's view – that the validity of the norm does not yet mean its application and compliance – cannot be denied. Kelsen stressed the *sine qua non* condition to enter a legal norm in force, that it must meet the requirement of any effectiveness.[61]

The simple addition to the provision content may completely change its application in practice – in accordance, moreover, with the likely intention of the legislator. It is enough to add one word – instead of 'access to information' the sentence should read 'access to secured information'.

The above examples show how easy it is to skew the legislator's intentions due to the incompatibility of technological and legal languages. The creation of the criminal regulations that pertain to the realm of new ICTs requires great precision. So it is even more important to seek the unification of criminal law terminology, so that the scope of protection does not raise doubts, e.g. Article 285 § 1 of the Polish Penal Code still uses the term 'pulse signal', although in the era of digital telecommunication companies refer to 'call units', which determine the time of a call; Article 278 § 5 of the Polish Penal Code uses the rather old-fashioned concept of an ATM card, while other Acts regulating various financial issues (*inter alia* the Act on Payment Services, the Banking Law) use much more general and broad definition of 'payment card'. In most cases, actions taken in cyberspace are no different from those made in the physical space. For example, legal actions carried out in cyberspace are different from those made in the real world only by course of action. The most common are information-society services, i.e. provided for remuneration, at a distance, by electronic means and made available through the data at the request of the recipient. A characteristic feature of legal transactions in the data communication network is a completely different form, in particular the lack of physical contact between the transaction parties, while not altering the content of the legal actions – the contract is still a contract, the administrative action is still an administrative action etc.

Activities in the virtual space, violating the law, in the vast majority of cases are nothing new, at least not in essence. Theft is theft, whether it be a bank robbery taking place in the premises of a bank office or an interference in the computerised banking system; fraud remains fraud whether a simple letter is sent, or the means of electronic communication are used. However, it is rather difficult not to notice the appearance of behaviours entirely new to us, and what's more requiring a totally new perspective and a different look at long-established concepts.

Identity theft, before the era of ICT, was not overly common and in most cases could be classified as fraud. The emergence of global information and communication systems resulted in a sharp increase in behaviours that allow the perpetrator to impersonate another person (in particular through the use of their digital profile) with the aim other than to cause strictly financial harm. Such a purpose is an inherent feature of fraud, so if there is no purpose to obtain financial gain, the perpetrator, even if hurting the victim badly, does not commit a crime from a legal point of view. Still, identity theft is not separately criminalised in most European countries. The exceptions are the UK, France and Poland. Sweden has also initiated intensive work to criminalise identity theft. Taking into account that identity theft has started to become a fairly common and global offence and an increasing threat not only to impersonated victims but also to the financials[62] (e.g. loans taken by imposters), in a not-very-distant future, adoption of appropriate European-wide solutions will be needed. Such need has already been recognised by the International Association of Penal Law.[63]

It would be worth considering starting a discussion in the near future on the criminalisation of impersonating somebody else for the sole purpose of hiding one's own identity (without the element of harm to the person whose identity is being used) including the creation of fictitious identities, to cause harm to another third party. The problem of creating a fictitious identity (especially digital profiles) to cause damage will most certainly increase in the future. An entirely new problem that the law will have to face is a phenomenon that might be called theft of virtual goods. On the one hand, it must be considered that virtual reality (not to be confused with cyberspace) is not an object of interest of criminal law. On the other hand, however, a discussion on the introduction of the concept of virtual goods ought to be initiated. Virtual goods, like property, should be protected by law. Notwithstanding the fact that these goods are intangible, they may represent measurable financial value (e.g. player profiles in computer games are often sold for considerable sums and, increasingly, are an object of unauthorised acquisition, including closing of the game by the owner of such rights, which sometimes may also in turn constitute a problem of a legal nature).

The discussion on methods of securing the rights of the individual in a situation of their violation in cyberspace should not be omitted as well. The problem of anonymity or, more precisely, the difficulty of identification of the person (and not only the IP address of the host) who is the cause of a law infringement is essential. Therefore the solutions that would enable the protection of rights of the individual, regardless of the possibility to determine the perpetrator, should be considered. It is important to consider, first of all, cases where the direct infringer cannot be determined (for example, when the IP address of the host is known, but it could not be conclusively determined who benefited from the terminal), or when the perpetrator can be determined, but the content that is of interest to the law, available in its jurisdiction, is physically located outside the country.

In view of the constantly evolving technology, it is difficult to talk about any anticipation of problems that can be encountered in the distant future, especially considering that the future that even a decade ago appeared to be distant is examined in terms of the past, due to the ongoing technological revolution.

Once again, as many times in the past, the forms of threat are continuously changing, while their content remains fairly constant. And the law, without changing its substance, must in the future adapt itself many times to a changing reality.

In this respect, one should bear in mind the words of Aristotle, who in his 'Politics' emphasised that 'there is one thing as vitally important as any: to keep a look-out against all lawlessness, and, more particularly, to be on guard against any of its petty forms'.[64]

Notes

1 Accessed 28/01/2015 at www.internetworldstats.com/stats.htm.
2 Barbara Mejssner, *Niezbite cyfrowe dowody [Irrefutable Digital Evidence]*, accessed 28/01/2015 at www.klubcio.pl/artykuly/321458/Niezbite.cyfrowe.dowody.html.
3 See Włodzimierz Wróbel in Andrzej Zoll (ed.) *Kodeks karny. Część szególna. tom II, Komentarz do art. 117–277 k.k. [The Penal Code. Special Part. Commentary vol. II, Commentary to the Articles 117–277 kk]*, Warsaw: Wolter Kluwers, 2008, p. 1287.
4 Andrzej Marek, *Kodeks karny. Komentarz [The Penal Code. Commentary]*, Warsaw: Wolters Kluwer, 2010, p. 570; Joanna Piórkowska-Flieger in Tadeusz Bojarski (ed.) *Kodeks karny. Komentarz [The Penal Code. Commentary]*, Warsaw: LexisNexis, 2012, p. 701.
5 See Małgorzata Dąbrowska-Kardas and Piotr Kardas in Andrzej Zoll (ed.) *Kodeks karny. Część szczególna. Komentarz, tom III, Komentarz do art. 278–363 k.k. [The Penal Code. Special Part. Commentary vol. III, Commentary to the Articles 278–363 kk]*, Warsaw: Wolter Kluwers, 2008, p. 25.

6 Attacks on internet providers take the form of such overload so that they are not able to fulfill their normal tasks, i.e. providing internet services.

7 Used, for example, in connection to *network weaving*, also called *connection laundering*, which is when somebody with the purpose to hide his or her identity reaches the host through several servers, each time changing identity (e.g. by altering the source address in the IP – hence *IP spoofing*); see Simson Garfinkel and Gene Spafford, *Bezpieczeństwo w Unixie i Internecie [Practical UNIX and Internet Security]*, O'Reilly & Associates, Inc., Warsaw: Wydawnictwo RM (Polish edition), 1997, p. 436.

8 Donn B. Parker, *Fighting Computer Crime. A New Framework for Protecting Information*, Chichester: John Wiley & Sons 1998, p. 117.

9 DNS spoofing is often used for this purpose, meaning an attack in which the DNS is using information originating from an unauthorised server.

10 Specific criminal liability under Article 130 of the Penal Code is intended for the person who, in order to provide foreign intelligence information that could harm the Republic of Poland, enters the IT system in order to obtain this.

11 Jerzy Skorupka, Wady oświadczenia woli w wybranych przestępstwach gospodarczych [Defect of intention in chosen economic crimes] in *Przegląd Sądowy*, 4 (2000), p. 45.

12 Oktawia Górniok, 'Niekorzystne rozporządzenie' i 'cudze mienie' jako znamiona przestępstwa oszustwa (na tle niektórych sposobów wyłudzeń nieruchomości) ['Adverse regulation' and 'Other people's property' as a crime of fraud (against some types of real estate scams)] in *Prokuratura i Prawo*, 9 (2002), pp. 11–12.

13 Robert Korczyński and Robert Koszut, Oszustwo komputerowe [Computer fraud] in *Prokuratura i Prawo*, 2 (2002), p. 17.

14 Bogusław Michalski in *Kodeks karny. Część szczególna. Tom II. Komentarz pod redakcją Andrzeja Wąska [Penal Code. Special Part. Volume II. Commentary edited by Andrzej Wąsek]*, Warsaw: C.H. Beck, 2010, p. 1174.

15 Robert Korczyński and Robert Koszut, Oszustwo komputerowe, p. 18; Piotr Kardas, Oszustwo komputerowe w kodeksie karnym [Computer fraud in the penal code] in *Przegląd Sądowy*, 11–12 (2000), p. 52.

16 See Bogusław Michalski, *Przestępstwa przeciwko mieniu [Crimes against Property]*, Warsaw: C.H. Beck, 1999, p. 220.

17 Bogusław Michalski in *Kodeks karny*, p. 1174.

18 Andrzej Adamski, *Prawo karne komputerowe [Computer Criminal Law]*, Warsaw: C.H. Beck, 2001, p. 116; Emil Pływaczewski in *Kodeks karny. Komentarz [Criminal Code. Commentary]*, Warsaw: LexisNexis, 2004, p. 786; Robert Korczyński and Robert Koszut, Oszustwo komputerowe, p. 35; Bogusław Michalski in *Kodeks karny*, p. 1181.

19 Piotr Kardas, Oszustwo komputerowe w kodeksie karnym [Computer fraud in the penal code] in *Przegląd Sądowy*, 11–12 (2000), pp. 72–73;

20 Lech Gardocki, *Prawo karne [Criminal Law]*, Warsaw: C.H. Beck, 2001, p. 57, item 96.

21 Małgorzata Dąbrowska-Kardas and Piotr Kardas in Andrzej Zoll (ed.) *Kodeks karny. Część szczególna. Komentarz, tom III, Komentarz do art. 278–363 k.k. [The Penal Code. Special Part. Commentary vol. III, Commentary to the Articles 278–363 kk]*, Warsaw: Wolter Kluwers, 2008, p. 141.

22 Stanisław Łagodziński, Przestępstwa przeciwko mieniu w kodeksie karnym (wybrane zagadnienia) [Offences against property in the Penal Code (chosen aspects)] in *Prokuratura i Prawo*, 2 (1999), p. 15.

23 Ibid.

24 Bogusław Michalski in *Kodeks karny*, p. 1110.

25 Oktawia Górniok in Oktawia Górniok, Stanisław Hoc, Michał Kalitowski, Stanisław M. Przyjemski, Zofia Sienkiewicz, Jerzy Szumski, Leon Tyszkiewicz and Andrzej Wąsek, *Kodeks karny. Komentarz* [*Penal Code. Commentary*], Gdańsk: Arche, 2002/2003, p. 1165.

26 Andrzej Adamski, *Prawo karne komputerowe*, p. 104.

27 Jerzy Barta, Paweł Fajgielski and Ryszard Markiewicz, *Ochrona danych osobowych. Komentarz* [*Personal Data Protection. Commentary*], Cracow: WoltersKluwer, 2007, p. 344.

28 The Act on Electronic Signatures also introduces criminal sanctions for falsifying documents. Article 47 of the Act imposes penalties on the use of data for the generation of a secure electronic signature that is assigned to another person. Certifying an entity issuing a certificate containing false information, as well as a person who uses such a certificate, shall be subject to criminal liability under Article 49 of the Act. It is also punishable, under Article 51 of the Act, to enable the qualified certifying entity to certify the signed data marking time (time stamp) other than at the time of execution of the service (false data).

29 Joanna Piórkowska-Flieger, *Fałsz dokumentu w polskim prawie karnym* [*Document Forgery in the Polish Criminal Law*], Lublin: n.p., 2003, after Andrzej Wąsek in Oktawia Górniok, Stanisław Hoc, Michał Kalitowski, Stanisław M. Przyjemski, Zofia Sienkiewicz, Jerzy Szumski, LeonTyszkiewicz and Andrzej Wąsek, *Kodeks karny. Komentarz. Tom I* [*Penal Code. Commentary. Vol. I*], Gdańsk: Arche, 2005, pp. 855–6.

30 Andrzej Wąsek in Oktawia Górniok et al., *Kodeks karny*, p. 856.

31 Ryszard Zakrzewski, Ochrona wiarygodności dokumentów w nowym kodeksie karnym [Protection of the credibility of the documents in new Penal Code] in *Przegląd Ustawodawstwa Gospodarczego*, 7–8 (1999), p. 6.

32 Mieczysław Szymczak (ed.) *Słownik języka polskiego* [*Polish Language Dictionary*], Warsaw: PWN, 1979.

33 See Joanna Piórkowska-Flieger, Przestępstwa przeciwko wiarygodności dokumentów w nowym kodeksie karnym [Crimes against credibility of the documents in new Penal Code] in *Przegląd Sądowy*, 10 (1997), p. 11.

34 Grzegorz Kopczyński, Pojęcie dokumentu i fałszu materialnego w nowym kodeksie karnym [Concept ot a document and forgery in new Penal Code] in Leszek Bogunia (ed.) *Nowa Kodyfikacja Prawa Karnego* [*New Penal Codification*], vol. II, Wrocław: Wydawnictwo Uniwersytetu Wrocławskiego, 1998.

35 Oktawia Górniok in Oktawia Górniok et al., *Kodeks karny*, p. 1151; Genowefa Rejman, Przestępstwa przeciwko dokumentom w świetle art. 270 i 271 kk. [Crimes against documents under Articles 270 and 271 of the Penal Code] in *Przegląd Prawa Karnego*, 19 (1999), p. 21.

36 Genowefa Rejman, Przestępstwa przeciwko dokumentom, p.20; Oktawia Górniok in Oktawia Górniok et al., *Kodeks karny*, pp. 1150–111.

37 Robert Zabłocki in *Kodeks karny. Część szczególna. Tom III pod red. Andrzeja Wąska* [*Penal Code. Special Part. Vol. III edited by Andrzej Wąsek*], C.H. Beck, p. 564.

38 See Genowefa Rejman, Przestępstwa przeciwko dokumentom, p. 25.

39 See Włodzimierz Wróbel in Grzegorz Bogdan, Kazimierz Buchała, Zbigniew Ćwiąkalski, Małgorzata Dąbrowska-Kardas, Piotr Kardas, Jarosław Majewski, Mateusz Rodzynkiewicz, Maria Szewczyk, Włodzimierz Wróbel and Andrzej Zoll, *Kodeks karny. Część szczególna, Komentarz do k.k. t.2* [*Penal Code. Commentary, vol. 2*], Cracow: Zakamycze, 1999, p. 1059.

40 Ibid., p. 1060.

41 Jerzy Skorupka, Przedmiot ochrony przestępstwa z art. 310 k.k. [Subject of protection of the crime under Article 310 of the Penal Code], *Palestra*, 7–8 (2002), p. 68.
42 Ibid.
43 Statement made by the payer or recipient addressed to his or her supplier, containing an instruction to execute a payment transaction – Article 2.36 of the Act on Payment Services.
44 Global standard (stands for Europay, MasterCard and Visa) defining the principles of cooperation of integrated circuit cards (chip cards), terminals and ATMs.
45 Mateusz Górnisiewicz, Radosław Obczyński and Mariusz Pstruś, *Bezpieczeństwo finansowe w bankowości elektronicznej – przestępstwa finansowe związane z bankowością elektroniczną.* [*Financial Security in Electronic Banking – Financial Crimes Related to Online Banking*], Warsaw: Polish Financial Supervision Authority, 2014, accessed 05/02/2015 at www.knf.gov.pl/Images/Bezp_finansowe_tcm75-39005.pdf.
46 Accessed 05/02/2015 at http://prawo.rp.pl/artykul/1173666.html.
47 According to CERT Poland Annual Report for 2013, p. 3, accessed 5/02/2015 at www. cert.pl/PDF/Report_CP_2013.pdf; CERT Poland is the computer emergency response team that operates within the structures of Research and Academic Computer Network (NASK, which operates national domain.pl registry).
48 Ibid., p. 5.
49 Ibid., p. 15.
50 Ibid., p. 13.
51 Ibid., p. 19.
52 Ibid., p. 21.
53 Ibid., pp. 11–12.
54 Ibid., p. 24.
55 Ibid., p. 25.
56 Ibid., p. 26.
57 Atak i obrona 2013 raport: Ataki i metody obrony w Internecie w Polsce [Attack and defense 2013 report: attacks and methods of defense on the internet in Poland] p. 12, accessed 19/10/2015 at www.cybsecurity.org/wp-content/uploads/2014/01/Raport_ AiO2013.pdf.
58 Ibid., p. 15.
59 Ibid., p. 25.
60 The law amending the Penal Code, and some other laws, was passed on 24 October 2008 (Journal of Laws, no. 214, item 1344).
61 H. Kelsen, *General Theory of Law and State*, Cambridge, MA: Harvard University Press, 1945, pp. 118–19.
62 For instance, in Sweden, according to the Ministry of Justice, in 2012 more than 65,000 people fell victim to identity theft, and the financial loss amounted to more than 3 billion Swedish crowns (over 30 million Euro).
63 See Resolution of the XIX International Congress of Penal Law 'Information Society and Penal Law' (Rio de Janeiro, Brazil, 31 August to 6 September 2014), accessed 10/02/2015 at www.penal.org/sites/default/files/files/Section%20II%20EN%20Rev%20 Final.pdf.
64 Aristotle, *The Politics*, Book V, Chapter 8, Oxford World's Classics ebook, Oxford University Press, 1995.

8   Dealing with cyber risk in Japanese financial institutions

*Ruth Taplin**

Introduction

There has been little acknowledgement in Japanese financial institutions and government organisations that cyber-risk threat and attacks are a reality and occurring. In Chapter 5, Motohiro Tsuchiya provides examples of Japanese bank security being breached by cyber attack. As mentioned in Chapter 1 of this book, banks in Europe and the United States have been reluctant to make public their breaches in cyber security, especially in terms of loss of cash and personal client data, as it is believed such adverse publicity will frighten off both savers and investors.

In Japan there appears even greater reticence in admitting or discussing such cyber security breaches in the banking financial sector. There might even be an element of dirty water or *kiru mizu*, the traditional Japanese phrase used to explain the cultural distaste for speaking out publicly about money matters. Curiously, despite the apparent lack of such cyber security breaches, a number of reports in Japan has been published recently that are very thorough in their assessment of how to combat, prepare and manage cyber attack in the financial sector.

The Council of Experts issued a recommendation report to the Center for Financial Industry Information Systems (FISC) entitled *Report of the Council of Experts on Countermeasures against Cyber Attacks on Financial Institutions* (hereinafter referred to as 'the report').[1] In the introduction the report of the Council recognises that cyber attacks have occurred worldwide and mentions in particular the case of South Korea, which was also cited in Chapter 5 of this book. The Council, which is comprised of experts from academia, financial institutions and government observers, came together to submit to the FISC a wide-ranging set of proposals to counter cyber risk. The Council report, while acknowledging that adequate security measures exist to combat phishing fraud for both customers and banks themselves, states that neither party has satisfactorily considered using these countermeasures because of the limited resources in terms of those who have the expertise to use them in the banking sector. Yet, as of the 2014 report, it claims that no such cyber attacks such as breaches of data and system shutdowns have occurred or been confirmed in Japanese financial institutions. The report, however, does provide a very thorough list and explanation of countermeasures to deal with and manage cyber attacks should they happen in Japanese financial institutions. This chapter will provide a summary of these countermeasures and assess if they can be adopted in Japan as well as being translated globally.

The definitions of the types of possible attacks in the Council report are very similar to those listed and explained in Chapter 2 of this book by Monica Lagazio. However the report's assessment of awareness in Japanese financial institutions is quite noteworthy.

Risk awareness

In Japanese financial institutions there exists a low awareness of risk of cyber attack for a number reasons as outlined in the report.[2] One reason, as mentioned above, is that such financial institutions do not think they will be attacked because of their belief in the low incidence of cyber attack and disruption experienced in Japan. Another reason is that these institutions mistakenly believe that they are safe because their systems are built on mainframe core banking architecture and with networks that operate as closed systems. Additionally, as outsourcing occurs and systems become more complex with less direct management from the parent company, there is an increasing unwillingness to be responsible for the whole operating environment.

It was also suggested that management teams find it difficult to keep abreast of rapidly changing technical systems, may not be well-versed in systems-related matters and give a higher priority to overall systems reviews.

Finally, government bureaucracy in Japan is both pervasive and burdensome. The rate of government-derived company acts is high and often overwhelms managers of financial institutions[3] who cannot also deal with cyber risks.

A number of suggestions was put forward in the Council report to make Japanese financial institutions both aware and at the forefront of managing cyber risk. One is to make it unequivocally clear to banking personnel in charge that if they do institute adequate security measures against cyber attack, they will be held responsible and accountable for breaches in security.

Supervisory agencies in tandem with financial institutions need to reinforce awareness-raising through training and human resource development and need to study how costs of these activities will be met. Concerned parties that exchange electronic data and files cross check with others that all are prepared and practise security measures against cyber attacks. It is also suggested that supervisory agencies carry out checks, audits and examinations against cyber attacks. The Council also demanded that the FISC includes more details in all its guidelines concerning how to manage and deal with cyber threat and attack. Within this process three steps were suggested including keeping written descriptions up to date in line with rapid changes to technology that can prevent and cause cyber attacks; putting the right amount of information within the guidelines so that they do not become overwhelming and confusing to users; and classifying responses according to their being required or desirable.[4]

Working cooperatively to limit cyber attack

Within the cultural context of Japanese society being encouraged to work collectively for the betterment of the overall society, which harks back to feudal times in which every villager was required to work hard and cooperatively to meet taxes in rice for the *daimyo* (feudal landlord),[5] sharing of information is encouraged. The report suggests that sharing incidents of cyber attack throughout the Japanese financial industry and working collectively to stop them is a viable countermeasure. This suggestion is tempered, however, by an understanding of the modern business environment in that the source of the information of the nature of the attack is kept anonymous and the best situation in which this information should be shared is when the public at large is unaware of it. Such sharing can be used to prevent other financial institutions from being similarly damaged. The process of communication should be similar to that used for risks and scandals in general. Through collation of pieces of information, especially in the case of targeted attacks, from individual financial institutions and expert organisations, it makes it easier to assess the motivation and methods of the hackers. As many companies outsource their operations, their systems will be operated by a shared system centre of some kind, which will be at relatively low cost coupled with high security.[6]

Although the idea of data pools to share cyber-attack information across financial industry in Europe and the United States has been mooted, the element of intense competition and mistrust of company rivals has mitigated against such information sharing. Despite competition occurring among and within Japanese companies, there is also a sense of Japan Inc. that exists, which supports collective information sharing and some sense of trust. This is reflected in the popularity of patent pools, which share innovations and inventions across companies as the R&D cost for a single company alone is prohibitive.

Such cost sharing with regard to a cyber attack could also be employed as part of what the report terms the creation of a joint-response organisation. The report states that the purpose of such a bespoke organisation for the financial industry could be twofold: one, sharing information on cyber-risk events particular to financial services and in tandem reinforcing countermeasures; and two, assisting small and medium-sized enterprises (SMEs) with preparedness for cyber attack. This could allow larger financial organisations, whether insurance or banking, to partake in such a joint-response organisation, which would help to stop security breaches entering their organisations through less well-resourced companies such as SMEs.

External measures

One of the most difficult attacks, as described in Chapter 2 by Monica Lagazio, is Distributed Denial of Service (DDoS) because it is unpredictable. The report suggests that the most effective way in which to manage DDoS attacks is again a cooperative one with effective joint surveillance. With the support of telecommunications operators, illegal traffic or controlling the bandwidth coupled with the introduction of a cloud mechanism to distribute the point of access could assist in repelling cyber attacks in financial institutions.

As Japanese financial institutions are a common target for cyber attacks from other countries, the report notes that measures of prevention against infection through maintenance contractors and vendors are paramount. Before applying software and version updates, preventative measures should be required, such as an electronic digital signature with updates to ensure that they are official. The maintenance contractor and vendor should also be required to block illegal programs from their equipment. The caveat is that remote maintenance will increase outsourcing costs and employees would have a heavier workload monitoring the sites. The report stresses that the financial institution should verify themselves that the external suppliers are fully prepared against cyber attack.[7]

Internal measures

The report notes that preparing for external cyber attacks is only a part of the countermeasures and that internal measures are of equal importance. Management of privileged IDs and passwords needs to be restricted by using such techniques as entitlement segregation of privileged IDs, restricting the number of holders and controlling the circumstances in which they may be used. It is also suggested that only one person should be allowed to use a privileged ID with the person's use monitored looking for patterns of use and, at appropriate intervals, assessment of such patterns of usage.

As there is a risk of coming under cyber attack when accessing the internet, it would be useful to completely separate the external and internal environments. However, separating these environments is not cost-effective. It would be less onerous and more cost-effective to introduce measures for blocking such as virtual environments for external connections. Yet, the report suggests that using this method to be effective needs to be bolstered by data exchanged between the two environments through devices such as USB sticks being properly controlled.

To counter the embedding of illegal codes and falsification of website contents, the introduction of a constant monitoring mechanism would be effective. The report moots the idea that, because it is expensive and requires particular skills and experience, a monitoring system in tandem with another financial institution operated by an external vendor could provide the solution. The report suggests that the financial industry in Japan could establish such an organisation to conduct monitoring services for Japanese financial institutions. The report outlines a number of procedures to respond to the risk of a cyber attack when studying in advance an effective response procedure that assesses the scope of damage, vulnerability to a particular attack, damage recovery and maintaining operations from a number of different aspects, which include: ascertaining who will be able to authorise the partial shutdown of a system; preserving evidence of the attack for forensic purposes; deciding on who will organise and what will be the nature of external and public communications; organising what the responses and the compensation to customers will be; and knowing how data and the system will be recovered.[8]

In addition to the above, it is suggested that response training particular to cyber attacks will be conducted in tandem with existing disaster prevention and system-fault response training. Officials responsible for cyber-risk issues would then be prepared in advance to respond effectively to events and related technical matters. This would all be part of raising officials' awareness of the risk of cyber attack and mobilising them for when it occurs to minimise disruption. A possible framework for such training could include joint training undertaken with concerned organisations, training solely internal to one financial institution or a combination of the two. Methods used in training include, among others, drills for checking the communication process, desktop training and forensic training. To lessen burdens on employees, it is suggested that existing training frameworks for other disasters such as system failures or earthquakes could be expanded and used.

Several existing training programmes, with some that are bespoke to managing cyber risk, are mentioned in the report with most being initiated in 2013. They include:

1   The Ministry of Economy, Trade and Industry, which offers bespoke cyber-risk training conducted by Mitsubishi Research Institute. The aim is to train in responses to actual cyber attacks targeting the suspension and damage of control systems used for critical infrastructure, to highlight awareness concerning security threats that attempt to seize control of systems and review countermeasures against them.
2   A joint training programme run by the Ministry of Internal Affairs and Communications with banks who request that their personnel need to be so trained. The training programme is called the Cyber Defence Exercise with Recurrence (CYDER). The aim of CYDER is the improvement of the event response capability of local area network (LAN) managers and LAN operators in agencies, ministries and private firms, and the development of skilled information system administrators who can manage cyber attacks that threaten ongoing system operations while taking daily operations into consideration.
3   Joint training organised by the National Information Security Center (NISC) since 2006. The name of the programme is CEPTOAR, which is an acronym for Capability for Engineering of Protection, Technical Operation, Analysis and Response. The NISC decided in 2005 in its Action Plan on Information Security Measures for Critical Infrastructures that a CEPTOAR would be created for each critical infrastructural area. There are 14 CEPTOARs including those for the financial sectors of banking, securities, life insurance, non-life insurance and medical services. The aim is to keep and improve the information-sharing system between CEPTOAR, NISC and critical sector-specific ministries and identify areas for improvement, issue resolution and checking the information-sharing system.
4   A joint training programme organised by three markets that is conducted by the Japanese Bankers Association, Tokyo Foreign Exchange Committee, and the Japan Securities Dealers Association where business continuity plans (BCPs) are exercised. The aim is to prepare the three markets through

training for potential disasters such as an earthquake striking Tokyo directly. It has been operational since February 2010.

5   Bank of Japan backup centre switchover training. This is aimed at training on switching over to backup systems and connecting customer computers based on the assumption of a system failure in Bank of Japan's network.

6   Cross-sector Critical Infrastructure Incident Response Exercise (CIIREX) 2013, conducted by NISC from 2006. The aim of this training is to improve the protection of essential basic critical infrastructure against any faults internet technology might be experiencing and to confirm responses to such faults, information-sharing systems and methods of initiating and carrying out BCPs.[9]

Cyber attacks on customers of financial institutions

Finally, the report addresses the need to prepare for and manage cyber attacks made on customers of financial institutions. The logic is that customers are the other side of the coin and, if not prepared adequately for possible cyber attack, all the efforts made by the financial institution will be mitigated. Customers need to be encouraged to take measures suggested by their financial institutions and each business segment should carry out measures that are both consistent and integrated.

A number of measures could be taken to improve IT literacy and to raise the consciousness among customers concerning security. The scale of cyber risk varies according to business segment and to what degree the financial transactions depend on internet usage. For example, financial institutions other than deposit-taking ones can take simplified measures such as offering free anti-virus software, depending on the extent to which internet-based services are utilised.

In line with the Japanese ability to be able to launch and implement nationwide campaigns,[10] it is suggested in the report that a campaign be launched and implemented similar to the one for remittance fraud termed in Japanese as *Furikome* or 'It's me' fraud. Accordingly, each industry group would play a central role in tandem with the police and the cooperation of supervisory agencies.

With reference to internet transactions, any promotion through branch networks may not be sufficient to persuade customers to adopt cyber-attack protection measures. More personal and directed measures can be used such as posting promotional material on institutions' websites and/or sending notifications by email directly to customers.

Financial-service providers can take a more personal and direct approach by asking customers when they open a new account what type of computers they rely on for financial transactions and explaining to them in detail about cyber risk. The explanations should include making the customer aware of the risks incorporated into internet transactions and the importance of countermeasures.

How to download software to prevent unauthorised programs being installed can be explained. However, the report highlights the point that, if these measures are to be effective, they all need to be launched in concert. If this is not done, it is noted that customers might all go to providers who offer both simple and quick procedures. For those financial institutions that only offer internet-banking services, website, telephone and email communication may need to be relied on to explain cyber risks to customers and what preventive measures they need to take. The above may increase the burden of financial institutions but is essential to keeping all online transactions safe and secure.[11]

Systematic response measures that are suggested include dissemination of computer software that will stop unauthorised programs being installed, providing one-time passwords, the introduction of transaction authentication and mechanisms for monitoring transaction content that will suspend on a temporary basis any that are suspicious or abnormal.

In the event that a customer does not implement or heed advice given, the financial institution can suspend the use by customers of online transactions unless the customer agrees to take full responsibility for the outcomes or it can refuse to open a new transaction account.

Smartphones and tablet terminals

As mentioned in Chapter 3 of this book by Cint Kortmann, smartphones and tablet terminals are increasingly linked to 'the network of things' (the Japanese name for the internet of things) and social media as well as companies through cookies. This leaves an open route to potential hackers. The report notes that smartphones and tablet terminals are being used increasingly in the financial industry in Japan because of their portability and the ease with which apps can be used and installed. Users of the devices and multitude of apps are often not aware, as mentioned in Chapter 3, that they are accessing websites that are suspect because a simplified type of URL can be displayed in their browsers.

It is suggested that to protect smartphones and tablet terminals measures need to be created from the point of view of applications management. Examples of measures that can be taken by users of these devices include: using only recommended applications supplied by the user's financial institutions; not allowing automatic connection to wireless LAN access points; downloading software to prevent unauthorised programs from being installed; and updating applications to the newest versions. Security measures can be imparted to customers from guidelines supplied by the Japan Smartphone Association.[12]

The report guidelines are thorough and point to the cultural specificities that are native to Japan including the tendencies to cooperation and the institutionalisation of resolutions to problems through other institutional organisations such as those listed in this chapter. The solutions are seen to be within the framework of Japan itself and the problems from largely non-Japanese sources. There is also a tendency to view the situation within the context of *tatamae* and *honne*. The former refers to how a situation should be and can be seen in the assertion that Japan has not been experiencing cyber attacks. The latter, however, refers to the reality of the situation and can be seen in the whole *raison d'être* of the report, which is to prepare Japanese financial institutions for cyber attacks and to suggest how to manage them. There is even a list in the report of cyber attacks that have been made on Japanese financial institutions.

In June 2011 there was the theft of authentication information for Internet banking from 53 Japanese financial institutions.

In October 2011 a phishing fraud occurred using the name of a Japanese financial institution. There was also a phishing fraud to steal passwords such as random-number list information for internet banking operated by a Japanese financial institution.

From October to December 2012 theft and illegal money transfers occurred through some infected computers owned by customers of Japanese internet-banking websites using a process that depicts a false screen and requests random list figures.

In addition crime notice and threats were posted to bulletin boards and sent through emails by spoofing from computers infected by illegal programs to facilitate remote control. Initially, the owner of the remotely controlled computer was arrested. It was subsequently discovered that the wrong person had been charged; the real culprit later admitted being responsible.

In December 2013 1,125 cases of illegal money withdrawal from bank accounts by stealing IDs and passwords for internet banking were reported from January through November. The total amount of damage was 1.2 billion yen (according to the National Police Agency).[13]

These examples show how serious attacks against Japanese financial institutions are becoming year on year. There are also many cases, in fact the majority, that are unreported.

Notes

* Mr Akio Ono and Mr Keitaro Oshima must be thanked for their contribution to this chapter.

1 *Report of the Council of Experts on Countermeasures against Cyber Attacks on Financial Institutions* [hereinafter *Report*], FISC, 26 February 2014.

2 Ibid., p. 4.

3 See work by Eiji Takahashi on changes to Japanese company law, both books and articles in the *Interdisciplinary Journal of Economics and Business Law*, www.ijebl.co.uk.

4 *Report* p. 5.

5 See Ruth Taplin, *Decision Making and Japan*, Abingdon: Routledge, 1991.

6 *Report* pp. 14–15.

7 Ibid., pp. 13–14.

8 Ibid., pp. 10–11.

9 Ibid., pp. 38–42.

10 See the description of the intellectual property awareness campaigns in Ruth Taplin, *Intellectual Property and the New Global Economy*, Abingdon: Routledge, 2010.

11 *Report*, pp. 16–18.

12 Ibid., pp. 17–18.

13 Ibid., p. 28.

Postscript

Ruth Taplin

The question concerning cyber risk/threat/attack/security and how it will be managed is not whether cyber risk/attack will abate. According to the *Daily Telegraph*[1], crime figures will rise by millions as cyber crime is added to the statistics, making it the most common offence in the UK. The future question is whether the private sector of financial services will universally accept the onerous task of protecting itself and its vulnerable customers through insurance policies and the training of its personnel in countermeasures. Managing cyber risk needs to become part of everyday routine across all departments in banks and insurance companies from human resources to accounts. As noted in Chapter 8 of this book, in Japan there is a mix of cyber-risk management countermeasures practised jointly by the government and private companies as the burden on banks and insurance companies would be too onerous to tackle cyber risk/attack on their own.

Criminal-gang plundering of individual bank accounts continues to be rife as the *Daily Telegraph*[2] noted with the latest malware, Dridex, a botnet, already accruing US$10 million from hacked US accounts through email attachment cyber attack. It has also been used in the UK and a 30-year-old Moldovan man, Andrey Ghinkul, has been arrested in Cyprus by the FBI, on suspicion of criminal conspiracy, bank fraud and unauthorised computer access with intent to defraud, among other charges in a nine-count indictment pending extradition to the US for trial. Yet, managing individual hackers seems to be less complicated than dealing with institutional/state cyber risk/attack.

So, the other question for future exploration is how governmental state institutions will deal with managing cyber risk/attack. It is a complex picture because of geo-political considerations such as one country attacking another through the state apparatus. On the one hand, when President Obama met the Chinese President Xi Jinping, the former promised that the US government would deal with cyber attack and risk. Yet, even to date, the US Senate has delayed voting on the final draft of the much-needed Cybersecurity Information Sharing Act on 2 August 2015 before the Senate recessed for summer.[3] As mentioned in Chapter 4, the House of Representatives passed its own cybersecurity bill entitled the Protecting Cyber Networks Act in 2015.[4] What is required to make the management of cyber risk/threat effective is a joint comprehensive House/Senate bill that is law showing a united front. The current situation is that after 19 October 2015, the Senate is set to reconvene and debate the bipartisan Cybersecurity Information Sharing Act. The aim is to create a bill that can be passed into law by the end of 2015 as many believe no substantive bills will be passed during election year 2016. Senate Intelligence Committee Chairman Richard Burr (R-NC) said: 'We have both pestered our leadership to death to bring this to the floor' and 'There's no more compelling reason for us to do that than the last attack, the one before, and the one to come.' One of the last major attacks was against the Federal Office of Personnel Management in early 2015, which resulted in the theft of personal information of roughly 21.5 million government workers, their family members and applicants for federal jobs.

The Cybersecurity Information Sharing Act is supported by both the chamber and the White House. Its intention is to encourage the voluntary sharing of cyber-threat information among private companies and between companies and the government. Companies will be protected from anti-trust laws if they share threats with one another. It also shields them from lawsuits by customers and stockholders for sharing data with the government.

Burr stated that the aim of the Cybersecurity Information Sharing Act is to limit data breaches by alerting companies and federal officials when a cyber attack has occurred so that measures can be taken to protect other businesses and government agencies.[5]

Chinese President Xi, on the other hand, while saying in a speech after his talks with President Obama that he will see that cyber attacks emanating from China will be dealt with without giving specifics, will also have problems delivering on whatever he intends to implement. According to Robert Atkinson (President) and Stephen Ezell (Vice President, Global Innovation Policy) of the Information Technology and Innovation Foundation, a Washington DC-based innovative technology think tank, China is pursuing a dangerous innovation mercantilism in which it uses any means including cyber crime on a state level to steal intellectual property and trade secrets to gain economic advantage and dominance for its own political aims. Such cyber theft/crime is pursued aggressively often through the Chinese government, breaking the rules that China agreed to when joining the World Trade Organization in 2001.[6]

The expanded use of cyberspace for nefarious purposes is increasing in the realm of the political with disastrous consequences. Since the Friday 13 November 2015 attack in Paris by the so-called 'Islamic State', the UK Chancellor George Osborne has on 17 November 2015 pledged £1.9 billion a year by 2020 for cyber security. The priority of targeting politically motivated cyber attacks despite severe budget cuts by the UK government points to the growing risk of cyber threat/attack. It is a further move towards another form of managing cyber threat/attack which includes an Institute for Coding, recruitment and training of promising young people to work in the cyber security sector and a Cyber Innovation Centre in Cheltenham for cyber start-ups, much like an incubator.[7]

Financial markets are also responding to increasing needs for tightened cyber security for reasons including terrorist money laundering. Cyber security issues were emphasised in the recent Securities Industry and Financial Markets (Sifma) annual meeting of 2015.[8]

Noteworthy is that A. M. Best, which has won awards many times over globally for being the best ratings agency, in December 2015 produced a special report underlining the importance of insurance companies, in particular, managing cyber security risk. The report states that while catastrophe insurance remains the major part of insurance company work, the severity and increasingly regular occurrence of cyber attack coupled with the difficulties of measuring its risk are a substantial threat to the insurance industry. As this book argues, both managing and understanding the value of losses due to cyber attack are an urgent priority for the financial sector as a whole. The report points to the recent frequency of losses due to cyber attack in the large managed healthcare industry. It estimates that the most likely maximum global loss because of cyber threat/attack amounts to US$31 billion per annum. This book argues that this amount of loss is rising at a ferocious rate globally at all levels of the financial sector.

Institutional state-backed cyber attack is probably the most difficult to eradicate and manage as a risk because the very protection of data privacy laws that citizens are entitled to by a democracy can be so easily compromised by state apparatus and, in the case of a totalitarian state, abused endlessly with no recourse for those abused domestically to appeal to the rule of law, with foreign individuals, companies and states being without any protection as well.

In fact a very difficult balance to create is respect and implementation of rule of law with regard to data privacy and countermeasures against cyber attack/crime especially within institutional frameworks. This is the nexus where more attention to managing cyber risk needs to be given.

Notes

1 *Daily Telegraph* (12 October 2015).
2 *Daily Telegraph* (14 October 2015).
3 'Cybersecurity bill is latest to be delayed in Senate', *New York Times* Jennifer Steinhauer, 5 August 2015, www.nytimes.com/2015/08/06/us/politics/cybersecurity-bill-is-latest-to-be-delayed-in-senate.html.
4 'House passes cybersecurity bill after companies fall victim to data breaches', *New York Times*, Jennifer Steinhauer, 22 April 2015, www.nytimes.com/2015/04/23/us/politics/computer-attacks-spur-congress-to-act-on-cybersecurity-bill-years-in-making.html.
5 'Cybersecurity information-sharing bill to get Senate vote in October', Erin Kelly, *USA Today*, 6 October 2015, www.usatoday.com/story/news/2015/10/06/cybersecurity-information-sharing-bill-get-senate-vote-october/73444240/.
6 'One hand tied behind our backs: why America must do more to curb China's dangerous innovation mercantilism', Information Technology and Innovation Foundation video event, 17 September 2015.
7 'George Osborne to double cyber crime – fighting funds', BT News online, 17 November 2015, http.//home.bt.com/news/uk-news/george-osborne-double-cyber-crime fighting-funds-11364016975920.
8 See report of the Securities Industry and Financial Markets (Sifma) Annual Meeting 2015, http://www.sifma.org.

Index

Where spellings, capitalisations, etc. differ between chapters, the majority styles have been used. Page references in italic type indicate relevant figures and tables. The abbreviation *n.* indicates a note.